Intercity Transport

Intercity Transport

Engineering and Planning

TOM RALLIS

Technical University of Denmark, Copenhagen

A HALSTED PRESS BOOK

JOHN WILEY & SONS
New York

First published in Great Britain 1977 by
The Macmillan Press Ltd

Published in the U.S.A. by
Halsted Press, a Division of
John Wiley & Sons, Inc.
New York

Printed in Great Britain

Library of Congress Cataloging in Publication Data

Rallis, Tom.
Intercity transport.

"A Halsted Press book."
1. Transportation. 2. Local transit. 3. Transit,
International. I. Title.
HE151.R27 1977   380.5'09   77–2351
ISBN 0 470–01394–X

Contents

Contents   vii

Preface

This book is for students in civil engineering who want to know something about intercity transport: its environmental, capacity and economic factors and its modes—shipping, railways, public road transport; air transport and pipelines. It describes the evolution of transport and transport systems, and discusses forecasting and evaluation. I also hope that, because it contains a considerable amount of background material, it will also be of interest to planners, designers, managers and consultants.

The book is a guide for an advanced course in transport. Students using it will have taken basic courses in road, railway and airport construction, road traffic engineering, urban traffic engineering and planning, advanced regional science, port construction, statistics and operational research, transport economy and investment analysis. Therefore brevity is both useful and necessary.

Many statistical data and examples are presented which should be useful in discussions and problem solving. Not all the data are from the most recent years, but this helps emphasise the changing values of intercity transport. I have been careful not to put too many Danish transport problems into the book; even so our problems at Great Belt and in Saltholm are very much like the problems of the Channel tunnel and the third London Airport. Even though these latter problems are postponed indefinitely, it is interesting to consider the evaluations. One day such problems will be solved. Perhaps air traffic has been somewhat overemphasised; however, according to my experience this is necessary because students know too little about this relatively new means of transport.

In recent years many transport problems have been treated in the literature, but to my knowledge, a book has not been published which offers a general, comparative description of transport, and which is applicable in practice to all service sectors of our transport networks.

Transport engineering is the science of measuring transport, the formulation of basic laws in relation to transport, and the application of this knowledge to the professional practice of planning, designing and operating transport systems.

I am indebted to the Technical University of Denmark and to the Directorate of Civil Aviation in Denmark for assistance, making it possible for me to visit the University of California, Berkeley, in 1962 and 1970, the New York Port Authority, the Federal Aviation Agency in Washington and General Motors in Detroit in 1965, and finally the South-east India Railways in Calcutta and the Tokaido Line in Tokyo in 1967. Without these connections, as well as those in Europe, including C.E.M.T. and O.E.C.D. in Paris and the University of Southampton, England, this book would never have been written.

Abbreviations, symbols, nomenclature and units have been used as consistently as possible, bearing in mind the variety of sources but any exceptions that may be found are entirely my responsibility. I should also like to draw attention to the comprehensive list of references included at the end of each chapter. Last but not least I wish to thank my former students O. Buskgaard, L. Denver, P. Bjorn Andersen and C. Wass for all their inspiration and help.

Tom Rallis

Technical University of Denmark
Copenhagen, 1977

Introduction

Elements and Problems in Transport

Life is movement. In civilised life this movement is transport, providing connections between individuals and communities. Transport, the movement of persons and freight from one place to another, dictates the rise and fall of cultures.

The main elements in transport are the network, the means of transport and the people. The main problems in transport are the environment, the capacity and the economy.

Transport and History

Some main elements of transport, such as road transport and sea transport, have been in use for several thousand years; others, such as the railways and air transport, have only occurred recently, in the nineteenth and twentieth centuries.

The people remain basically the same; the existing networks have been improved, both roads and harbours, and new networks, such as railways, and terminals, such as airports, have been established. However, the means of transport have improved markedly, the horsedrawn carriage and the sailing ship have been replaced by the automobile and the steamship, and new means of transport, such as locomotives and aircraft have been invented to increase speed. Some means, such as ships, railways and buses, trucks, pipelines and aircraft, are used mainly for long distance traffic and for public transport. These means of transport have, in the context of the main transport problems, the added features of better safety, capacity and economy compared with the individual short distance means of transport, such as the passenger motor vehicle.

Methods in Transport Engineering

To describe transport, three methods can be used: to give facts, to set up common laws for the comparison of facts, and to create facts in the form of planning, construction and simulation of transport systems. Normally the second method of comparing facts by the use of laws is the scientific method chosen. The laws of statistics and the theory of probability are used both for the solution of safety and queueing problems and for solving economic problems.

Aims in Transport Engineering

It is the goal of the transport engineer to reduce environmental disturbance caused by transportation, that is to reduce the number of people killed by accidents, disturbed by noise and air pollution, etc., to improve the layout, service and handling of passengers and freight, to locate and forecast the traffic distributed into regions, transport modes and transport networks and finally to use these facts to plan and construct better transport systems taking into consideration both constructional and operational costs. The planning also contains political, military, and sociological aims well as aesthetics, which are difficult to describe in technical—economic models. Often the transport engineer has to base his decisions on inexact models, and accommodate political motives.

1 Transport Evolution

1.1 Transport before 1500

Even if the hunting and agricultural life 15 000–10 000 years ago used the sledge and the canoe, it was not until 3000 B.C. that land and water transport really advanced, through the horsedrawn carriage and the sailing boat. Roads, canals and harbours could now be used for passenger and freight transport. Cities effected a mobilisation of manpower and communication over long distances in space and time, because of the developments in agricultural productivity. In particular, miners, merchants, soldiers and priests were travelling widely. Cities were built in great river valleys: on the Indus and the Ganges rivers in India, on the Nile and the Euphrates and Tigris rivers in the west and on the Hwang Ho in the east. World trade between these districts began because India was rich in food and spices, but poor in metals. Transport made it possible to distribute surplus products and to obtain access to distant markets. Urban markets provided the means of procurement, storage, and distribution. Other dynamic elements were the wars and the pilgrimages which were early mass transport systems. Some important cities had a precinct sacred to the gods, with ancient burial pits and sacred shrines and memorials to which pilgrims made their journeys from distant places.[1, 2] Powerful cities extended their frontiers and destroyed people who might block their trade routes.

In China, Persia and Rome, kings' roads or military roads were constructed. The Romans built a road network totalling approximately 100 000 km, some of it covered with stone pavements, and 7 m wide. At approximately every 6 km there were resting places, called mutations, where horses could be changed or rested, and every 48 km there were inns or mansions where people travelling could eat and sleep. These mansions were also post offices for the kings' post officers, the first public transport companies in the world. The first intercontinental route, the Silk Route, started in China near Canton; passing through the Gobi desert north of India, the Chinese tradesmen brought their caravans across to Samarkand and Babylon, and then via Alexandria to Rome. Their speed was 5–15 km/h. A speed of 15 km/h could only be achieved by the horses of the kings' post officers. Travelling by caravan from the

Euphrates to the Mediterranean, a journey of 360 km, took 10 days. A caravan could consist of approximately 1000 camels carrying about 300 tons of freight accompanied by 250 camel drivers and tradesmen.

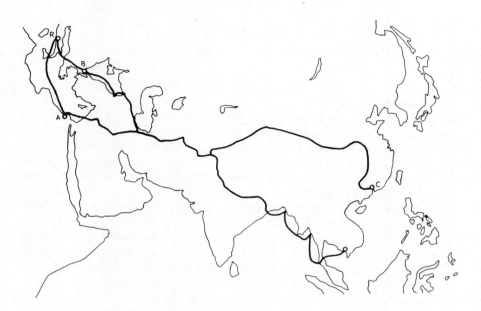

Figure 1.1 The silk route. B Byzantium, R Rome, A Alexandria, C Canton

Normally 10 such caravans passed through India each year on their way from China to Rome. The capacity of the trade routes was dependent on the capacity of the caravan stations, or serails. The big Sultan Han near Aksaray in Turkey could accommodate one caravan of 300 tons, made up of 1000 camels and 250 men. The stable yard was 30 × 50 m, and the main yard 45 × 60 m, with inn, mosque, warehouses and a well.

Other freight routes to Rome involved copper from Sinai, gold from Greece, silver from Spain and pewter from Britain. The export from Rome to India during the reign of Augustus amounted to approximately 100 million sesterce per year (about $8 million). Freight transport was expensive; an oil-press which Cato bought in Pompeii for 400 sesterce (about $33) cost him 300 sesterce ($25) to transport from the town to his farm, a distance of 100 km. The pavement of 1 Roman mile of road cost Hadrian approximately 100 000 sesterce ($8000), excluding the cost of bridge building and drainage.[3]

In 1278 a transport service from Rhuddlan in Wales via Chester to

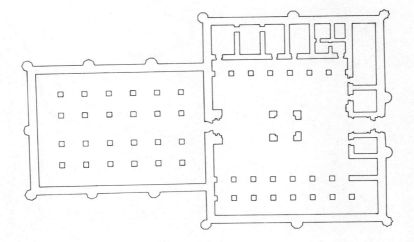

Figure 1.2 Plan of the Sultan Han

Macclesfield in England, a distance of 70 miles, was operating at an average cost of 6d per day per cart with two horses. Rogers found that service over long distances by common carriers cost $3\frac{1}{2}$d per ton mile but that the services of peasant carts were much cheaper, namely 1d per ton mile. This meant that 50 miles transport of grain cost 15 per cent of its value, but transport of wool only 1.5 per cent.[4, 25]

Major sea routes were established from Rome via Alexandria, through the first Suez Canal, and the Red Sea, via the Indian Ocean to the Bay of Bengal, and finally to the China Sea.

A sea voyage from Egypt to India could last 3 months, and to China 6 months, depending on monsoons. Sails and oars were used in ships which could be 30 m in length, and carry a cargo of 400 m³, or 100 men. Grain from Russia was sent to Greece during the Alexandrian period in volumes of approximately 20 000 m³ per year.[5,6,7]

The harbours of Ostia, Alexandria, Samos, Piraeus and Knidos are well known. Samos was the first port in the world constructed with a breakwater and a deep-water pier. The port of Alexandria could take 400 ships in the western basin of 2400 × 300 m equipped with a lighthouse. Canals and rivers were used for water transport in China, Egypt and Europe: the Rhine and the Danube were used by the Romans.

In Egypt, river transport was used during the construction of the pyramids. One pyramid constructed over a period of 20 years contained approximately 2 000 000 blocks of stone, each with an average weight of 2.5 tons. With

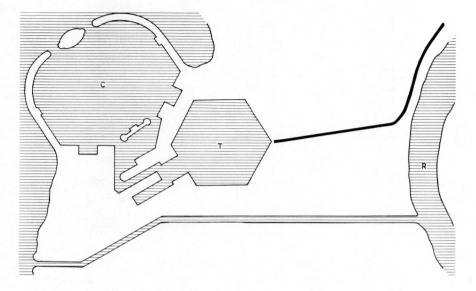

Figure 1.3 The harbour of Ostia. C Claudius, T Trajan, R River Tiber

100 000 blocks per year being positioned, 2500 gangs of men carried out the work: each gang handled approximately 40 blocks per year or 10 every 12 weeks.

In the harbour at Piraeus, the toll income during the Periclean period amounted to $30 000 per year (which was approximately 2 per cent of the goods' value handled). In Rhodes the toll income from the port during the reign of Caesar was $160 000 per year.[10]

In the thirteenth century sea transport was cheap. Gascon wine to Hull cost 8 shillings per tun or less than 10 per cent of its price in Bordeaux, while the costs of shipping wool from London to Calais worked out at 4 shillings per sack, or 2 per cent of its price in London.

It cost about 2 shillings to transport 400 pounds of coal from Newcastle to the Low Countries, but 200 tons of cargo shipped from Bergen-op-Zoom to London worked out at £20, or 2 shillings per ton.

The cost of packing and transport of one sack of wool from the Midlands to London including customs and subsidy amounted to £3; the price the English exporter paid per sack was £8, that is expenses of 40 per cent of inland price, which means that a wool merchant in Calais paid £11. The selling price of fine Cotswold wool in Bruges fluctuated between £12 and £13.

Bordeaux wine cost £5 per tun in London, that is 14 livres, of which 5 livres were paid for grapes, making of wine and brokerage; 1 livre was paid for transport to Bordeaux; 5 livres were paid for transport to London, and finally 3 livres for customs and dues. The export figures were as follows[25]

Export of wool from England per year (sacks)

1357–60	35 800
1402–05	10 800
1450–53	7 600

Export of wine from Bordeaux per year (tuns)

1308–09	102 700
1348–50	9 600
1379–81	7 800

1.2 Transport after 1500

After the fall of the Roman Empire the centre for world trade and transport was the Arabian part of Eastern and Western Europe, especially Turkey (Constantinople) and Spain (Barcelona). In the years after 1500 the discovery of America influenced trade and transport, so that Venice came to use Lisbon and Antwerp instead of Alexandria as transit ports. The Hansa period declined subsequently and Amsterdam and London became centres for overseas trade, whereas Paris, Frankfurt, Nuremberg, Leipzig and Moscow became centres of overland trade.

New merchandise, such as coffee, tobacco, potatoes and maize, came from America; sugar, cotton, leather, arms, rice, tea, paper and glass came from China and India. Europe produced timber, coal, wool, metal, furs, salt, wine, fish, grain and clothing.[8,9]

1.2.1 Land Transport

Roads

The Roman roads were used in the main part of Europe until approximately 1500 when monarchs began to build their own road networks. In about 1700 turnpike roads were introduced, on which not only the noblemen but also the farmers could travel, if they paid the toll.

In 1639, the king of England rode 260 miles in 4 days from Berwick to London. In 1658, stage coaches set out from the George Inn, London travelling to Salisbury in 2 days for 20 shillings, to Exeter and to Wakefield every Friday in 4 days for 40 shillings, to Plymouth for 50 shillings and to Durham for 55 shillings.[11]

In 1774 Woodforde paid £4 8 shillings for a journey by post-chaise from Oxford to Castle Cary in Somerset, a distance of 100 miles in 1 day. The wealthiest people made grand tours of France and Italy for 6 months to 2 years; English lords had almost the monopoly of tourist travel in Europe, and their requirements became the standard for post inns from Calais to Naples. In 1785, Gibbon was told that 40 000 English people were touring or resident on the Continent.[25]

Figure 1.4 Roman roads. R Rome, T Tarragona, M Milan, V Vienna, P Paris, L London
C Cologne

In 1830 there existed in Britain 1100 turnpike companies which owned approximately 22 000 miles of road in England (1 mile of road cost £1000 to construct). In the same year about 800 public transport companies handled passenger transport from London to other parts of England. In 12 hours a stage coach could travel 50–100 km (30–60 miles). Prices were 2–5p per mile per passenger. The number of coaches travelling from London to Birmingham was 22 per day. There were 16 passengers per stage coach, with only 4 accommodated inside. The fare for a trip from London to Edinburgh was £6 (riding inside). A big transport company, Chaplin, had 1500 horses and 64 stage coaches, and an annual income of £500 000. By about 1850 the railways had taken over most of the traffic from the roads.

The number of horsedrawn carriages in Great Britain in 1900 was about 500 000, but in 1940 there were only 20 000: the motor car had arrived. In 1920 there were 250 000 cars in Great Britain; by 1940 the figure was nearly 2 million, and by 1975 there were 10 million private cars. In the United States the numbers were approximately 6 million cars in 1920, and 80 million private cars in 1975.

Road networks were improved during these years: they were asphalt or concrete paved, and amounted to 150 000 km in Great Britain in 1970 and to 4 million km in the United States in the same year. The next international road network, after those of the Romans, the kings' highways and the turnpikes, has been built in recent years, namely the motorways. In England 700 km have been finished out of a planned total of 1500 km; in the United States 20 000 km have been finished out of a planned total of 65 000 km. Many of these are toll roads in the United States, and the service areas have petrol stations, motels and bus stations.[17]

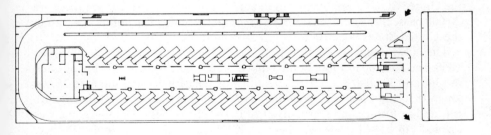

Figure 1.5 New York bus terminal—ground level, long distance

The bus station in New York near the Lincoln tunnel is the biggest in the world, 60 × 240 m with 8 floors. In 1964, there were 66 million passengers, and

2.5 million buses departing and arriving. This means 24 000 passengers per hour in 500 buses per hour at 165 bays.

A large road haulage centre near the New Jersey Turnpike covers an area of 360 × 60 m, with 160 truck-stands; it handled 1 million tons of goods in 1964.

In the United States, bus traffic amounted to 14 000 million passenger miles in 1964, approximately 20 per cent of the total public transport, but only 2 per cent of the total traffic on the entire transport network. The US truck transport companies represented 33 per cent of all road transport in that country in 1964, 300 000 million ton km, that is approximately 5 million tons of freight per day. The price per bus passenger mile was 2 cents; per truck ton mile it was 3 cents.[12]

Railways

In 1825, Stephenson's 30 h.p. steam driven locomotive took 34 cars with 100 tons of freight and 450 passengers the 40 km from Stockton to Darlington, at an average speed of 20 km/h. That was a sensation!

In 1850, steam locomotives of 380 h.p., fuelled by wood, ran at 64 km/h, but utilisation of the available energy was only 3 per cent. In 1900, 475 h.p. locomotives, fuelled by coal, ran at 80 km/h with 6 per cent utilisation; in 1960, 1000 h.p. diesel locomotives, driven by oil, ran at 130 km/h with 30 per cent utilisation. By 1964 Japan had 10 000 h.p. electric locomotives travelling at 200 km/h.

The width of the railway track in Europe is normally 1.43 m, the width of the cars 2.90 m, and the height above the track 4.30 m; car length is approximately 26 m, with each car taking about 100 passengers or 20–40 tons of freight.[14]

The number of locomotives in the world is very high; in the United States alone there are some 30 000, in Great Britain 6000. The number of wagons in the United States amounts to 2 million freight cars; in Great Britain there are 20 000 passenger carriages and 500 000 freight wagons. The number of staff in the United States is 500 000; in Great Britain the figure is 340 000.

The railway networks in Europe had 3000 km of track in 1840, 50 000 km in 1860, and 150 000 in 1960. In the United States there were 50 000 km of track in 1860 and 300 000 in 1960. In Great Britain the network amounted to 25 000 km in 1870 and 1960, with a maximum of 40 000 km in 1910. The same picture is found in France and Germany. The Paris – Bruxelles – Hamburg line was opened in 1848–50, together with those linking Vienna – Prague, Vienna – Berlin and Moscow – Leningrad. In 1851 the Paris – London rail route by ferry was opened; 1856 Paris – Frankfurt and Zurich as well as Vienna – Trieste (Semmering); 1860–70 Paris – Barcelona, Berlin – Moscow, Zurich – Rome (Brenner), and Paris – Milan (Mt Cenis). In 1884 came Zurich – Vienna (Arlberg) and in 1889 Vienna – Istanbul. Moscow – Peking

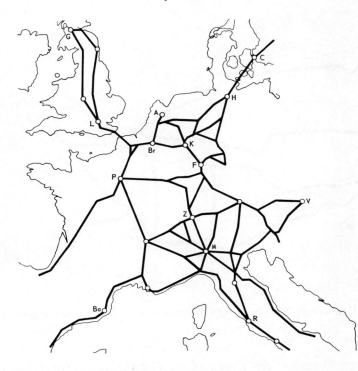

Figure 1.6 The European railway network. A Amsterdam, Br Brussels, R Rome, Ba Barcelona, M Milan, P Paris, L London, K Cologne, Z Zurich, V Vienna, F Frankfurt, H Hamburg, C Copenhagen

was opened in 1915, New York – San Francisco in 1869 (Central Pacific), Chicago – Los Angeles in 1881, and the North Pacific in 1893. In 1885 and 1915 came the Canadian Pacific railways, and in 1910 the Buenos Aires – Santiago routes.

In 12 hours a railway passenger could travel 400 km in 1860 and 800 km in 1900. In 1964 the 500 km journey on the Tokaido line from Tokyo to Osaka took just 3 hours!

There are approximately 2700 stations in Great Britain, a decrease from the 1962 figure of 5000. The great railway stations in London were not arranged in accordance with any predetermined plan. North of the Thames, Euston was constructed in 1837, with two platforms and four tracks, the platforms being 126 m long; it was followed by Paddington (1838), King's Cross (1852), St Pancras (1868), Liverpool Street (1874), and Marylebone (1899). Still north of the Thames, but serving the south of London, four other railway stations were

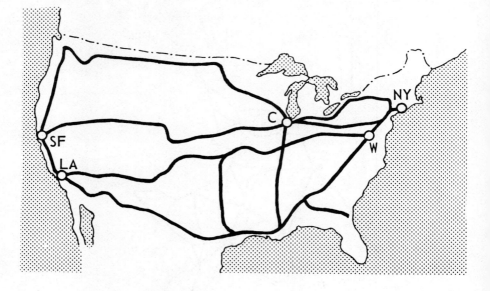

Figure 1.7 U.S. railways. NY New York, W Washington, C Chicago, LA Los Angeles, SF San Francisco

constructed: Victoria (1860), Charing Cross (1864), Cannon Street (1866) and Blackfriars (1864). South of the Thames there were two—Waterloo (1848) and London Bridge (1836). In 1966, the new Euston Station was completed with 20 platform tracks, the longest platform being 390 m. The first signal cabin at Euston, no. 1 box (1870), had 20 levers; no. 2 (1891) had 288 levers, mechanically operated; from 1906 it was electro-mechanical, and in 1952 a new box with 227 levers, all electrically operated, was opened. (Some 60 point levers and 130 signal levers.) Finally, in 1965 train describer equipment was introduced, allowing two signalmen to set up 755 routes.[15, 16]

Liverpool Street has been the station with the heaviest traffic; already by 1900 the number of journeys per year was 65 million (20 million season tickets, short distance); Waterloo, London Bridge, Victoria, Broad Street and Fenchurch Street had 30 million each (10 million seasons); King's Cross, Cannon Street and Blackfriars 15 million each (8 million seasons); Charing Cross, St Pancras and Paddington 10 million each (3 million seasons); Euston 5.4 million (2 million seasons) and Marylebone 500 000.

The number of trains arriving daily was: Liverpool Street 416 (380 suburban), Victoria 370 (306 suburban), Waterloo and London Bridge 293 (243 suburban), Charing Cross 187 (152 suburban), King's Cross and

Paddington 100 (40 suburban), St Pancras and Euston 78 (40 suburban), and Marylebone 13. In 1968, Liverpool Street had 200 000 daily passengers and 1000 trains in and out, that is 27 000 arriving passengers and 56 arriving trains per hour during peak periods. Waterloo, Victoria and London Bridge had nearly the same. Charing Cross had 120 000 daily passengers and 700 trains, that is 14 000 arriving passengers and 24 arriving trains per hour during peak periods; King's Cross and Paddington had 40 000 daily passengers and 300 trains; Euston and St Pancras had 30 000 daily passengers and 200 trains.

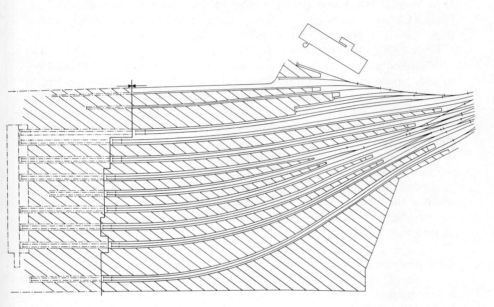

Figure 1.8 Euston Station, London

The Gare St Lazare in Paris handles approximately twice the Liverpool Street Station traffic on 26 platforms; the same goes for Pennsylvania Station in New York, with 21 platforms.

The establishment of railway stations in London caused great disruption: the St Pancras construction involved the demolition of 4000 houses. Between 1859 and 1867 some 36 000 London citizens were moved from their homes because of railway construction.

In 1845 18 per cent of railway passengers travelled 3rd class, compared with 1912 when the figure was 95 per cent. The price was then 1d per mile (2nd class cost 2d per mile). Wath's marshalling yard in London handled 7000 wagons of freight per day in 1910.

In 1850 the investments in railways in Great Britain were £40 million, or 25 per cent of total investments in Great Britain. Some 250 000 workers were employed on railway construction, and 1 million tons of coal were used for railway operations, or 2 per cent of total production.

The Birmingham – Manchester railway cost more than £23 000 per mile to build; London – Birmingham £50 000, and London – Brighton £60 000 a mile, and yet they brought in 6–10 per cent returns.

Three months after the opening of the London – Birmingham railway in 1838, regular coach services were reduced from twenty-two a day to four. From 1830 to 1850 the revenue from toll-roads in England dropped by one-third. The road became a feeder for the railway.

From 1870 to 1912 the railway traffic in Great Britain increased from 300 to 1300 million passengers, and freight from 200 to 500 million tons. From 1912 to 1940 railway traffic in Great Britain increased to 1800 million passengers only, because of competition from motor vehicles. By 1968 it had dropped to 800 million passengers. The freight traffic decreased to 300 million tons in 1940, and 200 million in 1968. British Railways deficit was £100 million in 1962.

In 1930 the railway traffic along the Rhine river in Germany, one of the world's most heavily used lines, was 15 000 passengers per day, both directions together. Munich, Frankfurt am Main and Cologne railway stations had 20 000 passengers per day in long distance traffic; Pennsylvania Station, New York, had 14 000. New York railways handled 80 million tons of freight in 1930.

1.2.2 Sea and Air Transport

Sea Transport
In 1492 Columbus's caravels, driven by wind, made the Atlantic crossing in 69 days, averaging 4 knots. A caravel weighed approximately 100 tons and had the following approximate dimensions: length 25 m, width 8 m and draught 2–3 m. It was the first full-rigged ship, with three masts, having large square sails on the foremast and mainmast, a lateen sail set on the mizzen, and a spritsail set forward of the stem. There were two sails on each mast, a large mainsail, and a smaller topsail. Guns aboard ship led to high ends, forecastle and aftercastle. During the seventeenth and eighteenth centuries, ships grew larger; the galleon of about 1200 tons was 70 m long with several square sails on each mast; ships of the line could make 8 knots. About 1840 the American T clipper ship sailed at 18 knots, with an extensive sail area and large crew of 100 men.

In 1807 Fulton drove his 40 m long, steam-driven vessel *Clermont* up the river Hudson from New York to Albany, a 240 km trip in 32 hours, about one-third the average time of sailing craft.

In 1838 a British side-wheeler, the 1300 ton *Great Western* crossed the Atlantic in 14 days; it was a sail — steamship made of wood. In 1870, an iron steam ship, the *Oceanic* (120 m long and weighing 3800 tons), crossed the Atlantic in 9 days, not faster than the clippers, but with 3000 h.p. In 1907 a steel, screw-driven, steam turbine ship, the *Mauretania* (240 m long), crossed the Atlantic in $4\frac{1}{2}$ days. Its engines produced 70 000 h.p. It weighed 32 000 tons, and carried 2300 passengers and 800 officers and crew; it had a speed of 25 knots, and was completely reliable in all seas and weather.

Cargo ships have developed rapidly. There are three main types: general cargo liners, bulk cargo ships and tankers. A general cargo liner can average 20 000—30 000 deadweight tons* and 10 000 G.R.T., be 140 m long, 20 m wide and draw 8 m, with 72 000 h.p. engine(s) giving a speed of 24 knots; the number of containers ($6 \times 2.4 \times 2.4$ m) carried can be 1200 (10 tons each).

A bulk cargo ship, for dry cargo, can be 40 000 D.W.T. and 25 000 G.R.T, 200 m long, 30 m wide, draw 11 m and have a speed of 16 knots. A tanker can be 100 000 D.W.T. and 60 000 G.R.T., 300 m long, 40 m wide, draw 14 m, have a speed of 16 knots and carry a crew of 30—40 men. River boats can be 20 m, 40 m or 80 m long, 4 to 8 m wide, and draw 2 m; they can carry up to 1500 tons.

After the decline of the Spanish empire the Netherlands dominated world shipping around 1600 with approximately 16 000 galleons. In 1840, the world merchant fleet amounted to 9 million G.R.T.; 33 per cent of the ships were British, and all were sailing ships. In 1900, the world merchant fleet had grown to 40 000 ships (of more than 100 G.R.T.) with a total of 30 million G.R.T.; still 33 per cent were British, but only 23 per cent of the total were sailing ships. In 1920, 1940 and 1967 the tonnage was 60, 70, and 180 million G.R.T. respectively, but the number of ships was still 40 000. In 1975 only 10 per cent of the ships were British, and all ships were steam and diesel driven. About 11 000 ships were cargo liners, 2000 were dry bulk ships, 4000 were tankers (if we look at ships of more than 1000 G.R.T.) and only 1000 were passenger ships.

Liberia, Great Britain, the United States and Norway dominate with about 20 million G.R.T. each, and with from 100 000 to 50 000 employed each (*cf.* the railways). The number of river barges in France is 10 000; in Germany there are 8000 and in Belgium 6000.

The discovery of America and of the route to India round the Cape of Good Hope at the end of the fifteenth century had far-reaching effects on world trade and ports.

---

* Gross Register Tons (1G.R.T. = 100 foot^3 = 2.83 m^3) give the total volume of the ship. Deadweight Tons are measured in imperial tons and give the cargo weight of the ship.

In 1553 the North-east Passage from London to Moscow was opened, and a Russian company formed. There were also companies such as the Turkey company, the African company, and the Virginia company. In 1601 the East India Company was formed; in 1668 came the Hudson's Bay Company, and in 1799 the West India Company.

The first sea chart printed as a separate sheet for use aboard ship was published in Venice in 1539. The navigating instruments, such as the clock, magnetic compass, and later the sextant helped ships to navigate the sea routes. The trip from Amsterdam to Leghorn (Livorno) took 5–12 weeks. Dutch and English traders went to the Far East (Indonesia) via the Cape route for spices.

By the end of the sixteenth century European merchant ships were carrying goods across the Atlantic, the Indian Ocean, and in small quantities across the Pacific. The two main routes were from Lisbon to India and from Seville to the West Indies. Goa was the chief oriental base on the Malabar coast of India; however, because of monsoons for three winter months, ships could seldom approach Goa, and for three summer months they could seldom leave it. Ships left Lisbon in March for arrival at Goa in September. They left Goa in January – February to reach Lisbon in August.

The caravels, of not more than 200 tons, sailed from Seville via the Canary Islands to Vera Cruz. The average annual tonnage increased from 10 000 tons in 1540 to 20 000 tons in 1580, representing about one-tenth of the total Spanish shipping capacity.

In 1593, of a total of 220 ships arriving at Leghorn, 73 brought grain; of these, 34 belonged to Hanseatic towns (Hamburg and Danzig), 12 were Dutch, 7 English, 4 Flemish, 2 Norwegian, and 1 came from Riga. At that time 60 ships used Seville each year.

In 1563, 7 ships were driven ashore at Nombre de Dios (Puerto Bello), 15 were wrecked in Cadiz, and 5 were lost in Campeche. From 1560 most shipping for the Indies sailed in convoy, escorted by 2 – 8 armed galleons. The heaviest losses occurred between 1620 and 1623 when of 34 ships sailing from Lisbon to Goa, 8 were wrecked, 2 captured, and 9 forced to return to harbour. Between 1550 and 1650 the total number of losses was not less than 100 ships. The earlier proportion of disasters was 1 : 8 and later 1 : 5.

Between 1630 and 1643 £200 000 was spent in conveying 20 000 British emigrants to New England in 200 ships and 40 000 emigrants to Virginia.

English merchant shipping increased from 90 000 tons in 1663 to 178 000 in 1688 and 261 000 in 1701, of which in 1688 about 28 000 tons were employed on the America trade routes. For comparison the Dutch shipping in that year amounted to 570 000 tons, of which 40 000 tons went to America.

The branch of American trade belonging especially to Liverpool was the slave trade, which was closely connected with the cotton manufacturing industry of Lancashire. In 1771, 58 slave ships sailed via London, 23 via Bristol, and 107 via Liverpool; they transported 50 000 slaves in that year.

The Spanish settlement of Manila became a principal market for the merchants of Macao, who sold Canton silk for American silver. The trans-Pacific trade had its Mexican terminal harbour in Acapulco. From Acapulco to Manila was a trade run of about 10 weeks; the return took from 4 to 7 months. Ships of 300 tons made two trips per year. Silk landed at Acapulco was packed across Mexico and re-exported from Vera Cruz to Spain or to Peru.

In 1597, the amount of bullion sent from Peru to Manila reached a value of 12 million pesos, a figure approaching the total value of the official transatlantic trade.[25]

In coastal waters piloting was improved by buoys, lighthouses, and so on. In 1863, the international rules of the sea were adopted. The width of sailing routes in heavily used waters was normally 8 nautical miles. The lengths of routes were shortened by the construction of sea canals. The Suez Canal, opened in 1869, shortened distances from Europe to India by almost 50 per cent. The North-east Sea Canal was constructed in 1896; the Panama Canal opened in 1914, and the St Lawrence seaway in 1956, with lengths of 100 – 200 km. The main routes from Europe to East America are now about 6000 km, Europe to South East America is 10 000 km, Europe to East Africa 12 000 km, and Europe to India 15 000 km, the same as the distance from Europe to the Western United States. Europe to eastern Asia is 20 000 km, the same as the distance from Europe to Australia. Today Rotterdam to Yokohama takes 40 days via the Panama Canal by conventional cargo liner, or 27 days by container ship.

Inland navigation is possible on rivers and on man-made canals. The invention of the pound lock made possible the development of large-scale canal systems, because it provided a means of changing the water level. The limiting factor in canal gauge is normally the size of the locks. Different vessels are used: narrow boats, barges, lighters, and tugs.

In Britain the connection between the Thames and the Severn was constructed in the eighteenth century; this was the Thames and Severn Canal, and the Kennet and Avon Canal from Newbury to Bath, in the east – west direction. The Oxford Canal and the Grand Union Canal connect the Thames with Birmingham and the North. From the river Trent, the route to Birmingham is by way of the Trent and Mersey Canal and the Coventry Canal. Thus Liverpool is connected with Birmingham, Bristol and London. From Birmingham to the Mersey there is also the Shropshire Union Canal. The British inland waterway system dates from 1761 when the Duke of Bridgewater opened the canal to carry coal from his mines at Worsley to Manchester where it was sold. The Bridgewater Canal was constructed by an

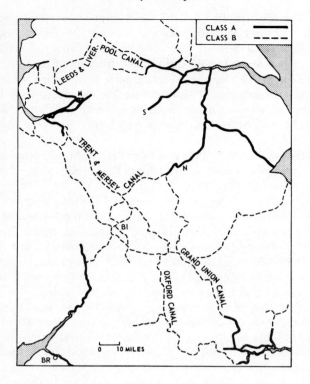

Figure 1.9 Inland navigation in Great Britain. L London, Bi Birmingham, Br Bristol, N Nottingham, S Sheffield, M Manchester

engineer named Brindley. The Manchester ship canal was opened in 1894, thus connecting Manchester and Liverpool. The Leeds – Liverpool Canal connects Liverpool with Leeds and Hull, through the Aire and Calder Navigation to the river Ouse. The Lancaster Canal was built to connect the Ouse to the Nene. In about 1850, there were 2000 km of navigable rivers and 4000 km of navigable canals in Britain. The railways took over inland transport after an inland waterway era lasting 100 years.

In China and the United States great canal systems were developed. The Erie Canal connecting Lake Erie with the Hudson river, was 500 km long and constructed in 1825. In 1833 the Ohio – Erie Canal was opened. In Europe the main rivers, the Rhine, Rhone and Danube are being connected by canals.

As during the fifteenth century ships grew larger, and the number of ships in ports therefore increased, the original medieval ports were extended beyond the old quay limits, first as a linear extension. Because of the great developments that took place during the reign of Elizabeth I, the Port of London was far ahead of other ports in 1560–80. Therefore, a quay elaboration, where large cuts are made in the river bank or jetties are extended into the water, was necessary (Billingsgate). The 20 legal quays in the Port of London were all situated on the north side of the river below London Bridge, stretching downstream as far as the Tower, with a total length of 450 m. To relieve congestion, sufferance wharves were introduced elsewhere on the river. The larger vessels of the East India company of 1612 anchored off Blackwall, and had their cargoes transferred to the legal quays by means of covered barges. [13,18]

About 1700 the value of London's foreign trade was approximately £10 million; in 1800 this had increased to £27 million; and in 1960 to £2700 million. The increasing trade in the eighteenth century produced overcrowding in the river and at the quays and wharves. It is recorded that 775 vessels were allowed to moor in the Upper Pool where there was only sufficient space for 545. As well as these ships there were 300 barges. Ships had to go wherever there was an empty berth and often they had to wait a week before loading and unloading. In 1802 new enclosed docks and warehouses, the West India Docks, were opened to restore order in the port.

The fourth era, the docks development of the Port of London began with tidal basins. The number of ships handled per year was 2800 in about the year 1700, and 5600 in about 1800; this had increased to 60 000 by 1960.

The advantages of docks lay in their speed of discharge, cutting by half the average time of 30 days, and in their security against theft. The tonnage of vessels moving inwards and outwards was approximately 10 million Net Register Tons (N.R.T.)* in 1870; in 1910 the figure was 20 million N.R.T., and in 1960 40 million N.R.T. This called for dredging of the river.

Within London's five dock systems, London and St Katharine, Surrey, India, Victoria, Albert and George V, and Tilbury docks there are 200 berths and a total of 35 miles of quay.† The Royal docks entrance locks, for example, can accommodate vessels up to 25 000 GRT, the water depths are 12 m, and they are served by rail with a marshalling yard with capacity for 1200 wagons. London's tug and barge fleet had decreased from 9000 to 6700 in the period 1936–60, because of truck traffic taking over small parcel traffic. Still the royal docks had a barge entering traffic of 27 000 barges per year in 1960. The number of port or dock workers was about 27 000 in 1960. In 1921 the fifth era, of simple linear quays, was introduced to London with the inauguration

---

* N.R.T. = cargo volume
† £ 150 million (at 1900 prices) were invested in the docks and harbours of Great Britain between 1860 and 1914.

of the 240 m long George V entrance lock. Specialised facilities, such as oil and container traffic installations, have now been provided. The tonnage of goods handled had increased from 2 million tons in 1820, 8 million in 1870 and 20 million in 1901 to 40 million in 1940, and 55 and 65 million in 1960 and 1970.

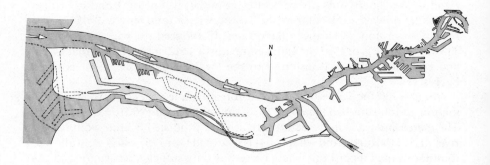

Figure 1.10 The port of Rotterdam, the old harbour is to the east

The Port of London is the biggest port in Europe after Rotterdam, where the number of tons of freight had increased from 40 million in 1940, to 75 and 150 million in 1960 and 1970, because of the size of the hinterland. However, 50 per cent of Rotterdam's freight is transit freight; 40 per cent of the total traffic is oil, 50 per cent other bulk freight, and only 10 per cent general cargo. New York Port and the Tokyo – Yokohama – Chiba Port system each handled 100 million tons of freight in 1960: Antwerp and Marseilles each reached 60 million in 1967.

This remarkable growth in harbour transport must be judged from the trade evolution in the world during the past 500 years. International trade freight handling by ship alone has increased from approximately 10 million tons in 1800, to 160 million tons in 1860 and 1500 million tons today. Of 1500 million tons of ship-borne freight, 1000 million is oil transport, 100 million coal, 50 million iron/steel and 20 million wheat.

Very heavy traffic is found in the English Channel, about 200 million tons per year. In the Suez Canal the traffic grew in the period 1930 to 1966 from 28 million tons and 5000 vessels to 240 million tons and 21 000 vessels. In the Panama Canal the figures were, for the same years, 28 million tons and 4000 vessels increasing to 80 million tons and 12 000 vessels, mostly the same as the Atlantic traffic. In the North-east Sea Canal (Kiel) the figures were, for the same years, 20 million tons and 60 000 vessels increasing to 60 million tons and 96 000 vessels. Shipping in the English Channel amounted to approximately

300 000 vessels in 1965, whereas Øresund and Great Belt in Denmark had 60 000 and 20 000 vessels, respectively, in the same year.

In 1930, the number of passengers carried by ship between Europe and the United States was 3500 per day; in 1957 1 million passengers sailed, and 1 million used aircraft. In 1930 45 million tons of freight were transported between Europe and the United States. Today this traffic is 80 million tons.

Coal carried on inland waters was not taxed, unlike the coal carried by sea. So coal cost only 5 shillings per chaldron (36 bushels) at the Tyne in about 1800, 30 shillings in London, and less in the Midlands. On Tyneside, wooden rails were used to run the trucks down to the river for loading; some 20 000 horses were employed in the transport of coal in the environs of Newcastle alone.

The cost of carriage on canals was from a quarter to a half of the cost by road. In 1825 the Trent and Mersey Canal yielded 75 per cent, the Mersey and Irwell 35 per cent, and the Leeds and Liverpool 16 per cent. A total capital of £13 million was used for canal construction in Great Britain.

A bitter struggle developed between railways and ships for internal traffic. The Trent and Mersey saw its dividend drop from 75 to 32 per cent between 1825 and 1839. The water traffic from Hamburg to Berlin dropped by two-thirds when the railway was opened. The river traffic from Cologne to Holland was only half of the railway traffic from Cologne to Antwerp.

From 1850 to 1870 traffic on the Rhineland railways increased almost twentyfold, while navigation on the Rhine increased only by a factor of three and a half.

In about 1850, transporting 1 ton of freight by canal cost 2d per mile. In 1908, more than half of the 4600 miles of canals in the United States had been abandoned. In 1900 the carriage of a bushel of wheat between Chicago and New York cost 4.42 cents by the lakes and 10 cents by train.

River traffic on the Rhine is very important for European inland waterways. At Koblenz 150 000 barges pass every year, and at the Germany – Netherlands border the freight traffic has grown from 50 million tons in 1930 to 90 million tons today. Traffic through the river port at Duisburg has decreased from 30 million tons in 1930 to 16 million tons today.

In 1914 maritime and land transport were in a state of equilibrium. The psychological shock and the material effects of steamers and railways had been assimilated. The Eastern United States and Western Europe were sectors with an excess of transport; they were over-equipped. In other sectors transport facilities were still not adequate to the needs of traffic, for example India. Still other sectors, for example China, were untouched by the revolution in transport.

Pipelines
The first pipelines were feeder lines to the oil ports in the United States. In 1865 the first line was opened in Pennsylvania. The first pumping line was constructed from Coreysville to Williamsport in 1879. In 1928 the pipelines were constructed from steel for high pressure work. In North Africa the first pipeline from the oil areas to Tripoli was introduced in 1934.

After the Second World War, in 1953, a 240 km pipeline was the first to be opened in Europe; it ran from Le Havre to Paris (diameter 25 cm) (a total of 12 parallel lines by 1970). Today 300 million tons of oil are transported through 13 000 km of pipelines in Europe, the products being both crude and refined oil.

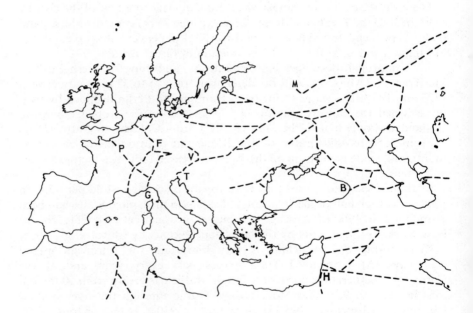

Figure 1.11 The European pipeline network. P Paris, F Frankfurt, G Geneva, T Trieste, V Vienna, B Baku, H Haifa, M Moscow

In the United States, 500 million tons of crude oil and 150 million tons of refined oil were transported through a 225 000 km network in 1957. In 1958 a 390 km pipeline was opened from Wilhelmshafen to Cologne (diameter 71 cm) carrying 22 million tons per year. In 1960 a 300 km pipeline was opened from Rotterdam to Frankfurt (diameter 61 cm) carrying 20 million tons per year. In

1962 a 780 km pipeline was constructed from Marseilles to Karlsruhe (diameter 86 cm) carrying 30 million tons per year; in 1964 this line was extended to Ingolstadt. In 1966 a 1000 km pipeline was constructed from Genoa to Ingolstadt (diameter 66 cm) carrying 18 million tons per year. In 1968 a 460 km pipeline was opened from Trieste to Ingolstadt (diameter 100 cm) carrying 54 million tons per year.

In England there is a pipeline from Liverpool to London; in Belgium, from Antwerp to Brussels, and in Spain, from Malaga to Madrid. For capacities of more than 6 million tons per year, pipelines can compete with inland water transport, for capacities of more than 20 million tons per year they also compete with smaller tankers.

Air Transport
One of the first propeller-driven aircraft in scheduled service, the Fokker F VII, had only one engine and carried 10 passengers when introduced in 1929. But by 1933 the three-engined Fokker F XII had been introduced with accommodation for 20 passengers. Table 1.1 gives data for some important aircraft produced between 1930 and 1970.

A bigger American supersonic aircraft should have a flying speed of 2900 km/h. Pegasus, an American rocket-driven aircraft is under consideration, with a flying speed of 12 000 km/h, being developed from the space programme; the flying height should be 100 km, and the start ramp 20×20 m.

The number of aircraft in the world increased from 100 000 and 4000 air carriers in 1956 to 160 000 and 7000 air carriers in 1970. In the latter year the number of airline companies was 180 with 800 000 employees. The big companies are Pan American Airways (formed in 1927) with 130 aircraft and 30 000 employees; British Airways Corporation, formerly BOAC and BEA (1939, 1946), with 140 aircraft and 40 000 employees; Air France (1933) with 90 aircraft and 14 000 employees: Lufthansa (1926) with 70 aircraft and 17 000 employees; KLM (1919) with 40 aircraft and 14 000 employees. Of other companies one should note Transworld Airways and United Airways in the United States (1930, 1931) with 120 and 300 aircraft and 35 000 and 42 000 employees, respectively, and the U.S.S.R.'s Aeroflot (1923) with 2000 aircraft and 400 000 employees.

In 1919 Alcock and Brown flew across the Atantic in an aircraft in 16 hours, and the London – Paris, London – Brussels and Amsterdam air routes began. In 1929 Imperial Airways opened a route from Genoa via Cairo, Baghdad, Karachi to Delhi, called the India Service. In 1932 a route from London to Cape Town was started, the African Service, travelling via Paris, Athens, Alexandria, Nairobi and Johannesburg, a total of 8000 miles in 11 days. In the same year Air France opened a route from Paris to Hanoi; 15 000 km in 5 days. This route had been flown by KLM since 1930. In 1934 the Imperial

TABLE 1.1 Specifications for some important aircraft built between 1930 and 1970

Aircraft	Date	Engines			Length (m)	Wing span (m)	Weight (tons)		Cruising speed (km/h)	Cruising altitude (km)	Maximum range (km)	Runway length (m)	Passengers
		No.	Type	Power			Unladen	Laden					
DC3	1930s	2	Prop.	2×1200 hp	20	30	8	12	300	2	2000	1200	30
DC6	1940s	4	Prop.	4×2500 hp	30	36	24	48	500	4	8000	1800	80
DC8	1958	4	Jet	4×6300 kg†	50	45	65	150	900	9	14000	2600	150
DC10	1970s	3	Jet	3×18100 kg	70	60	150	360	900	10	18000	3000	400
Concorde	1970s	2	Jet	4×17000 kg	60	20*	60	150	2300	18	8000	3000	150

* Delta wing

† Output of jet engines measured in kg thrust

Airways' India Service was extended to Sydney, a total route of 18 000 km.

In 1936, Air France started a service over the South Atlantic from Paris to Santiago, 15 000 km in 5 days, via Dakar – Natal (3000 km), the effective flying time being 65 hours. In the United States three companies served the main route from New York to San Francisco (4000 km).

In 1938 PAA opened the Pacific route San Francisco – Hong Kong via Hawaii and the Philippines (15 000 km) and the Atlantic route Lisbon – New York via the Azores and Bermuda, served by flying boats.

By 1938 Air France, Imperial Airways, KLM, and Lufthansa had networks of approximately 40 000 km each, and U.S. companies had 120 000 km.

Already by 1930 there were 140 airports in Europe and 150 in the United States. In 1954 there were 166 and 523. The number of airfields for private use was much greater; approximately 7000 in the United States in 1954, of which 3000 were controlled by the Federal Aviation Agency (F.A.A.), and 1000 were equipped with lighting and paved runways. Of these 150 were on important air traffic routes, 20 serving big cities, 40 serving provincial towns and 90 serving smaller towns. In Western Europe the 25 most important airports take 75 per cent of all air transport.

London's first airport was opened in Hounslow in 1919. A year later the traffic was moved to Croydon, a 1600-yard long grass aerodrome. In 1946 a military airfield, Northolt, with concrete runways was used together with Heathrow (1954) as the main international airport for London. At that time Blackbushe, Bovingdon, Croydon, Gatwick and Stansted also existed as airfields.

Heathrow, planned as a military airfield, was to have three runways arranged in a triangular pattern, with the main runway aligned east – west, and the other two S.W. – N.E. and S.E. – N.W. The runway layout as it now stands at Heathrow consists of three pairs of parallel runways, or one triangle reversed over another, but the central section of two of the runways has been withdrawn to leave four operative runways. In 1951 a new airport to relieve Heathrow was chosen; this was Gatwick, which was opened in 1958.

In the 1960s the discussion about a third airport for London arose. In 1971 a decision was taken to construct a new airport at Foulness instead of the alternatives: Cublington, Nuthampstead, Thurleigh and Stansted. This plan has since been cancelled.

From 1954 to 1970 traffic increased at Heathrow from 110 000 operations (85 000 scheduled) to 362 000 (262 000 scheduled), and the number of passengers from 2 million to 14 million; Gatwick had 5 million passengers in 1970.

Paris has two airports with intense traffic. Le Bourget which was opened in 1919 had 40 000 operations and 500 000 passengers in 1954; in 1975 it had 4 million passengers. Orly was opened in 1946 and had 50 000 operations and 1

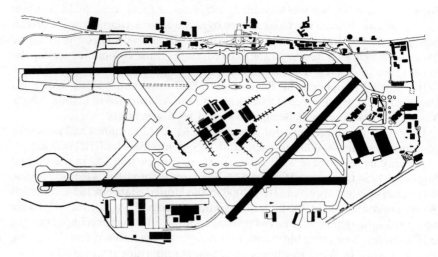

Figure 1.12 Heathrow Airport, London

million passengers by 1954; in 1975 the figures were 280 000 operations and 9 million passengers. A new third airport was opened (1973) at Roissy (The Charles de Gaulle airport).

New York had one airport in 1919, Hadley Field. In 1929 Newark was opened; in 1939 La Guardia, and in 1949 Idlewild, now known as Kennedy Airport. A fifth airport has been discussed for more than 10 years, but no decision has been taken, although the traffic has increased from 500 000 operations and 9 million passengers in 1954 to 1 million operations and 40 million passengers in 1970. Of these 40 million passengers, Kennedy takes 20 million.

Chicago had its first airport, Meigs Field in 1919. In 1927 Midway Airport was opened, and in 1956 that airport was relieved by O'Hare Airport (the airport with the most traffic handling in the world), 38 million passengers in 1974 and 700 000 operations with three parallel runways.

Los Angeles International Airport which was opened in 1927 had 20 million passengers in 1970 and 600 000 operations. Other airports near Los Angeles are Burbank, Long Beach and Ontario. A new airport in Palmdale has been discussed.[19]

It can be seen that the development in speed has been remarkable: the Atlantic crossing took 16 hours in 1919 (Alcock and Brown), 8 hours in 1959 (DC8), 4 hours in 1976 (Concorde), this will possibly be reduced to 2 hours by the U.S. supersonic aircraft, decreasing to half an hour by the proposed U.S. rocket.

The size of aircraft has grown in the same way: from 2 persons in 1919, to 200 persons in 1959, 400 persons in 1969, up to perhaps 800 persons in the future. These factors also influence airport runway lengths, noise and energy consumption. One DC8 uses approximately 7000 litres of fuel per hour.

Domestic routes had been established in Great Britain in the 1930s. From 1932 to 1938 the route mileage increased from 1000 to 5000, and the number of passengers carried from 3000 to 150 000. In 1938, the number of companies was 16 and the number of services was a maximum of 76 in 1935. The use of unsuitable aircraft, adverse climatic conditions, unsuitable airfields and inadequate ground organisation and navigational aids made punctual, all-weather day and night services impractical.

After the war, jet aircraft and navigational radar were important factors in increasing the number of air passengers carried by British airlines from 2 million in 1938 to 7 million in 1961. The number of domestic passengers in the United States had grown from 58 million in 1961 to 134 million in 1967.

After the Second World War an international civil aviation organisation, I.C.A.O., was started. I.C.A.O. co-ordinates all air navigation in the world. From 1950 to 1970 air traffic throughout the world increased from 30 to 300 million passengers; traffic on international routes increased from 7 to 75 million passengers. The budget of the airlines increased during 1960–70 from $5000 million to $18 000 million.

In 1967 there were 78 air route departures per day London – Paris, 55 Paris – Rome, 51 Buenos-Aires –Montevideo, 44 Copenhagen – Stockholm, 41 London – Frankfurt and 40 London – New York.

However, travel from airport to city centre and vice versa is still a weak point in aviation; it decreases the travel speed severely. The London – Paris (340 km) journey was done in 1921 at an average speed of 75 km/h; in 1950 this had only increased to 100 km/h, even though the aircraft speed had risen from 120 to 240 km/h. Even today, 60 per cent of the travel time is access and egress time. From London to New York (5600 km) this ground time amounts to 20 per cent of the total travel time.

1.3 Transport Systems

1.3.1 The Intercontinental Network

This network serves the whole world, an area of approximately 50 million km^2, with about 3000 million inhabitants. We can define 10 functional regions (nodes): Europe, N.E. America, N.W., S.E. and S.W. America, Australia, Africa, and East, South and Central Asia, connected by 15 links (see figure 1.13). In this network with link distances of approximately 13 000 km the passenger traffic is now mainly served by air, involving about 30 million journeys per year (0.6 journeys per inhabitant per year), 20 million journeys

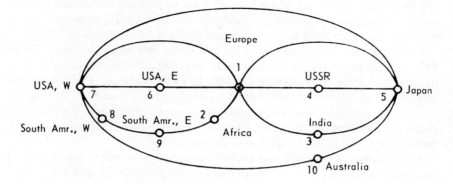

Figure 1.13 The intercontinental network

traversing Europe and 7 million journeys traversing the link Europe – N.E. America.

Frequencies vary very much according to the travel demand. By air London – New York had 40 connections per day in 1967, Paris – New York 20, Rome – New York 20, Frankfurt – New York 10, Amsterdam – New York 10, Tokyo – Honolulu 10, Tokyo – Seattle 10, New York – Los Angeles 50.

Fares between Paris and New York vary according to season, class, etc., from $200 to $300 for a single trip.

New York's international Kennedy Airport and London's Heathrow each have already about 20 million passengers per year. If these airports are not relieved of continental and domestic traffic by the railways, it will be difficult to handle the intercontinental traffic. Several airports in the systems' corridors should be used and passengers conveyed between airports and city centres by high-speed railways.

In 1975 the number of domestic passengers using Kennedy Airport was at the rate of 10 million passengers per year, whereas the number of domestic passengers using Heathrow was 3 million, with the London – Paris route handling about 7 million passengers per year.

World tourism amounts to approximately $10 000 million per year, distributed as shown in table 1.2 together with the national income per inhabitant. The transport budget was, on average, $360 per inhabitant per year in the United States, but only $100 in Europe.

The number of tourists per year had grown from 75 million in 1958 to 145 million in 1965, of which the countries mentioned below had 60 per cent.

The countries most visited are Spain and Italy (table 1.2). In 1980 the

number of visitors per year will be about 300 million, spending around
$30 000 million.

TABLE 1.2   World tourism and world trade

	1970 Income per inhabitant	1975 Income per inhabitant	1970 Tourist travel Number of tourists (millions)		1970 Trade import
	$	$	From	To	($1000 million)
United States	4700	6595	22	25	48
W. Germany	2500	6215	22	10	29
Great Britain	2000	3385	8	10	24
Canada	3500		7	25	16
France	2800	5390	10	10	16
Japan	1500	4115		4	14
Italy	1700	2700	3	21	12
Netherlands	2200		4⎱	10	12
Belgium	2200		4⎰		8
Sweden	3500	6840	2⎱	10	6
Switzerland	3000	7270	2⎰		5
Spain	700	2075		21	4
Denmark	2800	6800	2⎱	10	4
Norway	2200		⎰		4
Iran		1275			

TABLE 1.3   Intercontinental air passenger traffic (scheduled) 1970

From London to	× 1000
N. Africa	150
E.W.C. Africa	140
S. Africa	90
Middle East	170
India	90
Japan	80
S. Asia	50
Australia	140
Canada	380
United States	1250
C. America	100
S. America	50

World trade amounts to about $200 000 million per year, distributed as
shown in table 1.2. Freight traffic is mainly served by sea; approximately 1500
million tons of freight per year (0.5 tons per inhabitant per year): 1100 million
tons is fuel. Tables 1.3 and 1.4 give world air travel and world oil trade,
respectively.

TABLE 1.4 Oil traffic in 1968 (million tons)

To	U.S.A.	W. Europe	Japan
From			
S. America	86	39	4
Africa	7	159	—
Middle East	13	253	132
U.S.S.R.	—	45	2

Ships versus or combined with Rail Freight Transport Europe — Far East

Enormous transport growth, containerisation and the closing of the Suez Canal collectively provided a new impetus towards a 'land bridge' operation.

Take, for example, a route between the Far East and Europe. A typical time for movement of cargo from Yokohama to Rotterdam via the Panama Canal would be 40 days handled by bulk ships, 27 days handled by container ships and 23 days handled by container ships on the Pacific and Atlantic routes and unit trains across the United States.

The shortest land route would be the Trans-Siberian Railway; the question is whether this route will physically be able to handle a sustained movement with its existing operating scheme and capacity. Schedule reliability during severe winters presents another very real problem.

During 1966, 3 million tons were exported through ports on the Pacific Coast of the United States to the Far East in liners. It is estimated that 1.5 million tons could be containerised; in the reverse direction, the absolute volume of freight traffic is considerably less, but it is estimated that 1.5 million tons could be containerised. Between New York and Europe a similar pattern has developed. Half a million tons a year is transported to the Orient from Europe. Using a unit train price of $144 000 per round trip from San Francisco to New York, based on an 80-wagon train capable of handling 320 twenty-foot containers (10 tons) that is, 3200 tons per train, it would take 160 unit trains just to move this 500 000 tons.[20]

1.3.2 European Network

This network serves an area of about 5 million km^2 with about 300 million inhabitants. One can define 10 functional regions (nodes): Great Britain, France, Spain, Italy, W. Germany, Austria, Switzerland, Belgium, Netherlands and Scandinavia, connected by 15 links (see figure 1.14). In this network with link distances of approximately 500–1000 km, both passenger and freight traffic are served by different modes:

Sea—10 million passengers per year   200 million tons (+100 million tons via inland waterways)

Rail—15 million passengers per year   300 million tons
Road—40 million passengers per year   300 million tons
Air—15 million passengers per year
Pipeline—100 million tons
(This is approximately 0.25 journeys per inhabitant per year and 3 tons per inhabitant per year.)

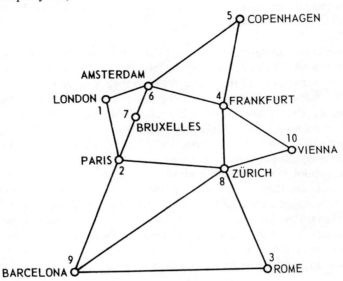

Figure 1.14 The European network

The most heavily used links and modes are for passenger traffic: London – Paris 7 million air passengers per year, London airport 10 million European passengers per year, Frankfurt – Cologne 6 million railway passengers per year, Frankfurt railway station 8 million passengers per year. The Frankfurt – Cologne motorway link carries approximately 6 million passengers per year.

Travel time for Copenhagen – Paris or Copenhagen – Zürich is about 15 –20 hours by rail or road, but only 2 hours by air; Copenhagen to Rome or to Barcelona is approximately 30–35 hours by rail or road, but only 3 hours by air. The rail travel times will diminish with an eventual Channel tunnel* and railway modernisation, for example London – Brussels from 7 to 2 hours, Brussels – Cologne from 2 to 1 hour, Cologne – Hamburg from 4 to 3 hours,

* The project has been postponed indefinitely.

Brussels – Paris from 2 to 1 hour, Paris – Milan from 9 to 6 hours through the Alps, and Milan – Rome from 5 to 3 hours. Cologne – Frankfurt will reduce from 2 to 1 hour, Frankfurt –Munich from 4 to 2 hours, whereas Munich –Vienna will remain at 4 hours.

In the same way frequencies would increase from London to the Continent by the Channel tunnel from 15 departures per day to 30 by land transport, whereas the air departures will be constant or diminish from 80 per day to Paris, 40 to Rhine – Ruhr and Ring City, Netherlands, 30 to Milan and 20 to Munich.

Second class rail fares are about 2 cents per km, for overland travel in Western Europe. When comparing the level of rail fares with that of air fares, it must be borne in mind that the actual distance covered between two given points is generally between 30 and 40 per cent more by rail than by air. The comparable rail fare per km is thus 2.6 cents, as against 6 cents for air travel in tourist or economy class. Including charges in respect of sleeping accommodation and meals on railways, the level of second class rail fares is approximately 50 per cent of the corresponding air fare; for first class rail travel it is about 75 per cent of the air fare in tourist class. As a general rule, car owners estimate their costs on the basis of fuel, running maintenance and repairs (excluding garage, insurance, depreciation and meals and lodging); this gives a cost per km of 2.5 cents, or 50 per cent of the air fare for one person. (This assumes a European car of average cubic capacity on intercity journeys—see chapter 4.) Tables 1.5 and 1.6 show traffic in Europe divided into road, rail and air as well as business, vacation and weekend travellers.

TABLE 1.5 Number of travellers (millions) per direction in 1970 and 2000 divided into road*/rail/air† travelling: more than 100 km per direction

		Germany	Great Britain	Italy	Spain
France	(1970)	5 /1 /0.4	0.7/0.4/1.0	1.9/1 /0.5	1.5/0.7/0.4
	(2000)	8 /3.5/2.6	1.1/1.1/5.8	5 /3.7/2.6	2.9/1.6/2.5
Germany	(1970)		0.3/0.2/0.8	2.6/1.1/0.5	0.8/0.1/1
	(2000)		0.4/0.3/2.2	3.4/2.2/2.2	1 /0.3/4
Great Britain	(1970)			0.2/0.1/0.7	0.8/0.1/1.7
	(2000)			0.3/0.1/2	0.9/0.3/3.8
Italy	(1970)				0.3/0 /0.2
	(2000)				0.5/0.3/0.6

Estimated by O.E.C.D., see chapter 5.
* Including bus traffic.
† Including charter traffic.

TABLE 1.6   Number of travellers (millions) per direction in 1970 and 2000 divided into business/vacation/weekend travelling: more than 100 km per direction.

	Germany	Great Britain	Italy	Spain
France	(1970) 1 /0.9/4.5 (2000) 4.3/0.9/9	0.5/0.9/0.7 2.3/1.3/4.4	0.6/0.9/1.8 2.3/1.5/7.4	0.2/1.5/1.0 1.1/3.0/2.8
Germany		(1970) 0.5/0.6/0.2 (2000) 1.6/0.7/0.6	0.7/2.9/0.7 1.8/4.3/1.7	0.2/1.8/0 0.7/3.1/1.6
Great Britain			(1970) 0.2/0.7/0 (2000) 0.8/0.9/0.8	0.1/2.4/0 0.4/4.2/0.5
Italy				(1970) 0.1/0.3/0 (2000) 0.6/0.7/0.2

Estimated by O.E.C.D., see chapter 5

Number of Private and Business Trips

The GETA study[23] found that the number of trips of more than 200 km per inhabitant per year in Europe was 0.5 (1965), and Lansing[21] found that in the United States the figure was 2 (1962). This indicates that the Americans travel four times as often as Europeans. With increasing wealth in Europe one may expect increasing intercity travel, both business and private.

The percentage of business trips of all trips in Europe was shown to be 38 per cent—in the United States it was 25 per cent. The trips were shared between air and surface systems as indicated in table 1.7.

TABLE 1.7   Number of trips per inhabitant per year for distances greater than 200 km

	Europe (1965)		United States (1962)	
	Business	Private	Business	Private
Air	0.028	0.002	0.088	0.060
Surface	0.120	0.400	0.436	1.440
Total	0.148	0.402	0.524	1.500

The number of trips per year and per inhabitant as a function of travel distance and transport mode for Sweden in 1958 is given in table 1.8 compared to the United States; it is seen that Americans travel 2.5 times as often as Swedes. Americans travelled only half as often as Swedes by public transport.

TABLE 1.8   Number of trips per inhabitant per year in Sweden and the United States (1958)

	Rail		Car		Bus		Air		Total		
> 400 km	0.43		0.20		0.05		0.04		0.72		
200–400	0.38	0.7*	0.76	10*	0.16	1.3*	0.03	0.3*	1.33	2.05	12.3*
100–200	0.59		2.24		0.54		0.02		3.40	5.45	

* U.S. figure

Trip Division by Modes in the United Kingdom and Europe

In the Southampton study[22] a division by modes for business trips was found for the United Kingdom. The investigation comprised 14 000 trips. Similar investigations were made in 1970–71 in other European countries. The study was made for Copenhagen, Cologne, Frankfurt, Zürich and Milan.

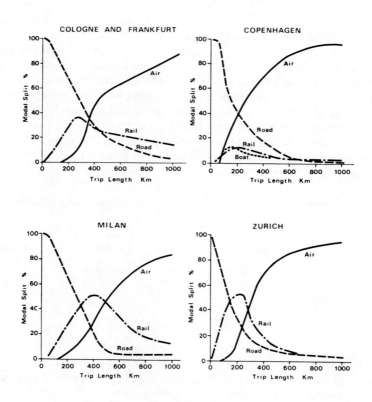

Figure 1.15 Trip distribution by mode for business travellers as a function of distance

In the United Kingdom the following distribution by modes was found for business trips in relation to trip length: these are shown in table 1.9 compared to European results (given in parentheses). The car is used especially for short trips and aircraft for long trips. The mode in relation to duration of journey was also investigated as shown in table 1.10. Here the car is used especially for one-day trips.

TABLE 1.9   U.K. business trip distribution by mode and distance (European figure in parentheses) for 1970.

	< 100 km (%)		100–500 km (%)		> 500 km (%)		Total (%)	
Rail	10	(19)	50	(30)	20	(9)	30	(22)
Road	90	(81)	25	(35)	5	(5)	60	(46)
Air	0	(0)	25	(35)	75	(85)	10	(30)
Total	50	(37)	45	(47)	5	(15)	100	(98)*

Shipping accounts for the other 2 per cent

TABLE 1.10   U.K. business trip distribution by mode and duration (European figure in parentheses) for 1970

	0 night (%)		1 night (%)		2 nights and over (%)		Total (%)	
Rail	14	(9)	7	(5)	9	(7)	30	(20)
Road	40	(34)	7	(7)	13	(9)	60	(50)
Air	4	(6)	3	(7)	3	(15)	10	(28)
Total	58	(50)	17	(19)	25	(31)	100	(98)*

Shipping accounts for the other 2 per cent

It was also asked why businessmen selected the various modes: Table 1.11 shows the results, and indicates that the minimum journey time is a very important point for all modes.

TABLE 1.11   U.K. business trip distribution according to reason for choice (European comparison in parentheses) for 1970

	Minimum Journey time (%)		Convenience of 'termini' (%)		Reliability or economy (%)	
Rail	50	(20)	20	(7)	30	(25)
Road	40	(40)	40	(7)	20	(6)
Air	80	(83)	10	(3)	10	(4)

Businessmen travelling from London were asked which means of transport to the terminal were adopted (see table 1.12). Here car traffic predominates for access to airports.

TABLE 1.12   U.K. business trip distribution according to access mode in London (European comparison in parentheses)

Main mode	Rail (%)	Taxi (%)	Car driver (%)	Car passenger (%)	Bus (%)	Walk (%)
Rail	40	20	15	10	10	5
	(7)	(20)	(19)	(11)	(27)	(15)
Air	10	10	50	20	10	0
	(6)	(23)	(42)	(17)	(9)	(2)

The people travelling were classified by socio-economic group, domestic and international trips, number of trips involved in a journey, purpose of journey, day of start, time of start, and so on. Thursday was the peak day, and peak hours related to the working day.

33 per cent of trips were made for the purpose of education/conference/ exhibition/research
25 per cent of trips were made for the purpose of professional and technical service
30 per cent of trips were made for the purpose of purchasing, marketing
14 per cent of trips were made for the purpose of administration.

Two-thirds of all trips started and finished at the home. Thirty per cent visited the destination city centre. The boundaries of a country did not produce a significant lowering of trips. For a time saving of more than 4 hours the choice of air travel was greater than 90 per cent. The mean value of time for Europe (1970) was £1.20 per hour.

Freight Transport
For freight transport the links with maximum traffic volume are the Rhine and the Channel (100 million tons per year), the Frankfurt — Ruhr railway line (60 million tons per year), as well as the nodes of Rotterdam Port (160 million tons per year) and the goods and marshalling yards in the Ruhr (60 million tons per year).

Other bottlenecks are the cross Channel connections.

In Germany and France the location of industry and natural products has meant that the average hauls have been longer than in other countries and this has favoured the railways. Table 1.13 gives the distribution of freight transport.

TABLE 1.13 Distribution of freight transport by means of transport (percentage of ton km)

Europe (1960)	Inland waterways	Railway	Road
Germany	29	43	28
France	9	60	31
England	—	44	56
Italy	1	28	71
Belgium	27	28	45
Netherlands	64	16	20

TABLE 1.14 Freight transport in Great Britain distributed by means of transport (million tons).

	Inland and coastal	Railway	Road	Pipelines
1960	52	243	1000	2
1973	50	194	1700	53
1973 (Percentage of ton km)	15	18	65	2

Great Britain

Since the 1950s there has been a steady increase in the demand for goods transport. Most of this has been sent by road transport, although a small amount of oil has been carried by pipeline. Rail traffic has declined mainly because of the fall in coal production. (99 million tons of coal + 35 million tons of iron + 60 million tons of other goods.) A major development in goods transport has been the growing use of containers. Table 1.14 gives freight transport distribution. Sea transport was used to transport 154 million tons of tanker cargo, 61 million tons of bulk dry cargo and 60 million tons of other dry cargo. In the Port of London 33 million tons was petroleum, 4 million tons coal and 19 million tons other goods. At London Airport 500 000 tons of freight were handled.

Some examples of freight transport mode distribution to Germany from some other countries are given in table 1.15. Air transport is not included because the percentage is less than one.

TABLE 1.15   Freight transport to Germany—mode distribution (1967)

From	Netherlands		France		Belgium		Italy	
By	million tons	%	million tons	%	million tons	%	million tons	%
Water transport (inland)	33	60	9	22	4	50	0	0
Pipeline	14	25	17	45	0.5	5	6	60
Sea	2	4	1	2	0.5	5	1	10
Rail	2	4	8	21	1	10	2	20
Road	5	7	4	10	2	30	1	10
Total	56	100	39	100	8	100	10	100

1.3.3 The American Network

The number of passenger miles per inhabitant has grown from 2500 in 1940 to 5000 in 1966. An American survey[21] showed that people spend 14—16 per cent of their (1960) household consumption on transport, increasing with increasing income.

Men tend to travel 20 per cent more than women by intercity transport. People between 18 and 64 years of age travel 90 per cent more than others. A breakdown of American travelling habits is given below for 1962.

(1)   34 per cent of adult Americans did not make any trips of more than 100 miles.

(2)   28 per cent of adult Americans took 1—2 trips or 9 per cent trips of more than 100 miles.

(3)   13 per cent of adult Americans took 3—4 trips or 10 per cent trips of more than 100 miles.

(4)   12 per cent of adult Americans took 5—9 trips or 17 per cent trips of more than 100 miles.

(5)   8 per cent of adult Americans took 10—19 trips or 22 per cent trips of more than 100 miles.

(6)   5 per cent of adult Americans took more than 20 trips or 42 per cent trips of more than 100 miles.

TABLE 1.16   Percentage of U.S. passenger trips by use of modes

	Rail	Bus	Auto	Air
Business	25	13	24	61
Non-business	75	87	76	39

It is seen that the travelling habits vary considerably. Twenty-five per cent of all passenger trips in intercity transport were business trips, but the use of modes of transport was as shown in table 1.16.

Between 1955 and 1962 the number of intercity passenger trips per inhabitant in the United States increased by 15 per cent. Within public transport the number of intercity bus and rail trips decreased by 40–45 per cent, while the number of trips by air increased by 35 per cent.

A statement of trips per person travelling split into business and non-business is given in table 1.17

TABLE 1.17   Business and non-business travel

		Rail	Car	Bus	Air
Trips per person travelling trips of more than 100 miles per year (1962)	Business	2.4	9	3	5
	Non-business	1.7	5	2	2
	Total	1.8	6	2	3
%Adults making trips	Business	1	10	1	4
	Non-business	6	61	8	8
	Total	7	64	9	11

The North-East Corridor in the United States

The passenger traffic on railway lines in the United States has been decreasing for many years. As there were difficulties with the very heavy road and air traffic along the north-east coast, and especially the overloading of the airports in New York, the U.S. Government set up an office of high-speed ground transportation in 1965.

This network serves an area of about 250 000 km² with about 50 million inhabitants extending from Boston via New York and Philadelphia to Baltimore and Washington (eventually combined with a finger to Pittsburg).

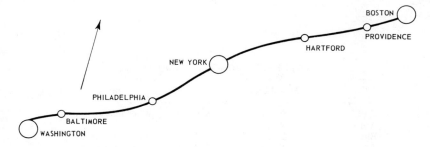

Figure 1.16 The north-east corridor in the United States

TABLE 1.18   Percentage distribution of 150 million trips by modes for north-east Corridor passenger transport (1970)

	Business 27%		Private 73%				
			High 14%		Medium 54%		
						Low income 5%	
	Short (<200 km)	Long (>200 km)	Short 11+11	Long 3+2	Alone 13	Group 41	Total
Rail	2	1	2	1	1	1	8
Auto	16	0	17	0	38	3	74
Bus	0	0	3	0	2	1	6
Air	0	8	0	1	0	0	12
Total	18	9	22	5	41	5	100

150 million trips were distributed to transport modes in the north-east corridor as shown in tables 1.18 and 1.19.

TABLE 1.19 U.S. transport (1970)

| | U.S. total | | | Percentage distribution of passenger km to modes | | |
	pass. km	ton km	Corridor	Boston – Washington (766 km)	N.Y. – Washington (350 km)	N.Y. – Philadelphia (150 km)
Sea	—	28	—	—	—	—
Rail	1	36	12	3	9	19
Auto	88 ⎫		68	43	45	74
Bus	2 ⎭	16	8	1	10	6
Air	9	0	13	53	36	1
Pipe	—	20	—	—	—	—

TABLE 1.20   New York – Washington

	Travel time	Fare	Frequency
Rail	180 min	$19	6 departures day
Auto	240 min	—	—
Bus	220 min	$14	20 departures day
Air	220 min	$38	60 departures day

Public transport is used more inside the corridor, than outside. Long distance traffic is 10 per cent of total traffic in the corridor. The service was as shown in table 1.20 in 1970.

The amount of freight transported per inhabitant per year has increased from 4500 ton miles 1940 to 9000 ton miles today. Three aspects of freight

TABLE 1.21   U.S. modal division of manufacturing tonnage by length of haul (1967)

	Water (%)	Rail (%)	Truck (%)	% of total tonnage
0— 50 miles	4	19	77	14
50— 100 miles	3	27	70	15
100— 200 miles	2	36	61	18
200— 300 miles	4	50	46	13
300— 500 miles	4	55	41	14
500— 800 miles	2	62	36	12
800—1500 miles	10	65	25	10
> 1500 miles	12	75	13	5

TABLE 1.22   U.S. modal division of manufacturing tonnage by shipment size (1967)

	Water (%)	Rail (%)	Truck (%)	% of total tonnage
0—10000 pounds	0	4	96	10
10—30000 pounds	0	17	83	13
30—60000 pounds	0	25	75	31
60—90000 pounds	0	74	26	11
> 90000 pounds	11	80	9	36

TABLE 1.23   U.S. modal division of manufacturing tonnage by commodity (1967)

	Water (%)	Rail (%)	Hired truck (%)	Private truck (%)
Food	3	56	19	22
Textile	0	9	60	31
Paper	2	55	28	15
Plastics, etc.	11	52	26	11
Petroleum, coal	79	6	10	5
Rubber	0	25	63	12
Wool	5	53	13	29
Furniture	1	20	53	26
Stone	2	36	44	18
Iron/steel	7	50	38	5
Machinery	1	32	52	15

transport are particularly critical in determining for which mode a shipment is suited. They are the distance, the size of the shipment and the nature of the commodity (see tables 1.21, 1.22 and 1.23). The first two tables exclude petroleum and coal products.

1.3.4 The Tokaido Corridor in Japan

This corridor serves an area of about 50 000 km² with about 50 million inhabitants, extending from Tokyo to Osaka via Nagoya and Kyoto (see figure 1.17).

Because of the heavy traffic it was decided to build a new railway line from Tokyo to Osaka which was opened in 1964. The travel time is 3 hours and the maximum speed is 210 km/h. As it paralled the existing line the new stations could be at intervals of about 50 km.

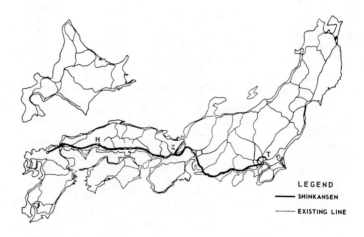

LEGEND

—— SHINKANSEN

—— EXISTING LINE

Figure 1.17 The Tokaido line in Japan. T Tokyo, K Kyoto, H Hiroshima

TABLE 1.24   Percentage distribution of passenger km/ton km by modes (1970 Japanese total)

Intercity	Passenger km (%)	ton km (%)
Sea	1	42
Rail	57	22
Auto	21	36
Bus	20	—
Air	1	—
Pipeline	0	—

The continuation of the Tokaido line, the new 500 km San-yo line from Osaka via Okayama to Hakata is already completed or under construction. The cost of the extension is £2 million per mile, 50 per cent of which is for tunnels, terminals, power supply and rolling stock. The traffic was as shown in tables 1.24 and 1.25.

TABLE 1.25   Tokaido corridor transport

	1966–67	1973–74
Rail passengers (million)	44	128
Route (km)	515	680
Trains per day*	60	113

* Each way, on week days by the end of the year

It is possible that other corridor networks will grow during the next years in the regions of densely populated areas, such as Calcutta – Ganges (India), Moscow – Dnepr (Russia), and Cairo – Nile (Egypt).

1.4 General Observations

(1) At its first appearance each new kind of transport is conceived as a way of complementing the routes prevailing at the time.

(2) During the next phase the new method of transport attains its own form and develops its own capacities to the full. It seeks to become predominant by asserting its complete independence. There is competition with other means of transport and no co-ordination. The new method of transport takes over types of transport for which it is not well suited, even if it means carrying them at a loss.

(3) When the need to renew equipment arises for the mode of transport which has so far been predominant, it tries to assume the characteristics of its more fortunate rival. If this fails, the independence is lost, and it becomes just another auxiliary form.

(4) This evolution in methods of transport occurs over a specific period of time in any particular geographical area. In those regions which are late in developing a transport system, a short cut is sometimes possible.

(5) Each form of transport still retains certain advantages, which prevent it from disappearing completely and can even give it the chance to stage a comeback. This provides an element of stability.

(6) It is necessary to consider the relationship between the main stages of development in transport on the one hand and the requirements of traffic on the other, because the capacity of older forms of transport carries with it the danger that the supply of transport may become excessive.

(7) The economic situation and political influences then combine with technical developments to determine the evolution of the means of transport. This evolution can be divided up into chronological periods as has been shown.[25]

These facts are used in chapter 5.

References

1. d'Avenel, G. (1919), *L'Evolution des Moyens de Transport*, PUF, Paris
2. Childe, G. (1942). *What Happened in History*, Penguin, Harmondsworth
3. Schreiber, H. (1961). *The History of Roads*, Barrie & Rockliff, London
4. Trevelyan, G. M. (1944). *English Social History*, Longmans Green, London
5. Ying-shih, Y. (1967). *Trade and Expansion in Han China*, University of California
6. Charlesworth, M. P. (1924). *Trade Routes and Commerce of the Roman Empire*, Cambridge University Press, Cambridge
7. Woolley, L. (1963). *History of Mankind*, 1, Part 2, Mentor, New York
8. Miller, K. (1888). *Weltkarte des Castorius: Peutingersche Tafel*, Ravensburg
9. Kretschmer, K. (1909). *Die italienischen Portolane des Mittelalters*, Institut fur Meereskunde, Berlin
10. Finch, J. K. (1960). *The Story of Engineering*, Doubleday and Co., New York
11. Dyos, H. J. and Aldcroft, D. H. (1969). *British Transport*, Leicester University Press, Leicester
12. Hay, W. W. (1961). *Introduction to Transportation Engineering*, Wiley, New York
13. Bird, J. (1963). *The Major Seaports of the United Kingdom*, Hutchinson, London
14. Rice, R. A. (1970). *Historical Perspective in Transport System Development*, Carnegie-Mellon University, Pittsburgh, Pennsylvania
15. Jackson, A. A. (1969). *London's Termini*, David and Charles, London
16. Berghaus, E. (1960). *Auf den Schienen der Erde*, Süddeütscher Verlag, Munich
17. Touring Club Italy (1963). *Le Autostrade in Italia e All'estero*, Milan
18. Grosvenor, J. (1957). *The Port of London*, Staples, London
19. Allen, R. (1964). *Great Airports of the World*, J. Allan, London
20. Bendtsen, P. H. and Rallis, T. (1971). Transport Outside Towns, Topic II, 2, *4th Int. Symp., CEMT*, Hague
21. Lansing, J. B. (1964). *The Changing Travel Market*, Ann Arbor, Michigan
22. University of Southampton (1972). *V.T.O.L. A European Study*, Vol I–III, Southampton
23. Marche, R. and Flaven, B. (1968). *Passenger Air Travel*, SETEC, Paris
24. Cheslow, M., *et al.* (1971). *Northeast Corridor Transport*, Final Report, D.O.T., Washington
25. Cambridge Economic History of Europe (1950–67). Vols II, IV and VI, Cambridge University Press, London

2 Environmental Factors in Intercity Transport

2.1 Accidents

One of the constraints associated with transport is risk. A unit of measurement for risk is required for use in the analysis of transport capacity. As there is no escape from death, the issue that can be dealt with is how to make the current expected life span (approximately 600 000 hours) longer and less uncertain. Traffic density and safety are often inversely related. Safety, however, does not enter into capacity problems explicitly, but through different rules, equipment, design, etc.

If a traffic control system handles a certain amount of traffic, it is with an acceptable standard of service, and first of all with an acceptable standard of safety. Starr suggested (1969) a unit of risk per hour of exposure.[1]

There is often a conflict between the validity of observations and detailed analysis because fatal accidents are so infrequent. Then an indirect measurement, such as 'near collision', which is a more frequent event, can be used.

The number of people killed in Denmark each year in road traffic accidents is approximately 1200. In Great Britain the figure is 8000 and in the United States 50 000. Compared to these high figures the number killed in Denmark in railway, sea and air accidents is low: approximately 25, 50 and 10 respectively. In Great Britain the figures are 200, 400 and 80, and in the United States 1250, 2500 and 500. The total number of traffic fatalities is approximately equal to the number of people killed in their homes and at work.

The ratios of numbers of injured to numbers killed differs between road and railway traffic: for railways the ratios are 5:1, whereas for roads they are 20:1.

Of the people killed in railway accidents 25 per cent are passengers, 20 per cent employees and 55 per cent other persons (35 per cent suicides, 20 per cent trespassers and vehicle passengers killed at railway/road crossings).

Often the number of people killed per 10^8 passenger km is given; for example, 0.2 people are killed in sea, rail, schedule air and bus traffic accidents, but 2.0 in private road traffic and 10.0 in private air traffic accidents.

Another measure, namely the number killed per 10^6 passenger hours, gives 0.2 persons killed in sea, rail and bus traffic accidents, but 0.9 in road traffic and 1.6 in air traffic accidents, compared to a death rate of 0.2 per 10^6 life hours for people in the 35–44 age group, 1 for people between 55 and 59 and 2 for people between 60 and 69 years.[2]

2.1.1 Safety at Sea

Some of the things covered in the international regulations for preventing collisions at sea are, for example, section 13 signalling by light, section 16 manoeuvring in fog, section 18–19 starboard right of way, section 20 sail right of way, section 21 action by stand-on vessel, maintain course and speed, section 22–23, action by stand-by vessel, speed decrease or stop, section 24 overtaking, section 25 narrow channels starboard right of way, section 28 signalling by sound, and section 29 that every vessel shall at all times maintain proper look-out by sight and sound, maintain safe speed, so that she can take effective action to avoid collision and be stopped within a distance appropriate to the prevailing conditions and circumstances. There are altogether 38 rules and 4 annexes.

Use of radar traffic separation schemes are incorporated in the regulations as well as a paragraph governing responsibilities between vessels; for example, a ship is restricted in her ability to manoeuvre, constrained by her draught, etc.

The Inter-governmental Maritime Consultative Organization (IMCO) under the auspices of the United Nations has been working on safety problems at sea since 1959.

Equipment for long-distance navigation includes for example, the Loran system, the Consol system and the Decca system. The first systems reach 700–1200 nautical miles with positional tolerances of 0.5–2 nautical miles. Decca reaches 100 nautical miles with an accuracy of 30 m. The first systems mentioned are used by the United States and NATO and cover the Atlantic and Pacific Oceans, whereas Decca is used in the North Sea, Baltic, Persian Gulf, Indian and Japanese seas. Port radar is used in the approaches to London, Rotterdam and Hamburg.

It has been necessary to regulate traffic in sea areas where shipping is dense. A commission has put forward proposals for channelling traffic in areas where the probability of collisions is high. One-way routes would be good in situations involving three ships, because the rules only apply to two-ship situations. However, current regulations only advise ships to follow such procedures; they are not mandatory. In the English Channel, the Øresund at Elsinore, at Gibraltar, etc. a separation zone has been established so that ships keep to the right-hand side. The zone should be a minimum of 12 nautical miles long and 2 nautical miles wide.

Turning through 180° demands a circle diameter of 2–5 ship lengths.

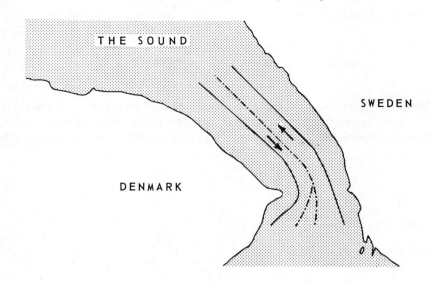

Figure 2.1 Traffic regulation in the sound at Elsinore

Tactical diameter, that is the diameter required when under way, is a little more, approximately 2.5–7 ship lengths for a full turn of 180°. Stopping distance is approximately 5–12 ship lengths from full speed. The corresponding time is about 15 minutes.[3] Tugs may be necessary to manoeuvre big ships in ports and a pilot is usually necessary in the approaches to a harbour.

Sailing ships suffered a loss rate of 4 per cent until they disappeared entirely from the high seas during the First World War. By 1913 the number of steamships lost at sea had fallen from 2 to 1 per cent of total world tonnage. In 1959 the figure was as low as 0.25 per cent of total tonnage, but since then the loss rate has gradually increased; in 1966 the figure was 0.5 per cent of total tonnage. 160 ships (> 500 G.R.T.) were shipwrecked in 1967, 15 of which were caused by bad weather, 61 by grounding, 10 by collisions, 33 by fire and 38 by other causes. In 1968, the number of Danish registered ships lost was approximately 7 per year; Greece, Liberia and Panama had 70 per year.

Liverpool Insurance Underwriters report the number of ships larger than 500 G.R.T. lost and broken up, tanker tonnage being 40 per cent of the world total, bulk carrier fleet 25 per cent and general cargo tonnage 35 per cent. In 1973 approximately 600 000 G.R.T. were lost from the general cargo fleet, approximately 300 000 G.R.T. were lost from the tankers and 200 000 G.R.T. from bulk carriers.[5] Lloyds Register of Shipping reports the number of ships lost and broken up per year for ships greater than 100 G.R.T. For the period

Intercity Transport

TABLE 2.1   The Number of ships totally lost or broken up (1965—69)

Japan	220	326
U.S.A.	71	639
Great Britain	62	553

1965—69 the number of ships totally lost or broken up was as shown in table 2.1. Kostilainen[39] analysed accidents in the Baltic using Lloyds' weekly casualty reports. He found the percentage of accidents as shown in table 2.2.

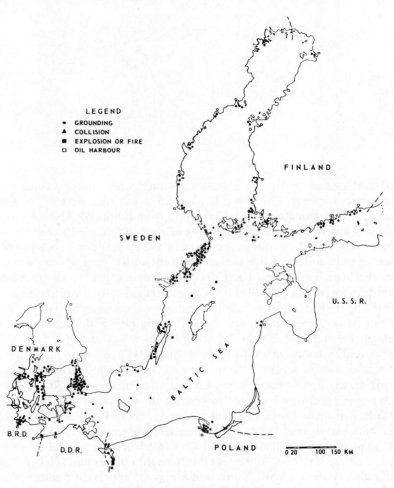

Figure 2.2 Collisions in the Baltic area

TABLE 2.2 Accidents in the Baltic

	All ships 1971–72	All tankers 1960–69
Groundings (stranding)	46%	56%
Collisions	35%.	35%
Fire	4%	9%

The Maritime Safety Agency, Japan, has reported the causes of casualties (2615 in 1973)[43] (table 2.3).

TABLE 2.3 Ship casualities in Japan and number of passengers and crew killed in Japanese waters (1973)

Ship casualities				
Operational mistakes	1231	Force majeure	249	
Mishandling of machinery	478	Mishandling of fire	138	
Structural defects	326	Bad loading	97	
Passenger/crew losses				
Overboard	99	Suicide	77	excluding fishing
Wound	46	Others	35	323 in 1973
Disease	32			

Statistics for 1955–60 show 2749 collisions at sea around the world, 72 per cent of which occurred in piloted waters. Of the 28 per cent in open sea, 608 were found in North European and Mediterranean Seas. The distribution was Dover, Texel, South England, Biscay 133, 70, 60 and 39 collisions, respectively; Sound, Route 1, Gibraltar, Skagen 27, 27, 24 and 13 collisions respectively. At Dover the bottleneck is between the Varne Lightship and the English Coast, a strip of water 5 nautical miles wide where ships travel in both directions.[46, 52]

Dr A Jensen[5] has shown that the ships at Elsinore arrive according to a Poisson* distribution in an area of 5×2 nautical miles. Radar observations over 10 days showed that approximately 40 near collisions occurred.

Methods of Estimating Sea Collisions[6]

Fujii, from the Japanese Ministry of Transport, has shown that the ratio, R, between the number of vessels in collision and the number of vessels registered increases with the length of the vessel. Shiobara, from the Japanese Association for Preventing Sea Casualties, gives a linear correlation between $\log R$ and $\log G$, where G is the gross tonnage. Sakaki, from the Japanese Maritime Safety Academy, was the first to seek a relationship between the

* See definition page 89

collision rate and the traffic volume, which he gave as a function of density, speed and tidal current.

A theoretical analysis by Fujii on collision rates and evasive action yields a general formula which can be used for estimating the number of collisions in a given waterway.

Because fatal accidents are so infrequent, accident reports should be studied. Fricker quotes a classic collision report.[53] The failure to follow the harbour advisory radar operated by the U.S. coastguard for the San Francisco Bay, coupled with neglect of the rules of the sea by two ships, resulted in a serious collision. Ship I left Estero Bay, California, at 12.30 on 17 January north-bound for San Francisco, where at 22.00 about 25 miles south of San Francisco the weather visibility became greatly reduced by a dense fog. At 00.49 on 18 January ship I heard ship II report to the harbour radar that she was leaving Long Wharf, Richmond.

At 01.04 ship I was in the main shipping channel, 2000 feet wide, on a course of 69° and travelling at a reduced speed of 13.5 knots.

At 01.20 the harbour radar advised ship I that ship II was passing north of Alcatraz Island, outward-bound. Ship I then changed course to 65° to line up with the channel under the Golden Gate Bridge. At 01.27 ship I observed a radar contact on the scope at a range of 6 miles. Ship I made several attempts to contact ship II on V.H.F. channels but without success. At 01.36 when ship I heard the signal located on the centre span of the bridge slightly to port, her course was 58° and speed 11 knots. At 01.39 ship I saw the port side-light of ship II on her starboard bow 200 yards away. Ship I went hard to port, stopped engines and at 01.40 her bow penetrated the port side of ship II.

At 00.48 ship II had reported her departure to the harbour radar on V.H.F. channel 18 and then shifted her receiver to channel 10, used for communications with the owners' office. As a result, neither the harbour radar nor ship I were able to communicate with ship II.

At 01.39 ship II switched her V.H.F. channel from 10 to 16 because the radar contact on the port bow was approaching rapidly.

Before that ship II had observed ship I at 01.33 and had decided on port-to-port passing. By 01.37 ship II was on a course of 270° at a speed of 4 knots. This collision was caused by faulty navigation on the part of both masters, because they navigated at immoderate speeds in dense fog within confined waters and failed to keep to the starboard side of the channel before the collision.

2.1.2 Safety on Railways

The probability of accidents due to human error on railways can be reduced by the provision of automatic, mechanical and electrical installations between railway tracks, signals and trains.

Signals and points are power-operated, and any failure in the signal circuits or power supply automatically causes the signals concerned to indicate STOP, whether the track is clear or not. The basis of train signalling is the track circuit system, by means of which the signal immediately behind a train is automatically set at danger, and remains so until the train has passed a safe overlap distance beyond the next signal.

Signal overlaps are often associated with trainstop, which takes the control of a train out of the hands of a driver if he should pass a signal at danger. The overlap is the distance in which a train can be stopped by an emergency brake plus a safety margin.

At the signal cabins interlocking of the levers is arranged so that the signalman cannot set up two conflicting routes, which would enable a collision to take place, or reset levers, back-locking.

An important development has been the progressive introduction of route control signalling, whereby the movement of a single lever clears the signals and sets the points for a complete route, by remote control. The levers have been replaced by push-buttons, where the circuits reset themselves automatically; also preselection is possible, that is a second move can be stored until the first move has been completed. Programmed machine signalling has been introduced, where control is effected directly from the working timetable, which is in the form of punched plastic tape.

Automatic train control (A.T.C.) consists of the following train-borne equipment: (1) Automatic train protection (A.T.P.) is a cab signal system that automatically enforces speed limits. (2) Automatic train operation (A.T.O.) is the automatic driver that controls tractive effort. (3) Automatic train supervision (A.T.S.) is the coordinator that monitors over-all system performance and maintains operation according to a plan or timetable.

A.T.C. can also involve track-side equipment, such as the following: (1) A.T.P. components include a conventional automatic block signal system. (2) A.T.O. requires markers or equivalent loops. (3) A.T.S. has a computer which continuously compares the loading of the system (from track circuits) with a timetable plan.

A track-circuit dependent system is used in the United States and Britain, but a track-conductor system is used on the Continent of Europe. The broadband systems used in Europe attain the same general objectives as the American and British narrow-band systems, but they use entirely different equipment. The conductors are approximately 60 bits* long, transmitted at a rate of about 1200 bits/second. The message comprises address (loop section number), accelerate/brake commands, speed and target braking distance.

---

* Amount of information equal to the logarithm of the numerical magnitude of the measurement to the base 2.

The European system does not require steel wheels on steel rails and it permits operation in which train spacing is determined only by the safe braking distance. While signalling often is technically correct, much signal receiving is still based on human reaction and causes many accidents. However, track and coach failures also occur. Table 2.4 gives the following statistics for 1971, according to the International Union of Railways (U.I.C.).

TABLE 2.4   Number of railway accidents by type 1971

	Collisions		Derailments	Numbers killed	
	Train/train	Train/car		Passengers	Staff
British Rail	39	109	351	49	59
Deutsche Bundesbahn	320	461	383	180	121
India	90	560	743	393	270
Japanese railways	6	1815	149	0	1
French railways	23	349	100	54	38

Because fatal accidents on railways are so infrequent, all accident reports should be studied. British Rail inquired into the derailment of the Hastings to Charing Cross passenger train on 5 November 1967 near Hither Green (Southern Region). The train, which consisted of two six-coach diesel-electric sets, was approaching Hither Green on the 'up' fast line at about 70 miles/h when the leading pair of wheels of the third coach struck a wedge-shaped piece of steel that had broken away from the end of a running rail, and became derailed. The train ran on for about 1/4 mile, when the derailed wheels struck a diamond crossing causing the general derailment of the train, killing 49 passengers and injuring 78. Most of the casualties occurred in the four overturned coaches.

The joint at which the fracture occurred was between two short closure rails. It had been made with fishplates and was supported by a timber sleeper, which had been placed there in June to replace a concrete sleeper that had cracked. The rail that fractured was new when it was laid in February and the fracture was caused by excessive working of the joint resulting from its unsatisfactory support condition: inadequacy of the bed of clean ballast, the absence of a rubber pad on the original concrete sleeper and the substitution of an ordinary timber sleeper. The joint had been pumping. The train itself was running within its permitted speed. The permanent-way staff were prepared to accept too low a standard of maintenance, and were responsible for agreeing to an increased speed of 90 miles/h in July, when the standard of track maintenance was not adequate. The practice of using such closures has now been abandoned.

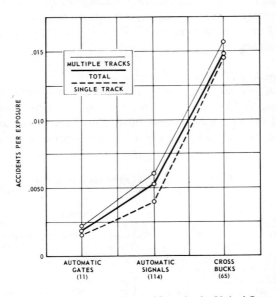

Figure 2.3 Railway crossing accidents in the United States

Railway level-crossing accidents account for 3 per cent of the total motor vehicle deaths in the United States. There are manual crossing, automatic half-barriers and unguarded crossings. The sequence of operation at an automatic half-barrier level crossing may be that the train strikes treadles and shorts a track circuit 1000 yards from the crossing, whereupon red lights flash to stop the traffic: after 8 seconds the barriers start to fall and reach the horizontal position 16 seconds after initiation.

TABLE 2.5   Accidents at level crossings

		Number of crossings	Number of persons killed per year
Britain 1961–67			
Manual		3 398	8
Half-barrier		205	1
Unguarded		16 609	14
Europe 1964–67			
Half barriers	France	2 215	24
	Germany	410	16
	Holland	345	23

The statistics relating to automatic crossings in Holland show that the traffic movement (road vehicles per day × trains per day) is exceptionally high, 3 million. In France a movement of 500 000 is a practical maximum for automatic crossings.

2.1.3 Safety on Roads

The number of persons killed in road accidents has increased very much since the Second World War. It is however important to divide the number into rural and urban accidents and further into car driver and passenger, pedestrians and two-wheeled vehicle drivers, as shown in table 2.6.

TABLE 2.6   Persons killed by road accidents[15]

	Total (1947)	In vehicles (1967)	Pedestrians (1967)	Two wheeled (1967)	of which in urban areas 1967 Number	of which in urban areas 1967 %	Killed per 10⁵ inhabitants (1970)	Urban population (%)
U.S.A.	32 582	42 270	9 950	2 560	16 000	30	—	
Great Britain	6 648	2 972	2 964	1 403	3 699	50	14	40
France	4 263	6 820	3 120	3 519	4 830	36	24	20
West Germany	—	7 865	5 822	3 299	7 318	40	31	30
Sweden	584	600	195	245	320	30	17	20
India	—	9 734			—		—	
Japan	—	16 038			—		—	
Denmark	334	354	350	373	455	40	25	35

The number of persons killed in urban transport accidents per 10^6 passenger hours is 0.02 for buses, 0.2 for automobiles and for pedestrians, but more than 1 for cyclists and motor cyclists. The dangerous part of travelling by bus is when the bus passenger is a pedestrian.

Vehicular traffic accidents in Denmark have been investigated by Thorson and Mouritzen, who described a coordinated electronic data processing system correlating information on 38 000 accidents on about 9000 km of rural and urban highways with road layout and traffic data for a five-year period from 1962 to 1966.[11] The relationship between the accident density (accidents per km), the accident rate (accidents per 10^8 vehicle kilometres), and the traffic volume for six types of roads (2-lane roadway under 6 m wide and over, 3-lane roads and 4-lane roads with and without central reservation, and finally motorways) and three types of intersections (cross roads, T junctions and forks) in rural and developed areas were investigated.

The total accident rate decreased from year to year; the same applied to personal injury rate and death rate.
Empirical formulae can be written as follows:

(1) The accident rate $A_r = a(N + b)^c$

(2) The accident density $A_d = a(N + b)^c N 365 \times 10^{-8}$

(3) The number of accidents $A = a(N + b)^c NL365 \times 10^{-8}$ (2.1)

where N is average daily traffic and a, b, c are constants. L is road length. The formulae can be used in an example:

For a 2 km section of a 2-lane rural road, more than 6 m wide, with a daily traffic of 3000 vehicles one gets:
Accident rate 59 accidents per 10^8 vehicle km
Accident density 0.65 accidents per km per year, and expected number of accidents 1.30 per year

The constants $a = 1.07 \times 10^5 / 365$, $b = 100$, $c = -0.2$ given from table 2.7

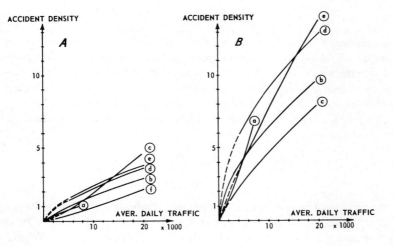

Figure 2.4 Road accident density in Denmark as a function of traffic. Left, intercity roads; right, city roads. a-f see the text.

Figures 2.4A and 2.4B contain graphical representation of rural and urban road accident density as a function of traffic. Three-lane roads are safer than two-lane roads in rural areas for daily traffic less than 8500 vehicles. Four-lane motorways in rural areas have the lowest accident density. In total the accident density in rural areas is lower than 5 accidents per km per year. The number of fatalities per accident in rural road sections was 0.1. The number of fatalities per accident in rural intersections was 0.08. Single vehicle accidents account for only 10 per cent of all accidents in urban areas, but for 80 per cent on motorways.

Between intersections the fatality rate was 6 per 10^8 vehicle km. At intersections the fatality rate was 1 per 10^8 vehicles in the flow.

TABLE 2.7   *a, b* and *c* values for different types of road sections

Type of road section	$\dfrac{365}{10^5}a$	$\dfrac{1}{100}b$	c
Rural areas:			
(a) 2 lanes, width < 6 m	0.87	1	−0.2
(b) 2 lanes, width > 6 m	1.07	1	−0.2
(c) 3 lanes	0.01	1	0.3
(d) 4 lanes without central reservation	3.59	1	−0.3
(e) 4 lanes with central reservation	3.79	1	−0.3
(f) 4-lane motorway	0.01	1	0.2

Jorgensen[13] states that for a large part of Danish road networks—for example, all 4-lane roads in rural areas—it has been shown that the frequency of the number of accidents per day could be represented by the Poisson* statistical distribution. This also applies to the number of accidents per year on shorter road sections, if major road intersections are excluded.

The probability that u accidents will occur for given mean value A is

$$P(u) = \frac{A^u}{u!}\exp(-A) \tag{2.2}$$

where, for example, A is given by equation (2.1) above, as 1.3 accidents per year. By means of equation (2.2) one can then compute the probability of observing given differences. If A is expected to be 5 and u is 11, a Poisson* table gives that $u > 11$ has a probability of 1.4 per cent. That road section would be considered a statistical black spot, at the 2.5 per cent level of statistical significance.

Ernst[14] has shown maps of accident rates for German freeways. The concept of the probability of danger of collision between vehicles was introduced by Harris (1964).[54] The probability represents the situation where

* See definition page 89

the inverse deceleration of the leading vehicle is less than the inverse deceleration of the following vehicle by more than $2(S-VT)/V^2$ where S is equal to the distance between vehicles, V velocity and T reaction time. If an average vehicle length is chosen, determination of average density and volume can be made. For about 2000 vehicles per hour per lane the probability of collision is more than 0.2, for 1600 less than 0.1 and for 1200 less than 0.05.

2.1.4 Air Safety

When the density of traffic flowing between two or more airports reaches a point where the pilots cannot be expected to take responsibility of deciding the correct action necessary to ensure a safe and expeditious flow of air traffic, a control area is established.

The various airports are then linked by control areas of various types, either in the form of airways or covering the whole of the airspace between the various points. Where the traffic is channelled an airway type of control area is most desirable.

A control area is delineated so as to encompass sufficient airspace to contain the flight paths of those flights or portions thereof to which it is desired to provide the applicable parts of the air traffic control service, taking into account the capabilities of the navigational aids normally used in that area (I.C.A.O. Annex 11).

The airways are channels of a width of 18 km, 9 km on either side of a line formed by radio beacons, and of a height of about 10 km, from 900 m above the ground to 11 400 m. Airway A9 leads from Milan via Zurich, Frankfurt, Hamburg and Copenhagen to Oslo. Airway R1 leads from London via Amsterdam and Copenhagen to Stockholm and Helsinki.

The primary navigation equipment associated with the airway system comprises the low-frequency non-directional radio beacon, N.D.B. (255–415 kHz), and the very-high-frequency omni-directional radio range, V.O.R. (112–118 MHz). The N.D.B.-routing and the V.O.R.-routing along the respective airways are performed by means of significant points. These significant points are specified geographical locations in relation to which the position of an aircraft can be reported (compulsory or non-compulsory). The spacing between two N.D.B. beacons must not exceed 57 nautical miles and between two V.O.R. beacons the spacing must not exceed 114 nautical miles, for an airway 18 km wide. (Maximum error 5° or 300 m in F.L. 150*.)[31]

Three types of rules are prescribed in I.C.A.O. Annex 2. These are the General Flight Rules (concerning protection of persons and property, avoidance of collisions etc.), the Visual Flight Rules and the Instrument Flight Rules. A pilot is required to comply with the general flight rules, at all times,

* 4250 m.

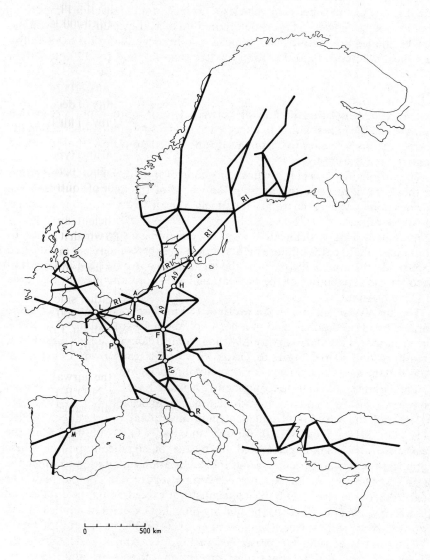

Figure 2.5 European airspace, lower routes. G Glasgow, L London, P Paris, M Madrid, R Rome,
Z Zurich, F Frankfurt, Br Brussels, H Hanover, A Amsterdam, C Copenhagen

and in addition, with either the visual flight rules or the instrument flight rules. A flight made in compliance with the general flight rules and the visual flight rules is a V.F.R. flight. The visual flight rules prescribe the minimum weather conditions (for example, flight visibility 5 km, distance from clouds 0.6 km horizontally, 0.15 km vertically) which must prevail for a flight to be made under those rules. A flight made in compliance with the general flight rules and the instrument flight rules is an I.F.R. flight. Aircraft must be equipped with suitable instruments and with radio navigation apparatus appropriate to the route to be flown.

Except when climbing or descending, an I.F.R. flight operating outside controlled airspace is flown at a cruising level appropriate to its magnetic track. An Air Traffic Control clearance must be obtained before operating an I.F.R. flight in controlled airspace. Such clearance is requested through the submission of a flight plan to an air traffic control unit. The time and level of passing each designated reporting point is reported by radio to the air traffic control unit.

For safety purposes it is necessary to maintain vertical or horizontal separation between all I.F.R. flights within controlled airspace. The minimum vertical separation between I.F.R. traffic is 300 m below an altitude of 8850 m and 600 m at or above this level. The cruising levels normally used by I.F.R. flights operating in controlled airspace are selected so that flights in one direction use even cruising levels, that is 4000 feet, 6000 feet etc. and those in the opposite direction use odd cruising levels, that is 3000 feet, 5000 feet, etc. There is sufficient space for about 30 aircraft to pass above one another at the same time within an airway of a height of 10 000 m, that is 15 aircraft in each direction. Because of meteorological conditions, crossing and intersecting paths of aircraft and considerations of economic cruising levels, it is, however, rare for more than 4—6 levels to be used simultaneously in each direction in any airway.

Horizontal separation covers lateral separation as well as longitudinal separation. If an aircraft is using a certain airway, the lateral separation is identical to half the width of the airway (9 km), that is aircraft must not overtake each other when in the same level. For aircraft using the same flight level longitudinal separation is necessary. This separation is normally 10 minutes for aircraft flying on the same track (if navigational aids permit frequent determination of position and speed). If an aircraft is maintaining a true airspeed ≥ 20 knots faster than the aircraft immediately behind it, and both aircraft have departed from the same airport or reported over the same reporting point, the longitudinal separation may be 5 minutes. For aircraft flying on crossing tracks there is a minimum of 10 minutes; for climbing or descending a minimum of 5 minutes.

The horizontal separation minima may be reduced to 2 minutes (8 km spacing) when radar-derived* information of an aircraft's position is available to the appropriate air traffic control unit.

Traffic Control

The objectives of the air traffic control service are to expedite and maintain a safe and orderly flow of air traffic according to the traffic rules. The Area Control Service provides the air traffic control service for I.F.R. flights, except for manoeuvres associated with arrival or departure. An Area Control Centre (A.C.C.) is established to provide area control service.

The A.C.C. is provided with information on the intended movement of each aircraft (flight plans) and the actual progress of each aircraft (position reports). The A.C.C. determines, from the information received, the relative positions of known aircraft to each other. It issues clearances and information in order to maintain proper separation between aircraft under its control and co-ordinate such clearance as necessary with other control units before transferring control of an aircraft to another such unit.

A centre clearance indicates: (1) aircraft identification (as shown in flight plan), (2) clearance limit, (3) route of flight, (4) level(s) of flight for the entire route.

The pilots' flight plan comprises information regarding: (1) aircraft identification, (2) type of aircraft, (3) time of departure, (4) airport of initial departure, (5) route to be followed, (6) airport(s) at which it is intended to land, (7) true airspeed, (8) cruising level(s), and so on.

Position reports comprise information regarding: (1) aircraft identification, (2) position, (3) time, (4) flight level, (5) next position, (6) estimated time of arrival and (7) meteorological information.

Two-way radiotelephony is used in air – ground communications for air traffic service purposes. In Copenhagen A.C.C. sector I, operating on 120.3 MHz, telephony and teleprinter facilities are used in ground–ground communications for air traffic service purposes. A long-range radar is also in use at Copenhagen A.C.C. operating at 118.6 MHz.

For air – ground messages, the conversation time of a position report is about 20 seconds and that of a clearance 24 seconds. For ground – ground messages, the conversation time of a position report is 12 seconds and that of a clearance 19 seconds. The signalling time per call is about 9 seconds. The typical call has a holding time (duration) of about 30 seconds, and there are about four such calls for each aircraft in flight in the Copenhagen control area, to which is added about 1–2 minutes' planning per aircraft.

Flight plans and position reports are placed on flight progress boards by

---

* Discrete Address Beacon System in which the blip includes identification, altitude, etc.

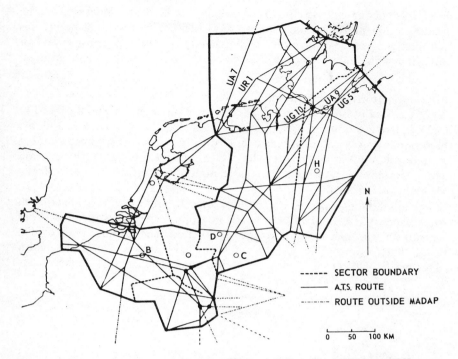

Figure 2.6 European airspace, upper air routes. B Brussels D Dusseldorf, C Cologne, H Hanover

means of handwritten strip cards from which the controller issues his clearances.

Radar equipment is a great help in improving safety, that is surveillance, and maintaining aircraft separations. The controller-handling speed cannot be increased, however, until automatic control units have been introduced.

Terminal areas are extended airways, cylindrical in ideal form, their axes passing through the main airport with a radius of about 100 km and a height of about 10 km, from 300–900 m above the ground to 11 400 m. To provide for the controlled airspace extending upwards from the ground (or water) in the vicinity of an airport, a control zone is established. It extends upwards from the surface of the earth to the lower limit of the terminal area. The radius of the control zone from the centre of an airport is approximately 8.1 nautical miles. With a runway length of 3000 m and an average slope of the vertical path of aircraft descending to land or climbing after take-off of 2.5°, the control zone contains the path of an arriving I.F.R. flight up to 300 m above ground level.

The primary navigation equipment associated with the terminal area are the holding point non-directional beams (383 kHz). These holding points are specified geographical locations in the vicinity of which the position of an aircraft in flight is maintained in accordance with air traffic control clearances.

Procedures (for inbound aircraft)
A.C.C. normally allocates aircraft at flight levels up to and including F.L. 140 (4.2 km) to a low holding, and aircraft at flight levels at or above F.L. 150 to a high holding. Aircraft required to hold must conform to specified holding procedures. A low holding pattern has: (a) holding point N.D.B., (b) holding axis, (c) 1 minute race-track pattern (1 minute flying time between turns), (d) right turn at facility.

The low holdings area is intended for aircraft holding with: (a) maximum true airspeed (T.A.S.) of 240 knots, (b) rate one turn (that is turning 3° per second), (c) windspeed (omni-directional) 60 knots. The holding area is oval in form: length of area is $240/60 + 2 \times 240/60 \times 7/22 = 6.55$ nautical miles, width of area is $2 \times 240/60 \times 7/22 = 2.55$ nautical miles. The length of buffer area is

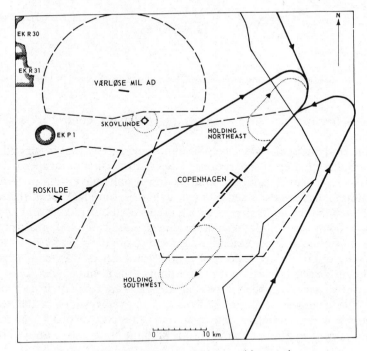

Figure 2.7 Copenhagen terminal area with central zones

based on cone of uncertainity, wind effect, pilot tolerance and safety cushion: 18 nautical miles (about 32 km), width of buffer area: 13 nautical miles (about 23 km).

A high holding pattern has: (a) two holding points V.O.R., or N.D.B., (b) holding axes, (c) holding between the two facilities, (d) right turn at the facilities, (e) 1 minute race track.

The high holding area is intended for aircraft holding with: (a) maximum (T.A.S.) of 360 knots, (b) rate half turn (that is turning 1.5° per second), (c) windspeed (omni-directional) 60 knots, (d) two nativational aids. The high holding area is oval in form: length is $360/60 + 2 \times 360/60 \times 7/22 = 13.64$ nautical miles, width is $2 \times 360/60 \times 7/22 = 7.64$ nautical miles.

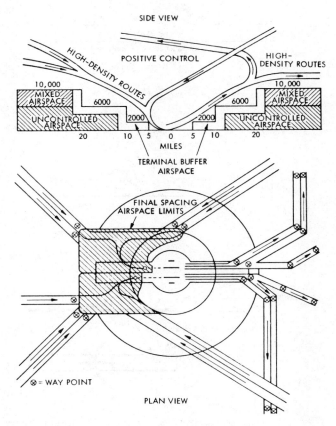

Figure 2.8 New control procedures for high density air routes

Experience with the established high holding area has shown, that an area based on a buffer of 5 nautical miles around the pattern should suffice, when using two navigational aids, that is length of buffer area 23.64 nautical miles (about 43 km), width of buffer area 17.64 nautical miles (about 32 km).

From the holding areas aircraft are either directed by radar to a position from which the final approach can be made or instructed by A.T.C. to carry out the appropriate approach procedure without radar control. Aircraft flying the intermediate procedure under radar control normally use 120, 140 or 160 knot indicated air speed (I.A.S.), according to type, and descend at a rate of at

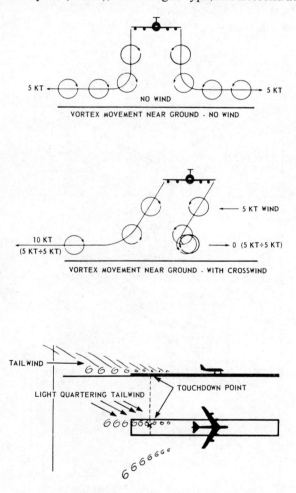

Figure 2.9 Air traffic turbulence

least 150 m per minute. Instrument approach-to-land procedures to the runway may be carried out from N.D.B.

Example
Under intermediate approach the beacon is left at the height of 1350 m on a track of 083° magnetic. 1350 m is maintained until a V.O.R. is on a bearing of 170°; then the pilot descends to 750 m. When due north of a N.D.B. (distance 9.7 nautical miles) the pilot makes a right turn to intercept and follow the final approach track, descending to 450 m. Final approach is carried out with the aid of the Instrument Landing System (I.L.S.) from abeam N.D.B. (runway distance 5 nautical miles, height 450 m) following the glide (descent) path with slope 2.75° or by aid of Precision Approach Radar (P.A.R.), V.O.R. or N.D.B.

The time interval between arriving aircraft is at least 3 nautical miles or 1 minute of flight along the final approach path. The time interval may be increased to 3 minutes to allow the aircraft to land in bad weather before the next aircraft descends. The reduced radar separation minima 5.4 km or 1 minute may be used under radar control.

The minimum time interval between departing aircraft is:

1 minute separation, if aircraft are to fly different tracks and lateral separation is provided immediately after take-off.

2 minutes, when (1) the preceding aircraft propose to follow the same track, (2) neither the preceding nor the following aircraft is cleared to execute any manoeuvre that would decrease the 2 minute separation.

5 minutes, at the time cruising levels are crossed, if a departing aircraft will be flown through the level of a preceding departing aircraft and both aircraft propose to follow the same track.

If an arriving aircraft is making a complete instrument approach, a departing aircraft may take off: (1) in any direction until an arriving aircraft has started its procedure turn leading to final approach, (2) in a direction at least 135° from the arriving aircraft, after the arriving aircraft has started procedure turn, provided that the take-off will be made 1–3 minutes before the arriving aircraft is over threshold.

The hazards of turbulent wake must be assessed when less than a 2 minute separation exists between a departing and an arriving aircraft or between two departing or arriving aircraft using the same runway, especially when a lighter aircraft is following a heavier one.

The Approach Control Service provides the air traffic control service for I.F.R. flights engaged in manoeuvres associated with arrival or departure. An Approach Control Office is established to provide Approach Control Service.

During the course of landing a pilot transmits about 114 bits. However, because of various contexts which give a redundancy of 81 per cent (information supplied by context/information transmitted in the channel), a trained controller receives only 22 bits of new information of which 16 are given by the quantifiers. The controllers on average, transmit 133 bits per landing with a redundancy of 78 per cent thus yielding to each pilot only 29 bits of new information. Of these, 21 bits are contributed by the quantifiers. Pilots and controllers speak at a rate of about 9 bits per second but they actually receive about 2 bits per second.

The typical call has obviously a holding time (duration) of about 30 seconds $(114 + 133) \times 1/9$ or $(22 + 29)1/2$ in the Copenhagen terminal area compared with the calls in the Copenhagen control area.

I.C.A.O.[21] published the number of fatalities in civil aviation for 1973 excluding China and the U.S.S.R., including both passengers and crew.

TABLE 2.8   Number of fatalities in civil aviation (1950–73)

		Large commercial aircraft	Small commercial aircraft (< 9 tons)	Non-commercial aircraft	Total
1973	Passengers and crew killed	1800	(including charter)	500	1900	4200
	(Aircraft crashed)	(60)		(300)	(1000)	approx (1400)
1970	Passengers and crew killed	1100	(including scheduled only)	—	1300	(U.S. only) 2400
1960	—	900		—	—	—
1950	—	550		—	—	—

Stratton (1974)[26] has investigated aircraft accidents for 1946–73. In these 28 years the average number of accidents in civil air transport was 186 per year; the number of fatal accidents was 59 per year; and the number of fatal accidents to I.C.A.O. scheduled service flights was 30 per year.

The risk of passengers being killed if involved in a fatal accident has fallen from 0.76 in the first half period to 0.53 in the last. Of the 59 fatal accidents per year 16 were collisions with high ground, and 3 were mid-air collisions.

Mathieu (1970)[25] has investigated aircraft accidents for the period 1959–69. In this ten-year period I.C.A.O. reports 326 accidents, 8917 killed; I.T.A. (Institut des Transports Aeriens, Paris) reports 525 accidents, 13 255 killed (including charter).

Methods of Estimating Air Collisions Rates

The basic structure of a risk evaluation model was developed by Marks and used by Reich for the parallel track problem over the North Atlantic Ocean. Approximations made for the sake of simplicity were the replacing of aircraft

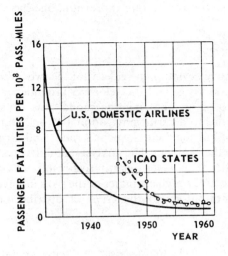

Figure 2.10 Air traffic accidents

by a rectangular solid with linear dimensions equal to that of the aircraft $(L_x L_y L_z)$.[12, 21]

If x represents along-track distance, y across-track distance and z altitude, the collision rate KF at a time t is given by

$$KF = N_x P_y P_z + N_y P_x P_z + N_z P_x P_y \quad r = (x, y, z)$$

where $N_r(t)$ is the rate at time t at which separations become less than L_r, P_r is the probability that at t the separation between aircraft in the direction r is less than L_r.

TABLE 2.9 Breakdown of aircraft accidents by country of accident (1959–69)

	Number of passenger deaths
United States	2516
Canada	235
Brazil	557
Columbia	493
Argentina	213
Great Britain	321
France	621
U.S.S.R.	277
Arab Republic	330
Japan	419
India	349
Philippines	264

Then using the level-crossing rate expression, one has

$$N_r = |\dot{r}| \times \frac{P_r}{2\,L_r}$$

where $|\dot{r}|$ is the relative deviation in velocity for the two aircraft, assuming that x, y and z separation losses and the velocities are independent.

The major problem in applying the model was obtaining the correct distribution functions to describe navigational errors. Data were difficult to find. Interaction of outside factors, such as radar and air traffic controllers, further complicate the problem. The analysis should attempt to compare the relative safety rather than exact quantitative results of collision risk probabilities. In order to give rough estimates of the risks involved, it is possible to make some assumptions as to the types of distributions that might be anticipated.

TABLE 2.10　Breakdown of aircraft accidents by accident type (Mathieu) (1959–69)

	Number of dead	
Collision with high ground	4619	35%
Collision with water	2323	18%
Airframe failure	1508	11%
Instrument failure	1101	8%
Fire	842	6%
Third party	837	6%
Control failure	726	6%
In-flight collision	548	4%
Runway overrun	361	3%
Crew failure	347	3%
Sabotage	316	2%
Power unit failure	268	2%

In Reich's study, it was observed that, for traffic over the North Atlantic, the experimental radar data seemed to fit an exponential distribution. He found

$$P_r = \frac{L_r}{\sigma_r}\exp\left[-\sqrt{2}s_r/\sigma_r\right](1/\sqrt{2} + s/\sigma_r)$$

where σ_r is standard deviation of separation in direction r and s_r is separation in direction r. For the parallel track problem, he found that reducing the lateral separation from 90 to 60 nautical miles would increase the theoretical collision rate about six times. Practical observations, however, provided correction factors.

Faison attempted to compare the relative safety of the current 5000 feet separation of parallel runways to possible closer spacings by use of Reich's model.

Steinberg found, evaluating risks in landings again, that a safe separation distance for parallel runways was less than 3000 feet, further that an acceptable missed approach rate could be maintained if the average spacing at the runway threshold was 50 seconds with speed control.

He included the term $(1 - P_r)$ in the formula because just before the loss of r separation, there is r separation. These terms were omitted in Reich's work, since in the North Atlantic case P_r is much less than 1. Steinberg used the Gaussian distributions.

Hockaday carried out a sensitivity analysis of parameters in Reich's model applied to aircraft landing on one runway and two parallel runways. He used the original model and Gaussian distributions. However, the calculation is sophisticated in relation to aircraft altitude and lateral separation as well as speed distribution.

Below is presented an example showing the use of formulae for collision probability in the Copenhagen terminal area, 3 June 1961.

At 1102 Sk 644 was abeam Bella holding at 7000 feet (2100 m) speed 210 knots. At 1105 Sk 632 was abeam Bella holding at 7500 feet (2250 m) speed 300 knots.

The longitudinal separation s_x can be calculated from the 3 minutes time separation $s_x = 3 \times 300/60 = 15$ nautical miles ~ 81000 feet

The standard deviation is

$$\sigma_x = 0.6 \times \frac{1}{60}\sqrt{(210^2 + 300^2)} \times 3 \times 1.8 \times 10^3 = 19\,800 \text{ feet}$$

if the uncertainity of time measurement is 0.6. With the length of the aircraft t_x equal to 200 feet, one obtains

$$P_x = \frac{200\sqrt{2}}{19\,800} \times \exp\left[-\left(\frac{81\,000}{2 \times 19\,800}\right)^2\right] = 7.8 \times 10^{-5}$$

The lateral separation s_y is equal to zero. The standard deviations are

$$\sigma_{y632} = \frac{10}{3} \times \frac{15}{57} \times 3 \times 1.8 \times 10^3 = 4740 \text{ feet}$$

and

$$\sigma_{y644} = \frac{2}{3} \times \frac{1}{3} \times 3 \times 1.8 \times 10^3 = 1200\,\text{feet}$$

If the uncertainty for N.D.B. navigation is $3\frac{1}{3}°$, minimum $\frac{2}{3}$ nautical mile

$$P_y = \frac{200\sqrt{2}}{\sqrt{(4\,740^2 + 1\,200^2)}} = 2.3 \times 10^{-2}$$

The vertical separation was 500 feet $= s_z$. The standard deviation is $\sigma_z = 2 \times 165 = 330$ feet at height of 7000 feet

$$P_z = \frac{200\sqrt{2}}{\sqrt{\pi \times 330}} \exp\left[-\left(\frac{500}{2233} \right)^2 \right] = 1.6 \times 10^{-1}$$

The collision probability $P = P_x \times P_y \times P_z = 7.8 \times 2.3 \times 1.6 \times 10^{-8} = 2.8 \times 10^{-7}$. With about 10^5 operations per year in the Copenhagen terminal area, this means three collisions per 100 years.

Stene[21] has investigated collision risk in I.C.A.O. circular 106-AN/80 (1972). The calculations were concerned only with altitude separations. In the following, the example of an accident report is given.

A Scandinavian Airlines System, Douglas DC8–62, of Norwegian Registry, crashed in Santa Monica Bay, approximately 6 nautical miles west of Los Angeles International Airport, Los Angeles, California, at approximately 1921 Pacific Standard Time, 13 January 1969. The aircraft was operating as Flight SK–933 from Seattle, Washington, to Los Angeles, California, following a flight from Copenhagen, Denmark. A scheduled crew change took place at Seattle for the flight to Los Angeles.

The accident occurred in the waters of Santa Monica Bay while the crew was attempting an instrument approach to runway 07R at Los Angeles International Airport. Of the 45 persons aboard the aircraft, 3 passengers and 1 cabin attendant drowned; 9 passengers and 2 cabin attendants were missing presumed dead; 11 passengers and 6 crew members including the captain, the second pilot, and the systems operator, were injured to varying degrees; and 13 passengers escaped without reported injury. The aircraft was destroyed on impact. The fuselage broke into three pieces, two of which sank in approximately 350 feet of water. The third section including the wings, the forward cabin and the cockpit, floated for about 20 hours before being towed into shallow water where it sank. This section was later recovered and removed from the water.

The weather at Los Angeles International Airport was in general terms: 1700 feet broken, 3500 feet overcast; visibility 4 miles in light rain and fog;

wind 060° at 10 knots; and the barometer setting was 29.87 inches of mercury. The weather in the accident area was reported to be similar.

The examining board determined that the probable cause of this accident was the lack of crew coordination and the inadequate monitoring of the aircraft's position during a critical phase of an instrument approach which resulted in an unplanned descent into the water. Contributing to this unplanned descent was an apparent unsafe landing gear condition caused by the design of the landing gear indicator lights, and the omission of the minimum crossing altitude at an approach fix depicted on the approach chart.

As a result of the investigation the board developed recommendations concerning DC8 failed indicator bulbs, altimeter setting procedures, and approach chart legends.

2.2 Noise

Noise is commonly defined as unwanted sound, and consists of a series of rapid pressure fluctuations which spread outwards from the source at the speed of sound. Hence, a measure of the amplitude of the pressure fluctuations is a measure of the sound level, which ranges from 2×10^{-4} μbar, the threshold of hearing, up to a level of 200 μbar. This range of pressure is rather unwieldy, so the decibel (dB) is used to describe the sound pressure level of a pressure fluctuation p in the form dB $= 20 \log 5000p$.

Some effort must be made to convert the actual sound pressure level into a subjective level heard by the ear. Therefore, noise is measured by an A-weighted sound-level meter, having modified frequency response which corresponds to the frequency response of our hearing; thus the dB(A) is a measure of the loudness of a noise. A twofold increase in the apparent loudness of a noise is produced by an increase of 10 dB(A) (instead of 6dB).

It is possible to define a single commercial index that sums up the over-all impact of a given pattern of noise. One calculates the decibel level of a steady noise that would give the same total energy over the same time period. This equivalent level is also called the average sound level, where L_x is the level exceeded x per cent of the time, for example, during a one-hour period. Thus L_{99} serves to define the background level, while L_{50} shows the median level and L_{10} indicates peak noise level. L_{eq} is sensitive to high peak levels.

A reasonable sound level indoors is approximately 40 dB(A) by day and 30 dB(A) by night. The sound insulation of windows in a building normally reduces sound levels from external to internal by approximately 20 dB(A), which means that outdoor noise level by day should be less than 60 dB(A), at night less than 50 dB(A).

2.2.1 *Railway Traffic Noise*[22] *and Sea Traffic Noise*

Railway noise is significant, because certain areas are exposed to high noise

levels on a continuous basis. The noise is produced either directly as motor
noise from the engine and ancillary equipment, or as sound radiation by the
vibration of the train structure caused by its motion and the interaction
between the wheels and the track. To eliminate the noise would require major
changes in the design of both the rolling stock and the track and, in fact, such a
process is under way.

Table 2.11 shows the sound of passing rail vehicles measured at 25 m
distance and 3.5 m above ground, with free sound dispersion and fault-free
rail surface and wheel treads, in dB(A) after Stüber (V.D.I.).[22a] Doubling of
the distance from train to measurement point results in a drop of 5 dB(A).

TABLE 2.11   Railway noise level measured in dB(A) distance 25 m.

Support		Speed (km/h)					
		60	80	120	160	200	240
Main line	ballast	80	84	90	94	98	100
	concrete slab	84	88	94			
	steel bridge	97	100				

TABLE 2.12   Railway noise level measured in dB(A), distance 25m, new electric train sets, on
support ballast.

		Speed (km/h)	
		120	200
D.B. ET 420 EML	West German train	79	
D.B. 403	West German train, high speed		88
J.N.R.	Japanese Tokaido line train		84
S.N.C.F. TGV	French, Tres Grande Vitesse, train		92

Table 2.13 shows the continuous noise level of equivalent energy, L_{50},
measurement as before, that is, distance 25 m, 3.5 m above track, free
dispersion, fault-free rail and wheel. Doubling the train frequency causes the
levels to rise by 3 dB(A). Doubling the speed causes the levels to rise by 3–7
dB(A). Doubling the length of the train causes the levels to rise by 3 dB(A).

At 200 km/h, modern electric train sets on level ground give rise to a sound
level of 84–88 dB(A) at 25 m distance. Ordinary passenger trains produce
levels around 98 dB (A). When trains run on embankments, viaducts, and
ballast-less steel bridges the noise levels rise by up to 15 dB(A) above the

TABLE 2.13   Railway Equivalent Noise Level, L_{50} (dB(A)) distance 25m.

Traffic flow: 10 trains per hour	Speed (km/h)			
	120	160	200	240
J.N.R. 12 and 16 car sets			68	
D.B.	70	80		
D.B.			75	80

Track on support ballast

normal level. Running in a cutting or behind sound barriers 1.5 m high withholds about 70 dB (A) up to a distance of 100 m.

There are no standards or restrictions for outdoor train noise level. The Danish State Railways follow the international legislation put forward by O.R.E. (Office for Research and Experiments under U.I.C.).

There are no official standards for noise from ships. However, under Danish health legislation motor boat use on lakes is restricted to approximately 200 m from the beach, and night use is forbidden.

2.2.2 Road Traffic Noise
The Nordic Building Regulation Committee gives the following noise characteristics for road traffic noise. Figure 2.12 shows the vehicle sound level as a function of equivalent number of passenger vehicles (1 truck $\sim$ 10 cars)

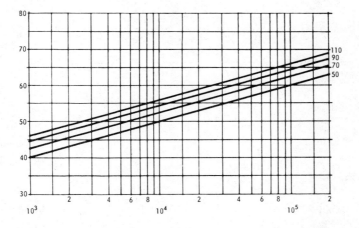

Figure 2.11 Noise levels near roads for traffic speeds 50–110 km/h. Ordinate, dB(A) at 100 m from centre of road; abscissa, traffic units per day (noise equivalents)

per day and vehicle speed, measured 100 m from the centre of the road in dB(A).

Under steady speed conditions vehicle sound levels increase with speed, that is 5–10 dB (A) for a doubling of speed, and also with traffic flow and composition, i.e. 10 dB(A) for a tenfold increase in vehicles from 100 to 1000 vehicles per day and 2–5 dB(A) for a doubling of number of heavy vehicles from 25 to 50 per cent. Both the character and levels of noise are affected by road intersections, pedestrian crossings, road gradients, road widths and road surfaces.

The fluctuation in noise level at intersections may exceed 20 dB(A). On a 1 in 11 ascending gradient, noise level increases by 6 dB(A) in traffic containing 20 per cent heavy vehicles; and halving the distance from the centre of the road from 100 m to 50 m increases noise level by 3–6 dB(A). A concrete surface gives about 1 dB(A) higher noise levels than asphalt for the same volume of traffic.

Reduction of vehicle noise could be obtained by reducing the cylinder pressure and bore size of the engine, altering its design, and ultimately by enclosing the engine and transmission and silencing the exhaust and inlet valves, engine cooling, and tyre and brake noise.

Noise propagation from the road may be reduced by screening with barriers or by constructing the road in cuttings; but ground absorption, vegetation and wind also play their part.

TABLE 2.14 Distance (m) from the centre of the road to obtain outdoor noise level of 55 dB(A) as a function of road type and screening

Screening	Number of lanes	Number of equivalent passengers vehicles per day	Average speed (km/h)	1 floor	3 floors	6 floors
Motorway						
Free	8	135 000	110	> 300	> 300	> 300
With vegetation				175	300	300
With barrier— height 5.5 m, distance 50 m from centre				200	225	250
Main highway						
Free	4	50 000	90	200	300	> 300
With vegetation				125	300	300
With barrier— height 4m, distance 40 m from centre				125	150	200

Johnson and Sounders found the number of dB(A) for a street as a sound level L_{50} exceeded 50 per cent of the time:

$$L_{50} = 46.5 + 10 \log\frac{N}{d} + 30 \log\frac{V}{6.5}$$

where N is traffic flow (cars per hour), V is speed (km/h) and d is distance (m) from edge of road.

Engine noise propagates outwards, falling 6 dB for each doubling of distance, whereas road and track noise is radiated from a line source and falls only 3 dB.

Table 2.14 shows the necessary distance from the centre of the road to obtain an outdoor noise level of 55 dB(A) measured as a function of vehicles per day (noise equivalents) and the average speed.[32]

2.2.3 Air Traffic Noise

In order to achieve a more precise numerical description of the relative noisiness of different types of jet aircraft compared with piston-engined aircraft, Kryter (1959) evolved a scale which gives more weight to high frequencies, the perceived noise level PNdB. It is assumed that levels expressed in dB(A) equal levels in PNdB minus 13.[23, 24]

An addition of 10 PNdB is again a doubling of annoyance. Taking into account the duration and pure tone contents gave a new scale, the effective perceived noise level, EPNdB.

Composite noise rating (C.N.R.) is a method of predicting the value of a single number rating of the cumulative noise that will intrude into airport communities at a specific time. The noise from one aircraft in PNdB can then include aircraft categories, distribution of aircraft types, number of aircraft per hour, runway utilisation, flight path, operating procedures and time of day. It is a calculated quantity; it cannot be measured.

The step-by-step procedure for estimating community reaction to noise from aircraft operations includes[27]

(1) collecting information on the nature of aircraft operations at the airport in question, types, number, utilisation of runways, flightpaths used, etc. for day (0700–2200) and night (2200–0700) forecasts.

(2) Selecting the appropriate sets of noise contours, which enable one to estimate the noise produced by one aircraft during take-off and landing by any of several classes of aircraft, for example jet.

(3) From these the perceived noise levels indicated for the area in question are determined. If the flight path is curved, the contours must be modified to conform to the curved flight path.

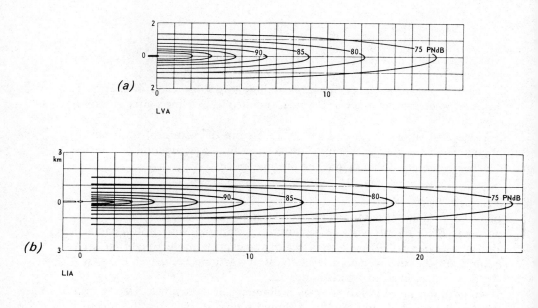

(a)

LVA

(b)

LIA

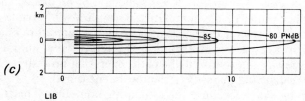

(c)

LIB

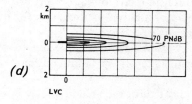

(d)

LVC

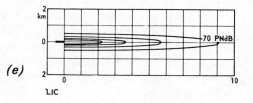

(e)

LIC

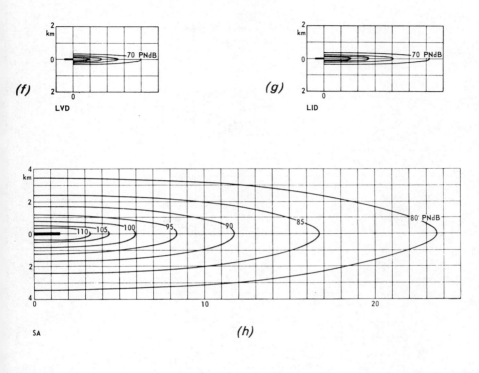

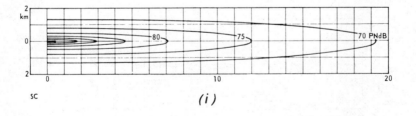

Figure 2.12 Airport noise from one aircraft, km from runway in PNdB *a*, Jet aircraft—visual
flight landing; *b*, jet aircraft—instrument flight landing; *c*, propeller aircraft—instrument
flight landing; *d*, light propeller aircraft—visual flight landing; *e*, light propeller
aircraft—instrument flight landing; *g*, very light propeller aircraft—instrument flight
landing; *h*, jet aircraft take-off; *i*, light propeller aircraft take-off

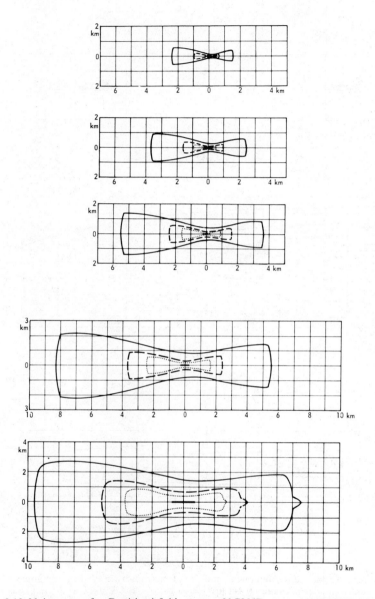

Figure 2.13 Noise zones for Danish airfields. ———90 PNdB; . . . . . . 100 PNdB. Class 1, 20–60 operations per day; class 2, 60–200; class 3, 200–600; class 4a, 200–600 with 15 per cent night traffic; class 4b, 200–600 with 10 per cent light jet traffic.

(4) Corrections are then applied to the perceived noise levels to take into consideration the number of operations, runway utilisation and time of day. The corrections for these factors are given in table 2.15.

(5) The composite noise rating for each type of flight operation is computed by adding algebraically the total of the correction numbers as determined by table 2.15 to the perceived noise level (PNdB) as determined. From these various values one C.N.R. must be chosen to apply to the area under study; normally the highest C.N.R. applies.

(6) An empirical relationship has been developed between C.N.R. and the expected response of residential communities (see table 2.16). The area in the vicinity of an airport can be characterised by three response zones, 1, 2 and 3.

The American airport noise indices are as follows

$$\text{C.N.R.} = \text{PNdB}' + 10 \log N - 12$$

where PNdB$'$ is the mean loudness of peak noises and N is the number of aircraft heard per day. Another one is called the Noise Exposure Forecast N.E.F., where

TABLE 2.15   Correction factors for composite noise rating (C.N.R.)

Correction	0700–2200	2200–0700	Number of operations per period N
−10	< 3	< 2	
− 5	3–9	2–5	
− 0	10–30	6–15	
+ 5	31–100	16–50	
+10	> 100	> 50	
			Runway utilisation (%)
− 0	31–100		
− 5	10–30		
−10	3–9		
−15	< 3		
			Time of day
+ 0	0700–2200 day		
+10	2200–0700 night		

TABLE 2.16   Expected Response and Composite Noise Rating (C.N.R.)

C.N.R.	Zone	Response
<100	1	no complaints
100–115	2	individuals may complain
>115	3	concerted group action complaint

$$\text{N.E.F.} = \text{EPNdB}' + 10 \log N - 88$$

It is seen that N.E.F. values are roughly C.N.R. values minus 70–75. The British index is called Noise and Number Index N.N.I., where

$$\text{N.N.I.} = \text{PNdB}' + 15 \log N - 80$$

This index does not take into consideration noise at night.

The comparisons between different measures equivalent to C.N.R. identify an upper boundary of acceptable noise exposure for residential use as being approximately 115 C.N.R. or 44 N.E.F. or 61 N.N.I. or 97 M (French unit) or 80 Q (German unit) for more than 500 operations per day.

At the lower levels of noise exposure, the equivalent C.N.R. is approximately 105, or 34 N.E.F. or 51 N.N.I. or 82 M or 60 Q.[32]

The C.N.R. values for some American airports are given in table 2.17 together with the complaints and annoyance.[28]

TABLE 2.17   Percentage Inhabitants Complaining and Composite Noise Rating (C.N.R.)

	Chicago	New York	Los Angeles
C.N.R.	107	115*	111
% annoyed	24	67	40
% complaints	5	22	12
% aware of noise before moving	21	25	40

* Area with C.N.R. > 115 is 10 000 acres for Kennedy Airport

For some years Denmark has had noise abatement procedures for Copenhagen Airport with a preferential runway system. The method for assessing noise exposure is composite noise rating. Two zones for land-use planning are defined: zone 1 with serious noise and no new building construction is defined as areas with 115 PNdB corrected and more; zone 2 with some noise and no new housing is defined as areas with 100 PNdB corrected, and up to a maximum of 115 PNdB corrected. (Zone 1 has approximately 15 000 inhabitants; zone 2 approximately 200 000.)

Figure 2.14 shows the zoning forecast for 1985. The restrictions for pilots using Kastrup Airport are controlled by a monitoring system. The noise abatement procedures cause a 10 per cent decrease in the capacity of the airport.

Figure 2.13 shows the Danish proposal for noise exposure areas for different types of airfield, with different types of aircraft, different traffic volumes and operation times (day and night). In this proposal, zone 1 is defined as 105 PNdB corrected and more, and zone 2 as land disturbed by 90

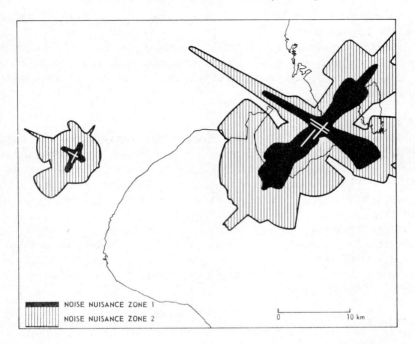

Figure 2.14 Airport noise zones for Copenhagen, to the east Kastrup (1985) to the west Roskilde. Black zone > 115 PNdB corrected, hatched zone > 100 PNdB corrected.

PNdB corrected and up to 105 PNdB corrected, that is, the criteria have been revalued by 10 PNdB compared to Kastrup Airport, since the tolerable noise level in rural areas with little background noise must be lower than that of the capital.

For airfields with no jet and no night operation and less than 600 general aviation operations per day this means a zone 1 length of approximately 1–1.5 km from the runway threshold. For 15 per cent night operations and the same data as before, zone 1 grows up to 2.5 km and for night jet operations up to approximately 4 km by day. The width is about 2 km.

Figure 2.14 also shows the proposed zoning around a new Roskilde Airport for 1985. This is one of the first land-use plans in Denmark taking into consideration aircraft noise from an airport not yet in operation.

The noise problems from aircraft are greatly influenced by the noise certification rules which are already being issued for aircraft by I.C.A.O. Annex 16, where the noise level 6.5 km from the take-off point in direct alignment with the runway should be less than 108 EPNdB for aircraft of more than 272 tons. Such certification should also be used for small aircraft. New types of aircraft such as the Boeing 747, are approximately 16 EPNdB quieter than the Boeing 707.

Aircraft already in use must be retrofitted, that is, the inlet and fan ducts of the engine are lined with sound-absorbent material, or the front fan section of the engine is removed and replaced with an acoustically treated fan of larger diameter.

2.3 Air Pollution

The carbon monoxide (CO) concentration in clean air is normally 0.1 parts per million (p.p.m.); however, motor vehicles and buses often pollute the air with up to 10 p.p.m., equivalent to 12 000 μg/m^3 or more, especially in urban traffic.[34, 35] The CO emission from road vehicles is approximately 3 g per passenger mile; for trains it is approximately 0.03 per passenger mile, so railway pollution can be neglected.

In New York State the ambient air-quality standards (12/69) require an acceptable air pollution service level of 30 p.p.m. averaged over an 8-hour period and 60 p.p.m. for a 1-hour period. The carbon monoxide concentrations depend on traffic volumes and meteorological conditions.[36,37] Table 2.18 shows some observations that have been taken in Frankfurt.[38]

TABLE 2.18   Motorway air pollution

	CO concentration (p.p.m.)	Side		% reduction of roadway concentration
		Leeward	Windward	
0 vehicles per h		4	4	30 m distance to
400 vehicles per h		6	4	edge of road: 20%
800 vehicles per h		8	5	30 m height
1200 vehicles per h		12	6	above road: 30%
1600 vehicles per h		18	8	

Windspeed approximately 2 m/s and measurement 3 m height above road

Table 2.19 sets out some observations that have been taken in the United States and in Denmark.

Modifications to motor vehicle engines to attain low pollutant emissions are: modification of induction systems, carburettor, combustion chamber, ignition system, etc., and the use of afterburners. Engine adjustments can reduce emissions from vehicles by 20–40 per cent for CO and 10% for hydrocarbons.

Direct CO concentration measurements made at 311 sites in Edinburgh and Coventry by Imperial College[33] yielded the following equation:

$$\text{CO(p.p.m.)} = 2.26 + 0.14R - 0.63A + \frac{Q}{V}\left(0.03T + \frac{2.368}{W}\right)$$

TABLE 2.19 Street air pollution (CO concentration, p.p.m.)

	Hourly				Weekdays	
					1-hour mean	8-hour mean
Detroit	Lodge/Ford	10	Copenhagen	Faelledvej	38–35	7–17
Los Angeles	Pico Boulevard	16		H.C. Anderson Boulevard	30	18
New York	Herald Square	18		Fredensg.	22	12
New York	East 45 Street	60		Lyngby Torv	35	10
				Lyngby Bus Station	40	34
				Roskildv Glostr.	30	17

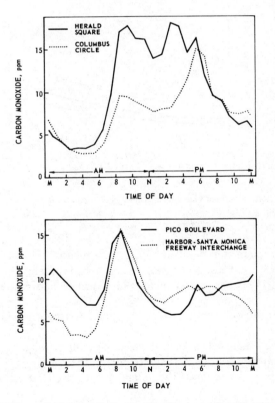

Figure 2.15 Air pollution in New York and Los Angeles

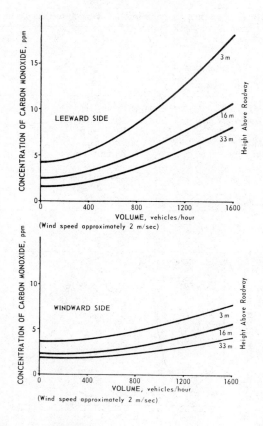

Figure 2.16 Air pollution from German motorways as a function of vehicles per hour, height above roadway and wind conditions

where R = ambient temperature (°C), A = mean windspeed (m.p.h.), Q = (two-way) vehicle flow, V = mean vehicle speed (m.p.h.), T = traffic arrival pattern index, W = road carriageway width (feet). The input required is:

(1) Number of vehicle miles of steady speed driving on the road link in an hour.
(2) The speed achieved in steady speed operation.
(3) The number of stops and starts during the hour.
(4) The number of seconds the vehicle is stopped and idling.

All of these measures are produced by the Dynamic Highway Traffic

Model (D.H.T.M.); but only (1) and (2) can usually be obtained from conventional transport planning analyses. The final product of the D.H.T.M. is a pattern of CO emission totals for each link, and the diffusion pattern of this CO must then be calculated in order to reduce the concentrations of CO at any given point.

Traffic is suspected to be the greatest single source of air pollution in most countries. This involves carbon monoxide (CO), hydrocarbons (HC) and oxides of nitrogen (NO_x); the latter can be a problem in airports. Tables 2.20 and 2.21 show some comparative data.

TABLE 2.20   Estimated emissions of air pollutants by weight for the United States (1969)

Source	Millions of tons				
	CO	Particulates	SO_x	HC	NO_x
Transportation	111.5	0.8	1.1	19.8	11.2
Fuel combustion in stationary sources	1.8	7.2	24.4	0.9	10.0
Industrial processes	12.0	14.4	7.5	5.5	0.2
Solid waste disposal	7.9	1.4	0.2	2.0	0.4
Miscellaneous	18.2	11.4	0.2	9.2	2.0
Total	151.4	35.2	33.4	37.4	23.8

TABLE 2.21   Pollutant emissions by transport mode

Mode	g per passenger mile		
	CO	HC	NO_x
Rail	0.03	0.2	0.2
Air	0.3	0.2	0.2
Road vehicle	3	0.2	0.2

Air Traffic Air Pollution

Although aircraft engines do not contribute greatly to the over-all air pollution problem, air pollution can be a problem for people living near airports. The new high bypass ratio engines powering the Boeing 747s, and DC101s already have achieved very low smoke levels.

A major retrofit programme is under way to lower the smoke level of DC9, B727 and DC8 aircraft. One of the technical advances is a redesigned combustion chamber, which soon will have reduced emissions of carbon monoxide and unburned hydrocarbons, especially in the new high bypass turbofan engines; however, the invisible pollutant, the oxides of nitrogen, has become an increasing problem.

In addition to the practical matters ranging from accidents to noise and pollution, there is the difficulty that so many vehicles and aircraft are now being used in urban areas that the results of congestion and delays are costing urban communities a great deal of money. This question is treated in chapter 3.

References

1. Starr, C. (1969). Social benefit versus technological risk, *Science*, **165**
2. Lawson, R. (1966). *An Analysis of Trends in Transport Facilities*, PB 185426, Washington
3. Tani, H. (1968). The reverse stopping ability, *J. Inst. Navig.*, **21**
4. Potts, C. E. and Roeber, J. F. (1972). Time/frequency and transportation, *Proc. IEEE*, **60**
5. Beer, W. J. (1968). Analysis of world merchant ship losses, *J. Inst. Nav. Arch.*
   The Liverpool Underwriters (1970). *Annual Report*, London
   The Lloyd's Register of Shipping (1970). *Annual Report*, London
6. Fujii, Y. and Shiobara, R. (1971). The analysis of traffic accidents, *J. Inst. Navig.*, **24**
   Government Report (1962). *Oresund Connection*, Copenhagen
7. Lloyd, T. I. (1970). Comparison of the safety record of British Rail and highways, *Accident Analysis and Prevention*, **2**
8. Pierick, K. (1971). Zur Problematik der Verkehrssicherheit, *Die Bundesbahn*, **45**
9. UIC (1971–73). *International Railway Statistics*, UIC Paris
10. Accident Reports (1968). *Railway Gazette*, **124**, October 4
11. Thorson, O. and Mouritsen, I. (1971). Report 6, Danish Council of Road Safety Research, Copenhagen
12. Raisbeck, G. (1972). Problems in the ratification of analysis of transport safety, *Accident Analysis and Prevention*, **4**
13. Jorgensen, N. O. (1972). *11th Int. Study Week Traf. Eng. Safety*, Brussels
14. Ernst, E. (1966). *8th Int. Study Week Traf. Eng. Safety*, Barcelona
15. United Nations (1973). *Transport Statistics*, New York
16. Highway Research Board (1970). *Factors Influencing Safety at Highway Rail Grade Crossings*, Special Report 50, Washington
17. Marks, B. L. (1963). *Air Traffic Control Separation Standards and Collision Risk*, Royal Aircraft Establishment, Farnborough
18. Reich, P. G. (1966). Analysis of long-range air traffic systems, *J. Inst. Navig*, **19**
19. Faison, W. E. (1967). Assessing separation criteria for approach to departing parallel runways, *IATA 17th Techn. Conf.*, Montreal
20. Steinberg, H. A. (1970). Collision and mid-air risks in high capacity airport operations, *Proc. IEEE*, **58**
21. Hockaday, S. (1969). *Separation of Landing Aircraft with Special Reference to Collision Risk*, ITTE, University of California
    I.C.A.O. (1972) *Circular-106-AN/80*, Montreal
22. The Pollution Committee (1972). *Noise, Roads and Railways*, Report 26, Copenhagen
    Stüber, C. (1974). *Railway Gazette International*, December
23. The Pollution Committee (1972). *Aircraft Noise*, Report 25, Copenhagen
24. Power, J. K. (1971). *Aircraft Noise Standards and Regulations*, DOT,Washington
25. Mathieu, E. (1970). *Regional Statistics on Safety*, ITA, Paris
26. Stratton, A. (1974). Safety and air navigation, *J. Inst. Navig.*, **27**
    National Transport Safety Board (1970). *Aircraft Accident Report*, January 13, 1969, Washington
27. Airforce Manual (1964). *Land Use Planning with Respect to Aircraft Noise*, no. 86–5, Washington
28. Plessas, D. (1973). Land use planning with respect to aircraft noise, *Land Economics*, **49**
29. Dienemann, P. and Lago, A (1971). Transport system technologies, *Transp. Science*, **5**
30. Rallis, T., Rasmussen, R. E. H. and Rydal, J. (1959) On dissipation of fog, *Ingenioren*, Int. Edition, Copenhagen

31. Rallis, T. (1963). Airports, *Acta Poly. Scand.*, **18**, Copenhagen
32. Rallis, T. (1973). Identification of critical parameters in transport systems and environment in Denmark, *Int. Symp. Transp. Enivron.*, University of Southampton, Southampton
33. Wigan, M. R. (1975). Some environmental impacts as part of the transportation planning process, T.R.R.L. *Suppl. Report 136 UC*, Crowthorne
34. Perkins, H. C. (1974). *Air Pollution*, McGraw Hill, New York
35. Sunn Pedersen, P. and Rasmussen, 1, (1973) *Luftforurening for Forbrendingsmotorer*, The Technical University of Denmark, Copenhagen
36. HRB, (1974). Air quality and environmental factors. *Transp. Res. Record 492*, Washington
37. Rummc, N. (1974). The effect of carbon monoxide, *J. Safety Res.*, **6**
38. (1973). *A Guide for Reducing Automotive Air Pollution*, PB 204870 and PB 204878, Washington
39. Kostilainen, V. and Hyvarinen, M. (1974). Ship casualities in the Baltic, 1971–72, *J. Inst. Navig.*, **27**
40. Kostilainen, V. and Hyvarinen, M. (1971). Casualties to tankers in the Baltic, *Report 5*, Technical University, Helsinki
41. Hara, K. (1974) Probability of collision in marine traffic, *J. Inst. Navig.*, **27**
42. Fujii, Y. and Yamanouchi, H. (1974). Frequency of accidents in marine traffic, *J. Inst. Navig.*, **27**
43. Maritime Safety Agency (1973). *Marine Accidents*, Japan
44. CLM Systems (1974). *Airports and their Environment*, PB 219957, Washington.
45. National Cooperative Highway Research, *Progress Report 133*, Washington (1972)
46. Wheatley, J. H. (1973). Collisions and strandings in the English Channel, *J. Inst. Navig.*, **26**
47. Beattie, (1963, 1966, 1968) Traffic regulations in the Dover Strait, *J. Inst. Navig.*, **16, 19, 21**
48. Fricker, (1961, 1973). Three classic collisions, *J. Inst. Navig.*, **14, 26**
49. Hargreaves, E. R. (1973). Safety of navigation in the English Channel, *J. Inst. Navig.*, **26**
50. Emden, R. K. (1975). The Dover Strait information service, *J. Inst. Navig.*, **28**
51. Foster, E. (1967). Safety at sea *J. Inst. Navig.*, **20**
52. Wylie, F. J. (1966, 1973). Regulations for preventing collisions at sea *J. Inst. Navig.*, **19, 26**
53. Diewald, W. J. (1974). Incorporating highway safety into level of service, *J. Proc. ASCE, Transp. Eng.*, **100**

3 Intercity Transport Capacity

It has become general practice to specify, by way of design standards, certain fixed values for the maximum traffic volume N at a route or terminal during a busy day or hour. These standards do not explicitly include the occupation time b of the route or terminal. One might therefore think of using the maximum traffic load Nb in a busy period. Such a standard would, however, be independent of the number of channels n (area) in use. The ratio of traffic load and the number of channels might then be used, the utilisation or service level Nb/n.[1]

Furthermore, if one were to use a maximum disturbance factor, that is, the rejection or delay in rush hours, one could ensure that all the relevant factors, namely the traffic volume, the separation between traffic units and the number of service stands or lanes in use, would be taken into account and that the number of traffic units affected by disturbance was expressed directly. A route or terminal ought thus to be expanded by another channel as soon as the rejection or the delay due to congestion exceeded a certain value. Such a traffic standard would, however, merely take theoretical and technical considerations into account, but would have no regard for economic considerations (*cf.* chapter 4).

The value of delay to be used for calculation of capacity will depend on the acceptable delay distribution. A long delay may be acceptable for long trips and for a special type of traffic. A complete delay analysis must include analysis of the delay build-up as the traffic volume increases. This may result in a temporarily overloaded route or terminal without exceeding acceptable delay criteria.

In choosing the tolerable delay the main criterion should be one of queue length, although other criteria such as safety and cost should be considered.

A purpose of routes or terminals is to ensure that the traffic units can make their trips without undue hindrance. Because of the rejection phenomenon and the waiting, however, a certain percentage of the units will be disturbed so that the desired speed is not obtained. If the routes or terminals are expanded, the capital invested for this purpose will yield a benefit; to quantify this benefit one should, in keeping with the purpose, use as a criterion the reduction in number of trips affected (*cf.* chapter 5).

In place of practical observation better results can be obtained by simulation, even though this is expensive in terms of time and money. However, comparative queueing theory investigations of the effect of future traffic volumes, future service times and future number of channels or stands in simultaneous use will presumably lead to good results, which could hardly be obtained from observations. Sometimes, it is impossible to use queueing theory; in such cases deterministic models can be used.

3.1 Sea Transport

3.1.1 Seaways

H. M. Petersen[2] published a thesis concerning the number of ships passing the Gedser lighthouse, located in the Baltic Sea.

In the year 1955, 40 434 ships passed the lighthouse, or an average of 3370 ships per month. The monthly variation was important; August had the heaviest traffic with 4344 ships and March the lightest with 2544. At that time the lighthouse was passed by 91 ships per day on average, 140 in August and 82 in March.

In the winter period, the average number of ships per day was 92, with a standard deviation of 22. In the summer period, the average was 139 (s. d. = 23). The numbers include westbound as well as eastbound ships.

The weekly variation shows that more ships are passing on Saturdays and Sundays (125) than on Wednesdays and Thursdays (102) compared with an average of 115 ships. The variation throughout the day shows that more ships are passing around midnight than around midday. The number of ships per day is therefore a function of the month and the day of the week.

The number of ships observed during a period in October 1955 was found to have a Poisson distribution*. The average speed was observed to be 9 knots, (s. d. = 1.9). The average distance between ships was 4 nautical miles.

When a waterway is so crowded that overtaking is almost impossible and vessels form into groups with almost equal speed, the traffic volume has reached capacity.

In a one-way channel and under ordinary navigation conditions for vessels of almost the same size L and speed V, the maximum traffic volumes N_{max} = $D_{max} \times V \times B$, where D_{max} is maximum density and B is width of the waterway.

D_{max} is determined by the size of the effective domain, the separation

* See page 89

between vessels, which is normally an ellipse having a semi-minor axis about $3\,L$, and a major axis of $7\,L$.

Fujii and Tanaka[3] found D_{max} to be $1.15/7\,L \times 3\,L$. If the width of waterway, B, is 2 km. we get $N_{max} = \dfrac{2V}{20\,L^2}$. For $V = 15$ knots (24 km/h) and $L = 0.2$ km

this gives $N_{max} = \dfrac{24 \times 2}{20 \times 0.2^2} = \dfrac{24 \times 2}{0.8} = 60$ vessels per hour

It can be seen that for $L = 180$ m the domain width $6\,L$ is 1000 m, that is, the vessels are using two fairways each with a rate of 30 vessels per hour, or 2 minutes separation per ship.

If six ships pass through the waterway per hour the traffic load $A = N/N_{max}$ is 0.1 corresponding to a service level A according to the levels used in the *Highway Capacity Manual**.

TABLE 3.1   Basic capacity in a 1 nautical mile wide channel as a function of G.R.T., length and speed

	Vessels per hour		
G.R.T.	100 000–20 000	20 000–3000	3000–500
Mean length (m)	235	127	67
Speed (knots)	14	14	12
Capacity (ships per hour)	50	150	450

3.1.2 Ports

Eddison and Owen[4] found delays to ships after they have entered the port. The delays arise because the ships have to wait for berths to be vacated by other ships. The distributions of arrivals of ore-carrying ships at British ports was effectively random. It was therefore possible to develop the theory of queueing to enable the average congestion delay per ship to be predicted for each port from a knowledge of the number of berths, the service time and the arrival intervals. The service time was determined by the size of ship (8000 tons) and the capacity of the unloading installation (8000 tons per day with 25-ton cranes). The arrival interval was determined by the annual tonnage of the total harbour (1 000 000 tons) and the size of ship (8000 tons).

If the total berthing time (including manoeuvring) is 36 hours constantly, and the arrival intervals are 72 hours exponentially distributed, then the delay is 1–18 hours for one berth (see table 3.2). One berth was most economic at tonnages approaching 1.5 million tons per year. Between 1.5 and 3.5 million tons per year it becomes more economic to have two berths, suitably equipped. From then on three berths are preferable. The cost of ships' time in

* See page 100

port must be compared to the cost of establishing a new berth, including cranes (see chapter 4).

Frequency Distribution for Arrival Intervals
It has been found that the arrivals at terminal sections are frequently random—independent of time and of previous arrivals, despite the fact that most of the traffic is scheduled. In terms of probability theory, this can be expressed by the following assumption. If the average number of arrivals per hour is termed N_a, the probability P that, for example, one traffic unit will arrive during the short interval dt is $N_a dt$, irrespective of the time at which the interval dt occurs, whereas the probability of two or more arrivals is $0(dt)$. The frequency distribution for the arrivals of the traffic units based on this assumption is known from statistical theory as Poisson's Law:

$$P_N = \frac{(N_a t)^N}{N!} \qquad N = 0, 1, 2, \ldots \quad (cf. \text{ chapter 2})$$

P_N is the probability that N units will arrive during the period t, when the normal average frequency of arrivals is N_a.

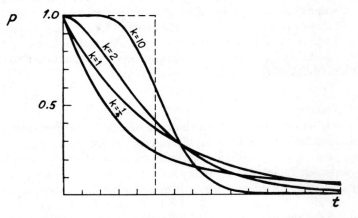

Figure 3.1 Probability distribution P with time t. $k = (\text{mean/s.d.})^2 = 1$ exponential, $k = \frac{1}{4}$ hyperexponential, $k = 2$ erlang

The sum of two Poisson-distributed flows is Poisson-distributed. A split-up of a Poisson-distributed flow gives Poisson distributions, when the split-up is independent of the actual traffic condition.

It can be shown that if the arrivals N have a Poisson distribution, the arrival intervals t will have an exponential distribution, that is they will follow the continued frequency distribution

$$P(t) = \exp(-t/a),$$

where $a = 3600/N_a$ and N_a is the mean value. In fact the completely random and the regular arrival patterns are the most commonly used, and it is only for these that mathematical solutions of any generality can be obtained.

Frequency Distribution for the Service Time

Supposing that the mean duration of normal handling operations in a section is b hours, the calculation may be based either, as a rough approximation, on a constant service time, or on simple and convenient formulae which apply to exponential distribution of the service time,

$$P(t) = \exp(-t/b)$$

where P is the probability that a handling operation lasts at least t hours. $N_b = 1/b$ is the mean number of handling operations per hour.

In traffic theory a queue system is characterised by a number of traffic units looking for a certain type of service at a service plant with limited access. By this limitation, the individual sections of the service plant may come to form bottlenecks whenever the number of arrivals, irrespective of time, exceeds the number of units handled, so that the units are, to some extent, in each other's way. This may be due to variations in the demand for service, irregularities in the handling, or disturbances from outside. Apart from the mutual interference of the traffic units due to such conflicts, the variations also result in incomplete utilisation of the traffic installations.

Delay Calculation

It is possible to work out the probability D of a delay encountered by those traffic units which arrive when all the stands are occupied.

As long ago as 1920 the Danish mathematician A. K. Erlang, employed by the Copenhagen Telephone Company, calculated the probability of delay D, if the traffic arrivals are governed by a Poisson distribution. A terminal layout with n stands, a constant traffic load $A = N \times b$, and an exponential distribution for the times required for passing through, or remaining in, the service section has the probability of waiting D. Thus

$$D = \frac{\dfrac{A^n}{n!}\dfrac{n}{n-A}}{1 + \dfrac{A}{1!} + \dfrac{A^2}{2!} \cdots \dfrac{A^{n-1}}{(n-1)!} + \dfrac{A^n}{n!}\dfrac{n}{n-A}}; \quad A < n, \; n = 1, 2, 3, \ldots$$

The average waiting time f for all units is:

$$f = \frac{Db}{n-A} \qquad A < n, \quad n = 1, 2, 3,$$

The mean number of units waiting in the queue can also be calculated as

$$E = DN$$

In the following, each queueing system will, in accordance with Kendall, be characterised briefly by three letters with an oblique line between them, for example $M/M/n$. The first letter indicates the arrival frequency distribution, the second letter indicates the frequency distribution for the holding time (service time) and the third letter indicates the number of service channels, stations, $n = 1, 2, \ldots$, being in use at the same time.

D signifies a regular, that is, constant frequency, distribution. M signifies a Poisson or negatively exponential distribution.

It is seen from table 3.2 that Eddison and Owen found

$$\frac{A}{n} = \frac{b}{a} = \frac{36}{72} = 0.5,$$

which for $M/D/1$ system gives $0.5 \times 36 = 18$ hours.

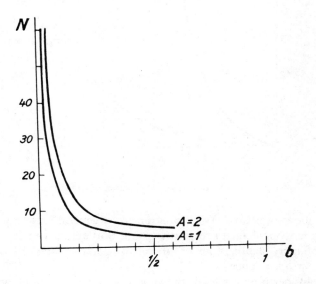

Figure 3.2 Traffic load A as a function of volume N and service time b

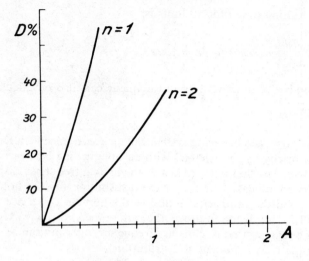

Figure 3.3 Probability of delay D

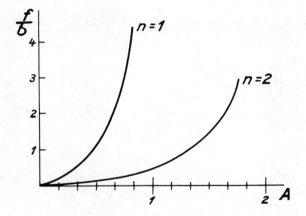

Figure 3.4 Waiting time as a function of traffic load

In the following a capacity calculation for a general cargo quay section 740 m long in Copenhagen Freeport is given. Bottlenecks can occur through shortage of quay depth, number of berths, cranes, gangs of dockers or warehouse or open space.

The mean berthing time at the quays was $b = 36$ hours with nearly exponential distribution.

TABLE 3.2 Mean waiting time/service time $=f/b$ for different traffic loads $A/n=(b/na)<1$ and various systems[5, 6, 7]

Constant $\dfrac{A}{n}$	0.1	0.2	0.3	0.4	0.5	0.6	0.7	0.8	0.9
$M/M/1$	0.11	0.25	0.43	0.67	1.00	1.50	2.33	4.00	9.00
$M/D/1$	0.06	0.13	0.21	0.33	0.50	0.75	1.17	2.00	4.50
$D/M/1$	0.00	0.01	0.04	0.12	0.26	0.48	0.88	1.69	4.18
$M/M/2$	0.01	0.04	0.10	0.19	0.33	0.56	0.96	1.78	4.26
$M/D/2$	0.01	0.02	0.06	0.10	0.18	0.29	0.49	0.90	2.14
$D/M/2$	0.00	0.00	0.00	0.02	0.06	0.16	0.33	0.71	1.98
$M/M/3$	0.00	0.01	0.03	0.08	0.16	0.30	0.55	1.08	2.72
$M/D/3$	0.00	0.00	0.02	0.04	0.08	0.15	0.28	0.54	1.36
$D/M/3$	0.00	0.00	0.00	0.01	0.02	0.07	0.17	0.41	1.21
$M/M/4$	0.00	0.00	0.01	0.04	0.09	0.18	0.36	0.75	1.97
$M/D/4$	0.00	0.00	0.01	0.02	0.05	0.10	0.19	0.38	1.00
$D/M/4$	0.00	0.00	0.00						

One gang of dockers can handle 20 tons per hour, that is 100 tons/h for 5 gangs or 200 h for a 10 000 ton ship. It is obvious that this old-fashioned way of cargo handling is not used. Better cranes, elevators, pallets and trucks can speed up the handling to 250 tons/h or 80 h for a 10 000 ton ship, if it is still both unloaded and loaded.

One gang consists of 8–10 men, that is 40–50 men per ship depending on the number of hatches and cranes.

However, using containers, 2 cranes can handle 40 containers of 10–20 tons per hour with only 2 gangs, that is 25 hours for a 10 000 ton ship with 500 containers. Bulk cargoes can be handled faster, up to 1600 tons/h for grain and 16 000 tons/h for oil. This means that a 100 000 ton dry bulk cargo can be unloaded and loaded in 125 hours, and oil cargo in 12.5 hours.

The number of ships arriving per day was $N=2$; the arrivals had a Poisson distribution.

The traffic load $A=N\times b=2\times 1.50=3$, table 3.2 and ref. 6 give:

Average delay f $=0.01\times 36=$ 0.4 h for $n=7$

$=0.03\times 36=$ 1 h for $n=6$

$=0.12\times 36=$ 4 h for $n=5$

$=0.51\times 36=18$ h for $n=4$

The utilisation A/n varies from 0.4 to 0.75 corresponding to service levels of A to C, D. This corresponds to a cargo turnover per metre of quay per year of $(2\times 10\,000\times 300)/740 = 8000$ tons/m/year.

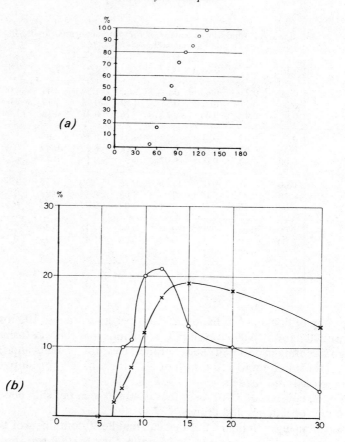

Figure 3.5 Frequency distribution of ship arrivals (*a*) and berthing time (*b*)
o, observed; x, theoretical

A container terminal with one berth, one container crane, and a 45 per cent utilisation of the berth, when it is kept in operation around the clock seven days a week, has been simulated by J. Buhr Hansen.[7a]

The terminal serves 75 per cent feeder ships (95 m long, 125 containers), and 25 per cent ocean-going ships (170 m long, 700 containers). Mean arrival time was 10 hours, normal distribution (s. d. = 4).

Mean service time was 4.5 hours (s. d. = 3.6). The service time is based on a crane operation with 20 lifts per hour, (s. d. = 4 following a normal distribution) with an additional stay at berth for 1 hour before and/or after the container handling. The turnover being 25 per cent of the ship capacity.

The delay of ships due to deviations from scheduled arrival hours was found by simulation to be 2.89 hours, by queueing theory to be 3 hours, the probability of delay being 0.45.

This calculation was for a yearly throughput of $2 \times 58\,000$ containers. Further simulation was done for $2 \times 118\,000$ and $2 \times 180\,000$ containers. The percentage of feeder ships was further varied from 75 to 50 and to 25.

As the traffic increases, the lengths of quays in use increase from 1 berth (200 m) and 1 crane to 3 berths (350 m) and 3 cranes, if the delay and utilisation are to remain reasonable.

When the terminal is open only during a limited number of hours a day the service time will increase, because a number of ships will have to stay overnight before handling is completed.

3.2 Rail Transport

3.2.1 Through Tracks

Recently, in Denmark, a single-track through line from Vordingborg to Rødby was constructed in connection with Rødby – Puttgarden ferry traffic. The line is approximately 34 km long with three stations for overtaking. The geometry is 7.2 km single line, 1.2 km double-track line, where running trains, for example, 835 m long freight trains can overtake each other. For a section of 8 km length covered at a speed of 80 km/h the service time is 6 minutes. The maximum traffic volume is theoretically 10 trains per hour, in both directions together; however, for 6 trains per hour in both directions together, the $M/D/1$ system shows a delay of 4.5 minutes, that is for a traffic load of 0.6—a service level B.

This is in accordance with the simulations made by Risberg (1963) and Law (1964), who for Swedish and Canadian single lines found 7 and 5–9 trains per hour to be the maximum traffic possible.[8, 9]

Double Track Lines

The longest of the minimum block interval times on the Copenhagen – Roskilde line applies to the block section nearest to Copenhagen Central, which has a length of 790 m.

The block interval time is calculated as the time required to cover a distance of 790 m plus the distance corresponding to the maximum train length for passenger trains (360 m), at a maximum permissible train speed of 50 km/h, plus an additional allowance for deceleration over a braking distance of 100 m (corresponding to the most unfavourable braking characteristic) from 50 to 30 km/h. An allowance must be made for the time required for the operation of the signals. Thus $b = 83 + 5 + 5 = 93$ seconds, almost constantly distributed.

This is about the same time as required by trains running at a maximum speed of 80 km/h over the longest block section of 2 km.

Data obtained concerning the working of trains over No. 1 track on the Roskilde – Copenhagen line during 8 rush hours at Easter 1961 showed that it is reasonable to assume a Poisson distribution, as Potthoff has shown to be the case near German railway stations. The line was used by 100 trains per direction per day including 60 passenger trains and 40 goods trains. The normal peak hour service was 6 trains per hour; however, this increased to 12 trains per hour during Easter, N.

The maximum traffic load on the line, $A = Nb$ was then $12 \times (1.5/60) = 0.3$, that is a service level A. The mean block delay was $0.2 \times 1.5 = 0.3$ minute.

For 24 trains, $A = 0.6$, that is service level B with delay $0.75 \times 1.5 = 1.1$ minutes.

For 36 trains, $A = 0.9$, that is service level F with delay $4.5 \times 1.5 = 6.8$ minutes.

At the same service level B a single track then takes 6 trains per hour in both directions, whereas a double track takes 48 trains per hour in both directions. The delay per kilometre of track is approximately 0.5–1 minute in each case.

3.2.2 Passenger Handling Stations

Copenhagen Central (1911) is a station with four through tracks which, on the approach lines, are used in the sequence, up – down – up – down. Two of the through tracks are used for long distance traffic, No. 1 and No. 2, respectively. These two tracks separate to make room for consecutive groups of depot and carriage sidings, eight groups with approximately ten sidings each. The innermost section between the inner home signal (0.75 km from the main building) and the platforms has a crossover and a set of points where the through line bifurcates to platforms, 1, 2, 3 and 4. There are eight parallel platform roads, which arriving and departing trains are able to use. The station serves as a terminus for a considerable number of trains both from the north and from the south-west. New signalling equipment with relay control and automatic route settings was introduced recently, and it is possible to arrange for 100 main route settings and 475 shunting route settings. It is possible to take a train to a platform via a shortened route setting; this means that a through platform road can be divided into two terminal platform roads, a northern and a south-western.

The points and crossings just south of the platforms are used by the following northbound movements: trains arriving from the west, trains from sidings to the platforms and shunting locomotives.

Southbound movements over the same points and crossings consist of empty trains directed into the sidings, shunting locomotives hauling trains from the platforms to the sidings, trains departing to the west and train locomotives going to the shed. The average occupation time for platform tracks was 10 minutes, including movements of locomotives, braking and starting times, and so on, exponentially distributed.

It is necessary to accommodate 12 trains arriving from the west during peak hours in the Easter period. The side for long distance trains thus accounts for 300 arriving and departing trains in 24 hours, including 150 trains from or to the west, or 100 000 trains per year and 9000 trains per peak month. A Poisson distribution applies in all these situations.

The traffic load $A = Nb = 12 \times 10/60 = 2$ for $n = 4$ tracks, or a utilisation of 0.5, that is a service level between A and B. The probability of delay is 0.17 or the waiting time is 0.9 minutes.

K. Smith of British Rail gives the following formulae for Victoria Station in London, which is a terminal station: $N = 30 \times n/(n+1) = 30 \times 4/5 = 24$ trains per hour and $b = 2n = 8$ minutes. This gives $A = 24 \times 8/60 = 3.2$ for $n = 4$ platform tracks, that is a utilisation of 0.8 and a service level of $C-D$, giving a delay probability of 0.60 or a waiting time of 6 minutes.[10]

A very heavily loaded track (No. 1) from Copenhagen Central to a marshalling yard in Helgoland 5 km north of Copenhagen was recently investigated for capacity problems by simulation. The problem was the combination of track and station capacity. If all trains stopped at two intermediate city stations, North Gate and Easter Gate, plus Helgoland, it was not possible with the existing signalling system to handle 20 trains per hour. The service time was in equilibrium at 220 seconds and the travel time over 5 km was 4.5 minutes more than normal. The stop time at stations varied between 40 and 80 seconds and the train lengths varied between 100 and 200 m.

By introducing two missing station arrival and departure signals for one of the stations, by using a constant train length of 200 m and shorter stop time at stations of 40 seconds, and using an Erlangian distribution, truncated with 9 degress of freedom, it was possible to obtain a service time of 135 seconds, when travel time was increased by only 45 seconds over the normal running time for 5 km (that is 27 trains per hour corresponding to service level B).[10a]

3.2.3 Goods Handling Stations

(i) Transit Goods Wagons at Marshalling Yards
A marshalling yard is a typical queue system, where the wagons arrive at the

reception sidings and are sorted in the line sorting sidings and the station sorting sidings to be picked up in the departure sidings.

Reception Group

Let the number of sidings be n_R, and the service time b_R be a function of profile, technical equipment, number of workers to handle uncoupling, technical inspection and paperwork, number of locomotives available, number of wagons per train, wagon speed and time required for the various operations. The number of trains per hour N_R is a function of the schedule. Rosteck, Gulbrandsen and Petersen have worked with these problems for Seelze near Hanover, Alnabru near Oslo and a marshalling yard in Montreal.[11, 12, 14]

For Seelze, a marshalling yard with hump and shunting locomotives, the number of sidings n_R was 10 and $b_R = 90$ minutes for one locomotive. The number of trains with 40 wagons per train was 3 per hour, that is 40 wagons every 20 minutes or 1 wagon every 0.5 minutes. This gave 72 trains per day, or 2880 wagons per day in one direction or a total of 5760 wagons per day.

However, the traffic load A_R was $3 \times 1.5 = 4.5$ for $n_R = 10$, that is a utilisation of 0.45 or a service level between A and B. The sidings should each be about 1000 m in length.

Line Sorting Group

For Seelze, the number of sidings n_L was 24, determined by the number of different lines from which goods trains were accepted; b_L was 270 minutes and the number of trains per hour, N_L, was 3. The traffic load A_L was $3 \times 4.5 = 13.5$ for $n_L = 24$, that is a utilisation of 0.56 or a service level between A and B.

The sidings should be 13.5×800 m $= 10\,800$ m plus 15 per cent extra length, that is approximately 12 km, with each siding 500 m in length.

Station Sorting Group

For Seelze, the number of sidings n_S was 10, determined by the number of different stations on the line to which the goods trains were dispatched; b_S was 12 minutes, and $N_S = 3$ trains per hour.

The traffic load A_S was $3 \times 12/60 = 0.6$ for $n_S = 10$, that is a utilisation of 0.06 or a service level A.

Departure Group

This can be treated in the same way as the reception group. The new marshalling yard in Maschen near Hamburg can take approximately 9000 wagons per day with 38 sidings in two station sorting groups. There will be 300 km of sidings and 800 points.

(ii) Terminal Wagons at a Goods Railway Station

If the number of tracks n is 24, the service time is 4 hours and the number of trains per hour is 4, it is possible to find the traffic load $A = Nb = 4 \times 4 = 16$ for $n = 24$, that is a utilisation of 0.66, or a service level of $B - C$.

The service time is made up of a loading and unloading time of 20 containers per hour, with 30 containers per train, and a manoeuvring time of one hour, that is

$$\frac{30 + 30}{20} + 1 = 4 \text{ hours} = b$$

Handling 750 000 containers per year, the number of trains per year is

$$N = \frac{750\ 000}{2 \times 30} = 12\ 500$$

or 34 trains per day with a peak hour of 4 trains.

Operating the terminal for 24 hours a day throughout the week it is possible to reduce N to 2 trains per hour, that is a utilisation of 0.33, or a service level A.

3.3 Road Transport

3.3.1 Highways, Motorways

The volume of traffic using a road, N vehicles per hour, is a function of the time b during which each vehicle occupies the safety distance L between two vehicles or the speed $V = L/b$, just as for ships in a waterway and trains on a track. The traffic load A is then $Nb = N \times L/V$, the volume/capacity as it is called in the American *Highway Capacity Manual*. By using the definition density $D = 1/L$, $A = N\ (1/DV)$ and, for n lanes in use, one finds a utilisation $A/n = N/nDV$, where V is the space mean speed.[13, 15].

It is a matter of common experience that the greater the number of vehicles present in a given lane, the slower they move. Speed will be high, when density is low. At low volumes high speeds prevail; as the volume increases, the speed will decline.

On the basis of the ideal capacity quoted in the 1950 edition of the *Highway Capacity Manual*, it is found that, on a multilane road a traffic flow of $N = 2000$ vehicles per hour per lane can maintain a speed of $V = 48$ km/h with a minimum spacing of 24 m, corresponding to a vehicle density of 42 vehicles per km. By definition the traffic load $A = NL/V = 2000 \times 0.024/48 = 1$.

The corresponding service levels are defined as $E - F$, queue, unstable-forced flow. The 'possible capacity' is said to be equal to this capacity, provided that there is no crossing traffic, the lane width is 3.60 m, the lateral distance from the edge of the lane to a fixed obstacle is 1.80 m, the sighting distance is 600 m, the gradient is less than 20:1000 over a length of 600 m and there are no heavy vehicles. The practical capacity in rural areas is stated to be reached at a traffic volume of $N = 1600$ passenger car units (p.c.u) per hour per lane at a speed of 70 km/h and traffic load 0.8, defined as service levels C–D; stable flow, however, at 1200 p.c.u. per hour per lane and 90 km/h traffic load is 0.6, defined as service level B; and at 800 p.c.u. per hour per lane and 100 km/h traffic load is 0.4, defined as service level A and called free flow.

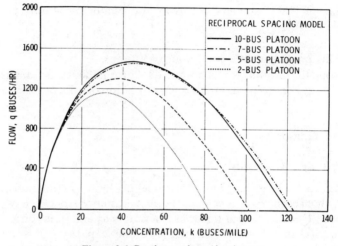

Figure 3.6 Bus lane volume/density curves

Restrictive lane width and lateral clearance, as well as alignment, are not a consideration on most highways and motorways, nor are intersections. Trucks and buses, being larger than passenger vehicles, take up more space, even in level terrain; therefore, their influence on motorway capacity must always be considered.

Passenger vehicle equivalents of trucks and buses and adjustment factors to be used in capacity analysis are given in the *Highway Capacity Manual*. At gradients of 6–7 per cent and passenger vehicle equivalents of 10, for 10 per cent trucks or buses adjustment factors as high as 0.50 are necessary.

Crowley[16] mentions that a bus lane could take 1000 buses per hour at about 35 km/h, with headway* of 3.5 seconds. Herman[17] found that the maximum

---

*The minimum time between one car and the next passing the same point.

number of buses per hour was 1400 at a concentration (density) of 40 buses per mile for groups of 10 buses.

However, at New York's bus terminal in 8th Avenue, two bus lanes together take 500 buses per hour; that is, $A = 250 \times 3.6/3600 = 0.25$ or a service level A.

3.3.2 Bus Stations

The long distance section of the New York bus terminal has $n = 65$ loading and unloading platforms and the normal berthing time for long distance buses is 20 minutes. Some 20 per cent of the buses are long distance vehicles. With a peak hour traffic volume of $N = 100$ buses, the traffic load is $A = Nb = 100 \times 1/3 = 33$, that is a utilisation of 0.5 for 65 platforms, giving a service level A. This corresponds to 1500 bus operations per day, or 500000 per year.[21]

3.3.3 Road Haulage Centres

Consider the conditions along 44 comb-shaped bays at Newark Union Motor Truck Terminal. The loading time is assumed to be 100 minutes per truck. On average 16 trucks leave during a peak hour.

The traffic load $A = Nb = 16 \times 1.6 = 25$ for $n = 44$, that is a utilisation of 0.57 giving service level A $-$ B.

This corresponds to 150 truck operations per day, or 50 000 per year.

3.3.4 Parking Areas

In front of Copenhagen Central Railway Station there is room for four lanes of vehicles, each holding 10 cars for passengers leaving the station. The mean time required for the loading of taxis is approximately 2 minutes; with 360 cars leaving in the peak hour, one has a traffic load $A = Nb = 360 \times 2/60 = 12$ for $n = 40$ stands, that is a utilisation of 0.3, giving a service level A. This is in accordance with Howlett's calculation at Euston Station in London.[18]

3.3.5 Toll Booths

Edie[19] has worked out delays at toll booths, near the George Washington bridge in New York. The number of booths open for traffic in one direction was four. The booth holding time was 10 seconds and the number of vehicles per hour 1200.

The traffic load $A = Nb = 1200 \times 10/3600 = 3.3$ for $n = 4$, that is a utilisation of 0.82, or a service level near D $-$ E.

If the arrivals were Poisson distributed and the holding times exponentially distributed, the average delay was $0.8 \times 10 \sim 8$ seconds.

In the same way it is possible to compare the probability of delay for 1, 2, 3 and 4 lanes in use on a motorway, if the arrivals are Poisson distributed and the headways are exponentially distributed. With 1440 cars per hour per direction, at a mean speed 72 km/h and a minimum headway 35 m for $n = 1$, we find[20]

			Service level
$A = 1440 \times \dfrac{0.035}{72} = 0.7$	$D = 70$ per cent		B – C
for $n = 2$	$U = 0.35$	$D = 6$ per cent	A
for $n = 3$	$U = 0.18$	$D = 0$ per cent	A
for $n = 4$	$U = 0.09$	$D = 0$ per cent	A

3.4 Air Transport

3.4.1 *Airways and Runways*

System analysis techniques were extended to include simulation by a digital computer by Bond in 1958.[22] An *en-route* air traffic control system using a reduced system of airways, area control, improved communication and navigation facilities and a 5-minute minimum longitudinal separation was postulated in the New York – Washington area, one of the busiest in the world. The system was analysed to determine its response to the expected 1965 traffic demand.

Samples of the expected traffic demand were prepared in terms of origin, destination, desired cruising altitude, aircraft type and desired departure time for each flight in the sample. Each sample flight was then assigned a particular route. Graphical simulation techniques were used in studying three route systems.

(1) Route V 140/A7 Washington – New York, 7 cruising altitudes and no radar.
(2) Route V 16 Washington – New York, 30 cruising altitudes.
(3) Airways to and from the Belle Mead intersection, south-west of New York

Simulation tests showed that route V 140/A7, under the postulated procedures, could handle rates up to 15–22 aircraft per hour, limited by the assumed proximity (17 miles to Washington) of its entry point.

Route V 16 appeared to be near its maximum usable rate for two-way traffic when the route was subject to approximately 65 aircraft per hour, including cross traffic at airway intersections.

A total peak rate of 50 per hour over Belle Mead intersection gave, with the controller's choice method (whereby the altitudes over the intersection are not subject to any prearranged system of altitude assignment), 0 minutes delayed climb, that is, the number of minutes outward bound planes are held at lower altitudes than desired after passing their entry point, and 11.7 minutes entry delay on the ground.

From the results of the postulated system, it was concluded that most of the traffic congestion occurred in the climb and descent portions of the airways, near the terminal areas.

In 1957 Manning[23] showed in the report 'General air – ground communication study' the number of aircraft passing over a reporting point (fix).

Altogether, data were obtained on 252 fixes in the high-density north-eastern area of the United States and it was found that, on average, there were eight crossings during the peak hour. The actual number ranged from a single crossing to a maximum of 31 at the Phillipsburg, Pennsylvania, reporting point, with 15 altitudes in use. The distribution of the number of crossings tended to follow the Poisson law.

3.4.2 Air – Ground Communications

The number of channels required can be calculated when the amount of air traffic is specified and the level of service stated. The level of service, as used in this type of discussion, is expressed as the decimal value of the probability that an attempt to make a call will not succeed and a delay will result. ($P = 0.5, 0.3, 0.2, 0.1, 0.033$.) The typical call has a holding time (duration) of about 32 seconds and there are about 10 such calls per hour for each aircraft in flight.

A report by Berkowitz and Fritz[24] summarises the delay suffered by aircraft landing at Washington National Airport. The delay was computed by queueing theory, graphical space – time techniques and dynamic simulation.

In all test groups the number of arriving aircraft per hour has been taken as 35, but the traffic load A varies from 1.17 to 0.91. The computation is based on only one runway being in use for landing. In some test groups, speed control is considered (that is the normal distribution of speed is cut off in 1.25σ, where σ is the standard deviation), in some cases with a headwind of 32 km/h; in the others neither speed control nor wind are considered.

Group 7: theoretical acceptance rate 31.6 aircraft per hour (speed control, 20 m.p.h. (32 km/h) wind)

Group 10: theoretical acceptance rate 36.1 aircraft per hour (no speed control, zero wind)

Group 6: theoretical acceptance rate 38.5 aircraft per hour (speed control, zero wind)

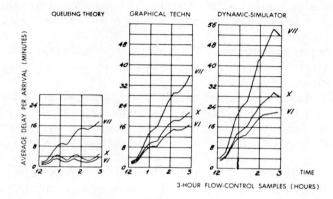

Figure 3.7 Queuing graphical and dynamic simulator delays for Washington Airport.

Test results from groups 6, 7 and 10 are shown in figure 3.7, partly to demonstrate that the waiting time is longest for group 7, which has the heaviest traffic load $A = 1.11$, partly to point out that the simulation waiting time is longer than the graphically calculated waiting time, which again is longer than the queueing theory waiting time. From the results it can be seen that when the traffic load $A > 1$, but near 1, the queue waiting time for the system $M/D/1$ is 15—35 per cent of the simulation waiting time, depending on the duration of the test. For $A < 1$, but near 1, the queue waiting time is 35—40 per cent of the simulation waiting time. Berkowitz and Fritz, who incidentally did not compare their results with the observations, did not take into account the efficiency factor which Warskow had observed. This is because, under peak traffic conditions, the control organs and pilots reduce the separation demands.

A mean separation of approximately 90 seconds applicable to 30 flight operations per hour is reduced to approximately 80 seconds with 50 flight operations per hour. The increase in the traffic load is thus not proportional to the traffic volume. Safety considerations are also taken into account by shorter final approach, speed control, more prompt departures from the taxiway and the assistance provided by computers and radar in estimating the separation requirements more precisely. Pardee[25] has also proved by simulation that two intersecting runways can deal with 64 landings and 61 take-offs per hour (rejections, that is overshootings, being 7–14 per cent).

It is interesting to note that the number of aircraft under control at any particular moment was found to vary according to the Poisson distribution.

Distribution of the time intervals between operations in the New York Terminal Area was exponential. This law was found to hold both for departures and approaches when considered separately and when the two are combined. The law also holds for each of the airports and for both V.F.R. and I.F.R.

In 1960 Warskow and Galliher[26] published a study of airport runway capacities in which airport operations at 15 U.S. civil airports were observed and measured. It was found useful to study airports by analysing operational delays due to various movement rates rather than maximum capacity ratings. Mathematical queueing formulae were tested. These studies demonstrated the importance and effect on operating rates of

(1) various aircraft populations
(2) runway lengths and turn-off layouts
(3) runway configurations
(4) I.F.R. or V.F.R. movements

The runway layouts were analysed from the standpoint of capacity by developing a curve of the operating rates of landings and take-offs and the corresponding delay to departures. Figure 3.8 indicates the effect that aircraft population has on V.F.R. runway capacity. At 6 minutes delay the number of movements per hour is respectively 35, 46 and 54 for one runway with turn-offs every 300 m.

The highest practical operating rate is obtained when the departure rate is high and the arrival rate is low. Figure 3.8 also indicates the effects of the spacing of turn-offs on V.F.R. runway capacity. Layouts 1, 2 and 3 assume right-angle turn-offs at spacings of 1000, 450 and 300 m. Layouts 4 and 5 assume 3 and 4 high-speed turn-offs. The relative practical capacity at 6 minutes delay is 35, 42, 46 and 48–53 for one runway with 20 per cent jet aircraft, measured in movements per hour.

With a short 1500 m runway for the twin-engined transports and light aircraft parallel to the long runway, a capacity of 35 + 65 movements per hour is reached. With a 3000 m parallel runway for take-off only, the capacity is 115 movements per hour.

Figure 3.8 shows how intersecting runways can increase V.F.R. capacity. The position of the intersection causes the operating rate at a 6 minute delay to vary from 78 to 47 movements per hour, for 3000 m runways with 300 m turn-offs and 20 per cent jet aircraft. Figure 3.8 also shows how I.F.R. movements decrease the capacity from 65 to 38 movements per hour.

If it is not desired to use a priority calculation, the traffic can be simulated as has been done by Jolitz.[27] He showed that this calculation can be carried out analytically by means of a non-equilibrium queue consideration, $M/D/1$. If the

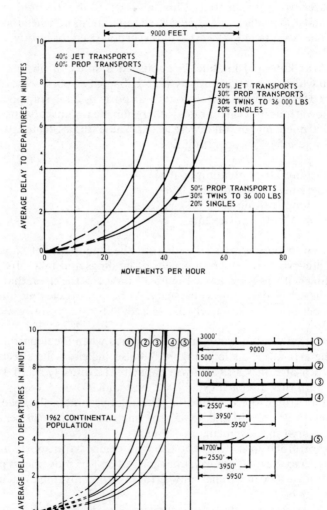

Figure 3.8 Runway capacity, V.F.R., I.F.R. and delays for different layouts and aircraft types

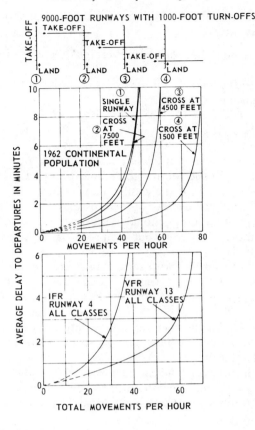

Fig 3.8 (contd.)

$M/G/1$ model is regarded as more correct, Khintchine's formula can be used.[28] O.N. Olsen[29] has shown that the two systems yield exactly the same result as the service time and scatter of results is insignificant.

There is sufficient space for about 30 aircraft to pass above one another at the same time within an airway with a height of 10 000 m, that is, 15 aircraft levels in each direction.

Because of meteorological conditions, crossing paths of aircraft and considerations of economic cruising levels it is, however, rare for more than 4–6 levels to be used simultaneously per direction per airway (n) (see chapter 2).

The horizontal separation minima may be reduced to 8 km, that is, $b=2$ minutes, when radar is available.

If the number of aircraft per peak hour per direction is $N = 40$, the traffic load for a one-way airway is

$A = Nb = 40 \times 2/60 = 1.33$ for $n = 5$ levels that is a utilisation of 0.26, or a service level A.

The maximum traffic load for the air traffic control has been described by Arad[30] and Rosenshine[31] as

$$A_C = Nb_1 + Nb_2 + Cb_3$$

where N is the number of aircraft under control, C is the number of conflicts (both per hour) and b_1 is the routine communication time, b_2 is the control communication time, and b_3 is the conflict control time.

The number of conflicts, overtaking or crossing, depends on the airway network geometry, and it is proportional to the separations, the speed and the square of the number of aircraft, but reciprocal to the area size and the organisation effectivity.

If, for a crossing, N_4 aircraft with separation b are crossed by N_5 aircraft with separation b, the traffic load $A_0 = N_4 b + N_5 b$ and $C = [(N_4 + N_5)A_0]/(1 + A_0)$; the conflict time b_3 can be 20 seconds per conflict.

$b_1 + b_2$ is about 430 seconds per aircraft, a controller transmits about 120 bits per aircraft and so does the pilot and they speak at a rate of about 10 bits per second (see chapter 2).

The air traffic control work load can be measured from the communication channels as the hourly percentage occupied by communication. If this traffic control work load reaches 0.6–0.8, that is a service level B – D, it is impossible to handle more aircraft.

In the United States' new National Airspace System and Automatic Radar Traffic Control System speed class sequencing and computer-aided approach spacing are used, and these improvements will lower the air traffic control work load. However, better airway geometry can also help, as shown by Slattery.[32, 33]

If $A_0 = 10 \times \dfrac{2}{60} = 0.33$,

then

$$A_C = 40 \times \frac{2}{60} + 10 \times \frac{0.33}{1.33} = 1.33 + 2.5 = 3.8 \text{ for } n_C = 6 \text{ channels.}$$

It is seen that the load per channel is 0.65 or near service level C.

For a terminal area it is necessary to split up arriving traffic to several holding points with only one departure route to the runway. If $n = 2$ points, separation $b = 2$ minutes and the traffic $N = 20$ aircraft per hour, one has a traffic load for each point of $A = 20 \times 2/60 = 0.66$ for $n = 1$ route of arrivals, that is service level C.

In runway capacity calculation one also has to take into consideration non-statistical equilibrium and preference rules.

Non-Statistical Equilibrium

Let us take the case where the traffic load A is greater than or equal to n, the number of service stands, and there is no equilibrium. In this transient system the probability that the queue will return to the order of magnitude of 0–1 becomes more and more remote.

Fritz[38] has, by extrapolation, adapted curves with the equation

$$E_t = C_0 t^{C_1} (\text{system } M/D/1)$$

for $A > n$, where C_1 is a function of A, and E_t indicates the size of the queue at time $t = t_0 b$. When there is no queue at $t = t_0$, C_0 is constant.

(C_0, C_1, A) is (0.3877, 0.7049, 1), (0.7226, 0.8929, 1.5) and so on

By integration the mean waiting time f is obtained over the whole period 0 to t from

$$f = E \times b.$$

For $n = 1$ runway in use and $N = 40$ operations per hour with an average separation time $b = 1.5$ minutes, then traffic load $A = Nb = 40 \times 1.5/60 = 1$ for $n = 1$, that is, a utilisation of 100 per cent, which means a service level F.

Fritz[38] gives the following delay for $A = 1, n = 1$, system $M/D/1$ and a time $t = 100b = 150$ minutes

$$f = 6.25b = 6.25 \times 1.5 = 10 \text{ minutes}.$$

TABLE 3.3   Mean waiting time/service time non-statistical equilibrium M/D/1

		A				
	0.5	0.7	0.9	1.0	1.2	1.5
$0 < t < 20b$	0.50	1.00	1.00	1.50	2.25	4.50
$20 < t < 40b$	0.50	1.00	1.76	2.75	5.00	9.00
$40 < t < 60b$	0.50	1.00	2.00	3.75	7.00	14.00
$60 < t < 80b$	0.50	1.00	2.50	4.75	9.50	18.50
$80 < t < 100b$	0.15	1.00	2.50	5.75	11.25	22.00
$100 < t < 120b$	0.00	1.00	3.00	6.25	13.00	26.00

DELAY *F b*

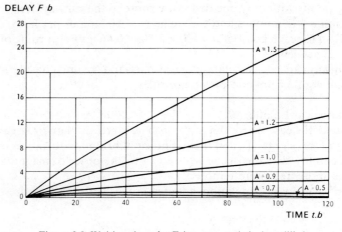

Figure 3.9 Waiting times by Fritz, non-statistical equilibrium
system *M D* 1

Queueing with Preference

Normally the traffic units use the service channel one at a time, the one waiting at the head of the queue being served either as soon as the preceding unit has left the service channel, or as soon as some other kind of service has been furnished.

If there are two queues, one of them, if it is composed of privileged traffic units, can be served before the other, or traffic units may be selected alternately from one or the other queue according to definite rules.

The number of arriving traffic units in the primary flow can be taken as N_L per unit of time with Poisson distribution, and the gap between two such traffic units to enable a unit from the secondary flow to be served between two primary ones to be at least G. It is also assumed that the number of traffic units per unit of time arriving at the common service channel from the secondary flow is N_S with Poisson distribution, and that the service time for a secondary traffic unit is fixed at b_S.

Arne Jensen[39] found the mean delay for all secondary units to be

$$f_S = \frac{b_S}{\exp(-N_L G + N_S b_S)}; E_S > 1, n = 1$$

The calculation is now based on the assumption that the intervals longer and shorter than G are independent of each other and statistical equilibrium is used to determine the frequency distribution for the number of traffic units waiting in the secondary flow, partly at a time where the gap shorter than G has just ended, and partly at a time where a gap shorter than G has just begun.

These times, which are conceived as points of equilibrium, permit the setting up of a set of equations for determining the probability of secondary traffic units being delayed by passing the common point.

TABLE 3.4 Mean waiting time/handling time, f_S/b_S for secondary flow in crossing traffic, b_S constant

Gap G (min)			4		3			2			1		
Primary N_L (units/h)	Secondary N_S (units/h)	b_S (min)	f_S/b_S	N_S	b_S	f_S/b_S	N_S	b_S	f_S/b_S	N_S	b_S	f_S/b_S
10	10	2.5	8	7	2.5	4						
20	10	1.0	8	6	1.0	4	1	1.0	2	12	1.0	2
30	10	0.6	33	10	0.6	8	10	1.0	10			

For $n = 1$ runway in use and $N = 40$ operations per hour, $N_L = 30$ landings and $N_S = 10$ take-offs, $G = 2$ minutes and $b_S = 1$ minute service time, one has according to Arne Jensen a take-off delay as follows $f_S = 10 \times 1 = 10$ minutes

Normal Queueing, Equilibrium
For $n = 2$ runways in parallel and $N = 80$ operations per hour with an average separation time $b = 1.0$ minute, one has a traffic load of $A = Nb = 80 \times 1/60$

$= \dfrac{4}{3}$ for $n = 2$, that is, a utilisation of 0.66, which means a service level C – D.

Erlang gives: $f = 1$ minute for $M/M/2$ (see table 3.2).

For $n = 1$ runway and $N = 40$ operations and $b = 1.0$ minute, $A = 0.66$, f = 2 minutes for $M/M/1$

For $n = 1$ runway and $N = 40$ operations and $b = 1.2$ minutes, $A = 0.80$, that is a service level C – D. $f = 5$ minutes for $M/M/1$.

For $n = 1$ runway and $N = 40$ operations and $b = 1.33$ minutes, $A = 0.90$, that is a service level E – F. $f = 12$ minutes for $M/M/1$, but $f = 6.0$ for $M/D/1$.

For $n = 2$ runways and $N = 80$ operations and $b = 1.33$ minutes $U = 0.90$. $f = 5.55$ minutes for $M/M/2$, but $f = 2.78$ minutes for $M/D/2$.

The ratios of landings to take-offs are of great importance, as well as aircraft population, turn-offs, runway pattern and weather. For a very high utilisation, the number of operations per hour can be tabulated as in table 3.5.

TABLE 3.5   Runway capacity under I.F.R. conditions (V.F.R.)

Landing/take-off ratio	1 runway	2 close parallel	2 independent parallel	4 runways
1:0	40	40	80	
3:1	40 (44)	48 (53)	80 (84)	
1:1	40 (48)	60 (80)	80 (96)	
1:3	48 (52)	60 (100)	96 (104)	
0:1	60	60 (120)	120	170
Average	40–50	70–80	90–100	150–170
With improved A.T.C.	60–70	80–130	130–170	250–500

Baran and Harris,[36] Mitre, give the improved A.T.C. figures shown in table 3.5 under the following conditions: lower separations, more control, etc. no wind, 6 nautical mile ILS-runway distance, 2 nautical mile landing − landing separation, 40 second take-off − landing separation, speed control, 5 seconds deviation (60 per cent aircraft 150 knots, 20 per cent 135 knots, 20 per cent 120 knots) (landing − take-off − landing −take-off).

Meisner[34, 35, 37] gives the delays corresponding to these conditions (see table 3.6).

TABLE 3.6   Calculated and observed delays

Operations per year	Calculated aircraft peak hour delay at airports (minutes)			
	1 runway	2 close parallel	2 independent parallel	4 parallel
200 000	29	9	7	0
300 000		22	15	6
400 000			29	10
500 000				15
600 000				23

For 1970	Observed peak hour delays per aircraft (minutes)	
500 000	Kennedy Airport, New York	110
700 000	O'Hare Airport, Chicago	80
600 000	International Airport, Los Angeles	40
400 000	International Airport, San Francisco	10

3.4.3 Apron
If the number of arriving and departing aircraft using an apron is close to the number using the runway pattern, that is, $N = 40$ aircraft per hour, and the

occupation time $b=90$ minutes, the traffic load $A=Nb=40\times1.5=60$. This means that at least 60 stands on the apron should be provided even to ensure a service level F.

A reasonable number can be found by P. V. Christensen's formula from telephony theory

$$n = A + k\sqrt{A} = 60 + 2\sqrt{60} = 76$$

where k is a constant close to 2.

The probability of rejection B can be calculated by Erlang's formula

$$B = \frac{\dfrac{A^n}{n!}}{1 + \dfrac{A}{1!} + \dfrac{A^2}{2!} \cdots + \dfrac{A^n}{n!}}$$

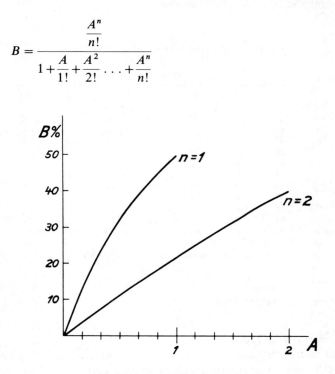

Figure 3.10 Probability of rejection B

Table 3.7 shows the values of B when A and n are known.

In proving the formula for rejection B, it is not necessary to presuppose anything about the distribution of the service times, or the distribution of traffic on each of the service channels or stands. However, it is presupposed that the traffic units leave the system, when they find all channels or stands occupied, and that arrivals are Poisson distributed.

In some sections of terminals, the traffic problems can be treated as rejection (loss) problems.

It must be assumed that we consider a time of the day when traffic conditions are stationary, that is when traffic is neither increasing nor decreasing, a consistently busy hour. The number of disturbed arrivals per hour is $N \times B$. The arrivals rejected accumulate immediately after blocking has occurred, and cause a prolongation of the critical condition. The variation in traffic volume will also cause the actual blocking to become greater than that calculated on the basis of average peak traffic.

When $A = 60$ and $n = 76$ B is 0 per cent.

TABLE 3.7   Probability of rejection, B (per cent)

Traffic load A	Number of service channels n							
	1	5	10	20	30	40	50	100
1	50	0.3	0	0	0	0	0	0
2	67	4	0	0	0	0	0	0
3	75	11	0	0	0	0	0	0
4	80	20	0.5	0	0	0	0	0
5	83	28	2	0	0	0	0	0
10	91	56	21	0.2	0	0	0	0
20	95	76	54	16	0.8	0	0	0
30	97	84	68	38	13	1	0	0
40	98	87	76	52	30	12	2	0
50	98	90	80	61	42	25	10	0
100	99	95	90	80	70	61	51	8

'Rejection' implies no queueing; 'delay' implies queues are allowed.

3.5 Passenger and Freight Transport

Passengers Per Traffic Unit

A passenger liner from Great Britain to Australia may carry 1700 passengers and a liner between Copenhagen and Oslo may carry 1000 passengers. A railway train with 13 cars of 80 passengers also carries about 1000 passengers and a jumbo jet carries 300–400 passengers. An intercity bus may carry 50 passengers and a helicopter approximately 25.

Freight Per Traffic Unit

The weight of 300 containers in a container ship is about 6000 tons. Container ships are now planned with 3000 containers with a weight of 60 000 tons. A goods train on the Danish state railways may have a weight of up to 1200 tons of which about 800 tons will be the weight of the goods. In the United States goods trains carry up to 3000 tons. A big road truck with trailer may carry 40 tons, the same as an air freighter.

Running Speed
The speeds indicated below are running speeds from station to station or from airport to airport and do not include access time to station or airport.

The Copenhagen – Oslo liner mentioned above has an average speed of 35 km/h. The running speed of railways, 100–140 km/h, has been increased in recent years; the permitted maximum speed on some lines has been increased to 200 km/h. For the Japanese Tokaido line, speeds are now up to 210 km/h and for the extension of these lines up to 260 km/h. The speed of buses and cars on motorways depends on the number of cars on the road and the service level, but the average speed is 50–100 km/h. For the moment speeds for aircraft are between 800 and 1200 km/h, reaching 2000 km/h for supersonic aircraft.

3.5.1 Passenger and Freight Capacity
Inland waterways can handle approximately 60 million tons per year. Ship canals and busy straits such as the English Channel handle up to 400–500 million tons per year.

The port traffic capacity depends on the ships' time in port so that container-ship berth capacity is 2 million tons per year, whereas non-container ship berth capacity is only 0.1 million tons per year for general cargo.

For bulk cargo a berth takes 10 million tons of dry cargo per year, but up to 100 million tons of oil per year. A big port takes 100 million tons per year.

Pipelines can handle 30–60 million tons per year depending on diameter and type of material transported.

If each train carries 1000 passengers or 1000 tons of freight that means that a railway line can carry 12 000 passengers per track per hour, that is 60 million passengers or 60 million tons of freight per year.

Marshalling yards take 6000 wagons per day or 36 million tons of freight per year. A passenger railway station handles up to 60 million passengers per year (of which approximately 60 per cent are long distance travellers).

A motorway may carry 1000 cars per hour per lane (service level A). With three lanes in each direction that means 6000 cars or 3000 trucks in both directions. With 10 per cent rush hour traffic we get 60 000 or 30 000 trucks per day. Theoretically, that works out at 18 million cars or 9 million trucks per year, and with 1.5 persons per car one gets 27 millions passengers a year. Usually 10 per cent of the traffic consists of trucks, so 9 million tons per year (with 10-ton trucks) plus approximately 24 million passengers per year is the observed capacity.

Road haulage centres take approximately 2500 delivery cars per day or 1 million tons of freight per year. A bus station takes up to 70 million passengers per year (of which approximately 10 per cent are long distance).

An air route takes 6 million passengers per year. Airport capacity is normally taken as runway capacity, that is 40 aircraft per hour, 400 per day and 120 000 per year, which means that an airport with only one runway can take about 12 million passengers per year. A large airport may handle up to 30 million passengers per year.

TABLE 3.8   Service level and capacity for railway, runway and motorway

Service level	Traffic load	Railway — Runway			Motorway lane		
		Volume (units/h)	Headway (min)	Speed (km/h)	Volume (units/h)	Headway (s)	Speed (km/h)
A	0.4	16	4	160	800	4.5	100
B	0.6	24	3	140	1200	2.7	90
C – D	0.8	32	2	120	1600	2	70
E – F	1.0	40	1.5	80	2000	1.8	50

Maximum 40 000 rail passengers	≡	Maximum 3 000 passengers/ hour at level F (i.e. 1 railway track = 13 motorway lanes)
Maximum 8 000 air passengers/ hour	≡	(i.e. 1 runway = 2 – 3 motorway lanes)
Maximum 40 000 tons railway freight/hour	≡	Maximum 20 000 tons freight/hour (difficult comparison, mixed traffic)
Maximum 12 000 cars in railway/hour (500 cars per train)	≡	(i.e. 1 railway track = 6 motorway lanes) (level B) (level F)

Table 3.8 shows capacity comparisons for different modes calculated in passenger or freight units. It is seen that 1 railway track equals 13 motorway lanes, 3 runways or 1 seaway, at the same service level F. It is also seen (Table 3.9) that the service level can be calculated for Kennedy Airport and compared to passengers' delays instead of aircraft delays. The aircraft delay is supposed to be constant, 4 minutes per aircraft both in 1970 and 1985; however, runway capacity is increased from 75 aircraft per hour to 130 aircraft per hour, and passenger capacity is increased from 75×0.75 (percentage air carriers) $\times 0.65$ (percentage load factor) $\times 130$ (passengers per aircraft) to $130 \times 0.75 \times 0.65 \times 210$ (see table 3.9 for explanation).

TABLE 3.9 Service level and capacity for Kennedy Airport (corresponding to 4 minute aircraft delay)

Service level	Traffic load	Average volume (passengers/h)	Average delay (min/passenger)	Year	Aircraft/h	Passenger/ aircraft†
A	0.4	2 000	9	1970	75	130
B	0.6	10 000	45	1985	130	210
C–D	0.8	15 000*	160			
E–F	1.0					

* 10 per cent of the days of the year or 10 per cent of the passengers of the year. It is obvious that these peak delays in 1985 are unrealistic.

20 million passengers/year	3 million passenger hours 40 000 aircraft hours per year	1970
88 million passengers/year	70 million passenger hours 500 000 aircraft hours per year	1985

† percentage load factor 0.65 percentage aircarriers 75

Practical capacity is found as the hourly traffic volume, at which the average delay reaches a specified level. In the north-east corridor project Mitre used a deferred traffic model to establish passenger delays at Kennedy Airport, New York[40]

On 10 per cent of the days of the year some passengers will get nearly 3 hours delay in the airport in 1985, with a forecast of 90 million passengers per year; this is, however, unrealistic and must be altered due to airport planning. It is not realistic to calculate that 70 million passenger hours will be lost per year in 1985; today (1970) this figure is only 3 million passenger hours lost per year.

Service Levels of Goods and Passenger Flows
The area for loading and unloading should be 0.200 m² per ton of cargo per year for goods from transit sheds; 0.125 m² per ton of cargo per year for goods from open storage space.

The warehouse area should be calculated from tons of cargo as
0.180 tons/m² floor area for transit goods
0.390 tons/m² floor area for long period storage

TABLE 3.10   Traffic loading of freight centres

	Area (m²)	Traffic units per day (tons)	Goods Storage time (hours)	Traffic load (%)
Copenhagen Free Port No 2 warehouse	15 000	100	480	66
Copenhagen Road Haulage Centre delivery bays	1 500	1050	6	42

The loadings and service levels of freight centres are shown in table 3.10. The calculation is as follows for road haulage:

$$A = 1050 \times 3 \times \frac{6}{12} = 1575$$

to be compared with $1500 \times 2.5 = 3750$. The traffic measured in tons can be converted into cubic metres by using 1 ton = 3 m³. The goods are stored up to a height of 2.5 m.

Waterloo Station, London, has 21 platforms. In 1954 (summer) 1600 trains and 224 000 passengers per day were handled, with 36 000 passengers per peak hour. In 1958, Hankin and Wright of London Transport studied[41] the flow of passengers on the Underground (subway). The results were as shown in table 3.11, and suggest that, for a width of 8 m, 720 passengers per minute may be the maximum flow.

Jackson[42] published in 1952 an article concerning the new railway station at Johannesburg. Actual observation shows that a train with 700 passengers can be cleared completely through two stairways, each 3 m wide, in 120 seconds or an average of 60 persons/m/minute. This figure compares

TABLE 3.11   Traffic loading of passenger terminals

Passengers	V Free speed (km/h)	N Max Flow of passengers (persons/m/min)	T Density (persons/m^2)
Level subways	5.8	90	0.9
Upward stairs	2.9	60	1.2
Downward stairs	3.5	70	1.2

favourably with the American Railway Engineering Association's estimate of 60 persons/m/minute. The number of persons/m/minute handled by escalators is 120.

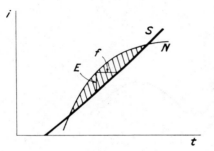

Figure 3.11 Number of waiting units *E*, as a function of arrivals and time

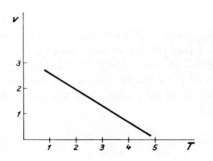

Figure 3.12 Speed *v* as a function of traffic density *T*

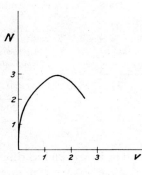

Figure 3.13 Volume N as a function of speed v

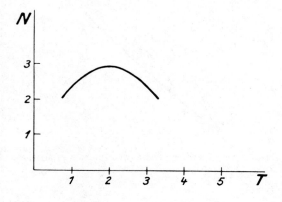

Figure 3.14 Volume N as a function of traffic density T

Nielsen[43] gives N_{max} number of passengers per second at the platform with width W m, density T persons per m² and speed v m/s

$N = W \times v \times T$, $W = 8$ m, $v = 1.5$ m/s, $T = 2$ persons/m²,

$N = 8 \times 1.5 \times 2 = 24$ persons per second = 90 000 persons per hour. This calculation was, however, based on urban railway passengers (1440 passengers per minute). Thus

$$A = Nb = N\frac{l}{v} = \frac{N}{WvT} = \frac{720}{1440} = 0.5 \text{ (service level B)}$$

In 1963 Operational Research note 152 concerning passenger handling capacities was published. The queueing problems in the passenger handling area were discussed by Knowler[44] who, on 14 July 1961, calculated and observed the queue lengths at London Airport No. 1 passenger building; with 17 desks in use, the queue theory $M/M/17$, and the simulation, $G/E_6/17$, showed a saving (in the simulation) of no more than 5 per cent of the desks.

Normally each sector of a terminal or line should take approximately the same number of passengers or tonnage of goods. In practice this is not always possible; Bambiger and Vandersypen (North-western Transport Centers) mention[45] that for Los Angeles International Airport they found the following possible maximum flows per section for 1969:

(1) Runway capacity   80 million passengers per year
(2) Apron capacity   80 million passengers per year
(3) Internal road systems   52 million passengers per year
(4) Parking area systems   52 million passengers per year
(5) External road connection 40 million passengers per year

The total capacity is then controlled by the external roads, that is not more than 40 million passengers per year. Sectors 4 and 5 could take more passengers by use of a railway line.

3.5.2 Transport Mileage Capacity
With 8760 hours per year and the speed quoted, the number of kilometres per year per transport unit is, dependent on utilisation, terminal time, etc. as shown in table 3.12.

TABLE 3.12   Transport mileage capacity

	Approx. hours/year	Speed (km/h)	km/year/unit 50% utilised
Ships	10 000	25	125 000
Trains	10 000	100	500 000
Cars	10 000	50	250 000
Aircraft	10 000	1000	5 000 000

If we want to arrange transport for 1 million passengers per year or 1 million tons freight over a distance of 6000 km (Copenhagen – New York, or Copenhagen – Teheran), we calculate either the number of passenger km (6000 million passenger km per year) or the number of ton km (6000 million ton km per year).

Taking a ship of 1000 passengers and 125 000 km per year per unit, that is 125 million passenger km per year, one gets:

$6000/125 = 48$ trips per year or 96 trips per year in both directions with 50 per cent load factor.

As one ship uses $6000/25 = 240$ hours per trip, one ship can operate 5000 hours/250 hours $= 10$ double trips per year (assuming 5000 hours in a year) (excluding port time) and 250 hours per trip (including delays due to bad weather); it is therefore necessary to use $100/10 \sim 10$ ships to make 100 trips per year.

This brings up problems like scheduling, reserve capacity and crew planning, which are treated in chapter 4.

References

1. Rallis, T. (1967). *Capacity of Transport Centres*, Fr. G. Knudtzon, Copenhagen
2. Petersen, H. M. (1956) *Working Paper*, Copenhagen (unpublished)
3. Fujii, Y. and Tanaka, K. (1971). Traffic Capacity, *J Inst. Navig.*, **24**
4. Eddison, R. T. and Owen, D. T. (1953). Discharging iron ore, *Operational Research Quarterly*, **4**
5. Brockmeyer, E, Halstrøm, H. L. and Jensen, A. (1948) *The Life and Works of A. K. Erlang*, ATV, Copenhagen
6. Jensen, A. (1950). *Moe's Principle*, KTAS, Copenhagen
7. Kendall, D. G. (1953). Stochastic processes occurring in queues, *Ann, Math. Stats*, **24**
   Buhr Hansen, J. (1973). On the planning and operation of container terminals, *23rd Int. Navig. Congress*, Ottawa
8. Risberg, J. (1963). Railway simulation, *IBM News*, Stockholm
9. Law, E. (1964). *Operational Research Papers*, Dalhousie University, Halifax, Nova Scotia
10. Smith, K. (1962) *Redevelopment of Victoria Station*, British Rail Operational Research Group, London
    Berg-Kristensen, P. (1975) *Working Paper*, Danish State Railways, Copenhagen
11. Rosteck, W. (1961). *Die Bundesbahn*, **35**, Leistungsf. von Rangierbahnhöfen, Berlin
12. Gulbrandsen, O. (1965). Alnabru Skiftestation, TØI, Oslo
13. Ashton, W. D. (1966). *The Theory of Road Traffic Flow*, Methuen, London
14. Petersen, E. R. (1971). *Bulk Service Queues and Train Assembly Times*, Queens University, Ontario, Canada
15. HRB (1965). *Highway Capacity Manual*, Washington
16. Crowley, E. (1963). An analysis of car – bus relationships in the Lincoln tunnel, *Traffic Eng.*, **33**
17. Herman *et al.* (1964). Single lane bus flow, *J. Oper. Res. Soc. Am.*, **12**
18. Howlett (1951). in (ed. D. G. Kendall) Some problems in queues, *J. Royal Stat. Soc. B.*, **13**
19. Eddie M. McCloskey (1956). *Operational Research for Management*, vol. II, Johns Hopkins University Press, Baltimore
20. Rallis, T. (1964). Operational research and design of roads, *12th PIARC Congress*, Rome
21. Jennings, N. H. and Dickins, J. H. (1958). *Management Science*, **4**
22. Bond, A. (1958). *ATC Systems*, Armour Res Foundation Report for Air Navigation Development Board, Chicago
23. Manning, E. (1957). *Air Ground Communication*, Bell Telephone Laboratory, New York
24. Berkowitz, S. M. and Fritz, E. L. (1955). *Techn. Dev. Report 251* Franklin Institute for CAA, Indianapolis
25. Pardee, G. (1963). *Automatic Terminal Environment Simulation Study*, F.A.A., Atlantic City
26. Galliher, H. P. and Warskow, M. A. (1960). *Airport Runway and Taxiway Design*, Airborne Instrument Laboratory for F.A.A., Washington
27. Jolitz, G. D. (1963). *Simulation of Factors Affecting Runway Congestion*, F.A.A. Washington
28. Khintchine, A. (1932). *Matem, Sbornik*, 39, Paris

29. Olsen, O. N. (1962) *Working Paper*, Copenhagen (unpublished)
30. Arad, B. A. (1964) *Measurement of Control Load and Sector Design*, F.A.A., Washington
31. Rosenshine, M. (1965). Application of automation to the solution of ATC problems, *3rd Symp Automation in ATC*,
32. Bates, M. (1969). *Stationkeeping and Cluster Control as Aids to Effective Airspace Utilisation*, D.O.T., Washington
33. Faison, W., Meisner, M. and Slattery, (1970). *Simulation Study of New York Metropolitan Area Air Traffic*, AD 702779, F.A.A., Washington
34. Meisner, M. and Faison, W. (1967). *Reduction of Delays in Terminal Areas*, FAA, Washington
35. Alexander, B. (1969). *Report of Air Traffic Control*, D.O.T., Washington
36. Baran, G. and Harris, R. M. (1969). *Airport Capacity*, M.I.T. for F.A.A., Washington
37. Carlin, A. and Park, R. E. (1970). A model of long delays at busy airports *J. Transp. Econ. and Policy.*, 4
38. Fritz, E. L. (1955). *Transient Steady State Delays in Airport Traffic*, C.A.A., Indianapolis
39. Jensen, A. (1957). *Ingeniøren, Int. Edition*, Copenhagen
40. Rallis, T. (1973). Intercity transport capacity, *1st Int. Conf. Transp. Res.*, Bruges
41. Hankin and Wright, (1958). Pedestrian flow in subways, *Operational Research Quarterly*, 9
42. Jackson, E. (1952). *Trans Inst. Civil Eng*, Johannesburg
43. Nielsen, O. (1952) *Ingeniøren*, No. 38 Copenhagen
44. Knowler, E. (1963). *Operational Research Note 130 and 140*, Ministry of Aviation, London
45. Bambiger, M. S. and Vandersypen, H. L. (1969). *Major Airports-Evaluation of Potential*, North-western University, Chicago

4 Transport Economy, Policy and Location

4.1 Economy and Transport

The European Common Market Commission has estimated the percentage of the total working population in the E.E.C. engaged in transport at about 6 per cent, but this figure only includes carriers for hire or reward. When adjustments were made for private transport, and if subsidiary transport activities, such as railway construction and maintenance, were included, the figure was 16 per cent of the total working population.[53]

The transport contribution to the gross national product (G.N.P.) for 1960 is shown in table 4.1

TABLE 4.1   Contribution of transport to gross national product

1960	G.N.P. (factor cost)	Transport as a % of G.N.P.
France (Ffr 1000 million)	286	6
Germany (DM 1000 million)	240	7
UK (£ 1000 million)	22	8

The transport contribution to the balance of trade for 1966 is shown in table 4.2

TABLE 4.2   Contribution of transport to the balance of trade

1966	Credit	% of total	Debit	% of total	Balance
France (US $ million)	238	3	279	4	− 41
Germany (DM million)	1205	2	1367	3	− 162
UK (£ million)	152	3	536	9	− 384

In the Netherlands the 9 per cent credit more than compensated for the 5 per cent loss on the balance of trade.

Table 4.3 illustrates the transport contribution to investments (1960), as a percentage of gross capital investment (G.C.I., *cf.* table 4.16)

TABLE 4.3   Contribution of transport to investments (percentage of G.C.I.)

1960	Inland shipping	Railways	Roads	Total
France	0.4	3.1	16	19.9
Germany	0.5	4.0	18	22.9
UK	0	4.5	23	28.3

Transport also contributes to government income. In 1960 about 11 per cent of the total ordinary revenue in the United Kingdom resulted from taxation levied on all forms of transport.

Transport is an important user of energy. The share of transport in overall consumption in France and Germany was 19 and 16 per cent, respectively, in 1960.

In 1960 the total expenditure on transport in Great Britain was about £3000 million, which was equal to about 50 per cent of the government's gross budgetary receipts and just under 33 per cent of the G.N.P.

In Denmark the G.N.P. does not include net profit from road investments, nor net profit from private passenger transport. The transport percentage of the G.N.P., 9.6 per cent, is therefore underestimated.

For the United States the G.N.P. in 1966 was $740 000 million of which transport represented about 20 per cent: $140 000 million divided into passenger transport [£90 000 million (£75 000 million roads)] and goods transport [£50 000 million (£40 000 million roads)].

4.2 Costs and Investments

An examination of the nature of the costs of operation is essential to the understanding of the functioning of transport systems. The cost of operation may be classified under:

Capital costs
Fuel and other material costs
Labour costs
Land use costs

4.2.1 Capital Costs

Production of transport services presupposes the use of capital structures and equipment, such as means of transport, transport lines and transport terminals. The costs are maintenance costs and depreciation costs.

Some illustrations of capital costs[72] in sterling are provided in tables 4.4, 4.5 and 4.6.

TABLE 4.4

Means of transport	Capital costs 1968
12 000 D.W.T. vessel (1957)	£ 1 million
1 freight train	£ 1 million
10 ton lorry (1967)	£ 3 000
Coach (1967)	£12 000
1 Boeing 747 Jumbo jet	£10 million

TABLE 4.5

Transport network	Capital costs		1968
1 mile of sea tunnel	£1 million	1 harbour berth	£2.5 million
1 mile of twin track	£1 million	station (1967)	£0.5 million
1 mile of 6-lane rural motorway	£1 million		
1 mile of pipeline	£0.04 million	airport	£10 million

TABLE 4.6

Maintenance costs per year			1968
1 mile of twin track	£10 000	station	£50 000
1 mile of 6 lane rural motorway	£ 1 000	airport	£1 million

Depreciation and maintenance costs vary from 25 to 40 per cent of total operational costs, if labour costs are excluded.

TABLE 4.7   Cost structure for different transport systems in 1960 (Sweden).[8]

	Shipping	Railways	Roads	Scheduled airlines (U.S.A.)
Staff wages	40%	63%	53%	45%
Fuel power	15%	12%	13%	15%
Service, supply	39%	21%	28%	30%
Depreciation	6%	4%	6%	10%

4.2.2 Fuel Costs

Costs for fuel and power are going to be a most important cost in the future. One of the more important characteristics of ships is their very low installed power, only between 2 and 3 hp per ton displacement. This implies a weight/drag ratio of 100 to 200 at 20–30 knots. There is, however, a very large increase in drag with increasing speed. New types of vessels, such as hovercraft and hydrofoils have weight/drag ratios of the order of 10. This is the same ratio as for aircraft. The weight/drag ratio for a train is higher than that for a truck. The energy consumption for a train is about 250 kcalorie per passenger km; for motor cars it is three times that amount; for aircraft the factor is six. Propulsive force must be available to overcome wave, track, road or drag resistance.

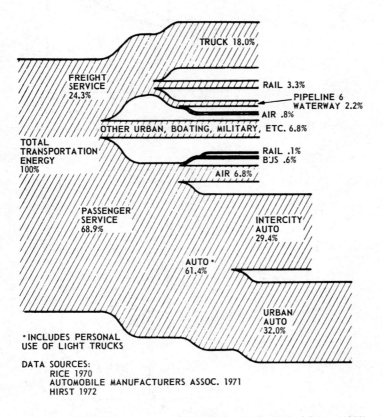

Figure 4.1 Transportation energy distribution in the United States (1970)

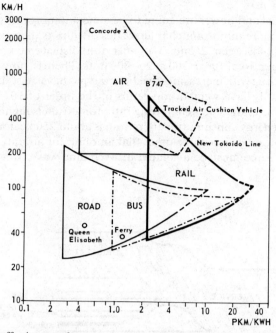

Figure 4.2 Energy effectiveness of passenger transport. Speed as a function of passenger km per kWh

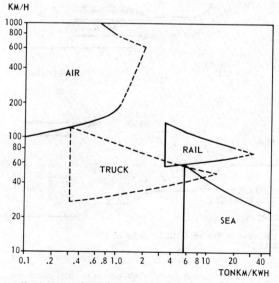

Figure 4.3 Energy effectiveness of goods transport. Speed as a function of ton km per kWh

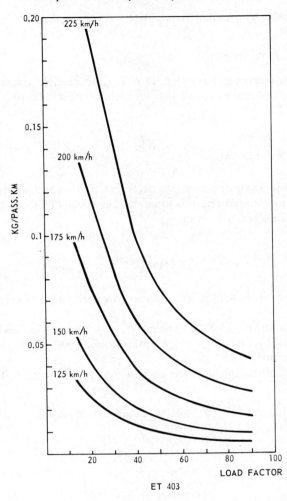

ET 403

Figure 4.4 Energy consumption for trains. Distance between stops 100 km

TABLE 4.8 Energy consumption

Mode	kcalorie/ passenger km	kcalorie/ ton km	Speed (km/h)	hp/ net tons	hp/ passenger	Gallons/ km
Train, ship	250	10–100	20–160	3	30	0.38
Car	750	300	80	9	60	0.06
Aircraft	1500	6000	800	600	240	2.5–5

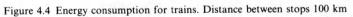

The energy used by a tanker is calculated as

$$\frac{\overline{hp}}{v \times D.W.T.}$$

where hp is horsepower, v is speed, D.W.T. is deadweight tonnage. If 1 hp is calculated as 2000 kcalorie, one gets for a ship with 48 000 hp, 28 km/h and 425 000 D.W.T.

$$= \frac{48\,000}{28 \times 425\,000} \times 2000 = 10 \text{ kcalorie/ton km}$$

Train resistance is proportional to its weight, friction and air drag, the cross-sectional area of wagon and the square of the speed. This can be calculated according to Sauthoff's formula

$$M = (105 + 0.025v)G + 11(2 + n \times 0.25)A \left[\frac{v}{100} \right]^2$$

where v is speed, G is weight, n is number of wagons and A is cross-sectional area.

For $v = 200$ km/h, $G = 250$ tons, $n = 8$, $A = 10\ m^2$, $M = 29\,000$ N; for a distance of 310 km, the energy consumption is $29\,000 \times 310\,000 \times 9 \times 10^9$ J $= 2 \times 10^6$ kcalorie.*

It is now possible to calculate the cost for fuel and power (see table 4.9).

TABLE 4.9   Cost ($) of 1 gallon (fuel) petrol[67]

	April	
	1973	1974
Germany	0.96	1.33
Great Britain	0.71	0.97
France	0.93	1.36
Italy	0.97	1.51
Switzerland	0.75	0.95
United States	0.45	0.60

4.2.3 Sea Transport

Thorburn[7] gives the following sea transport costs for a speed of 20 km/h:

* 1kJ = 0.278 kWh = 0.024 g petrol.
  1 kWh = 859.680 kcalorie.

0.4   Sw.øre per available ton km,   20000 ton km/h, 1000–1500 D.W.T.
0.1   Sw.øre per available ton km,   300000 ton km/h,   ~ 15000 D.W.T.
0.05 Sw.øre per available ton km, 2000000 ton km/h,   ~ 100000 D.W.T.
that is about 0.1 cent per ton mile (0.1–0.5d) (1968). Detailed information is given below.

Today a 16 000 ton tanker costs $200 per D.W.T. to build, whereas a 300 000 ton tanker costs only $70 per D.W.T. The operating costs of a 300 000 ton tanker per D.W.T. are only 10 per cent of those of a 16 000 ton tanker, that is the giant vessel has only 100 per cent greater costs than the 16 000 ton tanker, while crew and provisions costs are about equal. Only insurance and maintenance costs are higher for the giant vessel.

Bulk cargo ships cost a little less than tankers, but general cargo liners cost eight times more than tankers per D.W.T. A containership costs $25 million in construction and $1 million per year in operating costs for a 1200 container vessel. A conventional general cargo ship discharges only 20 tons per hour per hatch and spends 45 per cent of the year in port, a containership handles 400 tons per hour and stays in port 20 per cent of the year. The same figures for a bulk cargo ship are 1600 tons per hour and 15 per cent of the year in port and for tankers up to 16 000 tons per hour (pipeline) and 10 per cent of the year in port.

To ship 1 million tons of freight per year the 10 000 nautical miles from London to Sydney, therefore, once took 26 general cargo liners, but now takes only 14 containerships.

The distribution of capital investment for ports is shown below as an example.[90]

Quays, basins, breakwaters   30%
Tracks   7%
Roads and open storage   7%
Transit sheds etc.   33%
Installations   7%
Mechanical devices   16%

Saggar investigated conventional cargo liners on the United Kingdom–India run in 1970, one of the unprofitable general cargo routes.[91] Cargo liners are ships plying fixed routes according to a predetermined schedule and offering cargo space at fixed rates. Major proportions of costs are fixed, for example, ship insurance, maintenance and repairs, crew's wages, crew's provisions, stores and supplies, administration, port dues and fuel costs. The remainder, the variable costs, are cargo handling costs, cargo insurance and port dues for berthing periods greater than the scheduled time. The round voyage time is taken to be 180 days. This schedule is rarely realised;

the average round voyage time is 220 days or 110 days per single voyage. This means only three single voyages per year. If ports of call are reduced from 12 to 4, ships could be used for 8 single voyages. The total cost per freight ton would then fall from £14 to £6

TABLE 4.10   Operating costs for a cargo liner, London–Calcutta

Fixed costs	£1000 per year
Capital costs*	234
Fuel costs	21
Labour costs	110
Land use costs including administration	30
	395
Variable costs	
Loading, discharge	39
Harbour and insurance	44
	83
Total	£478
per ton	12

* Including depreciation, maintenance and insurance

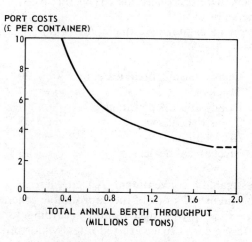

Figure 4.5 Port costs (McKinsey)

McKinsey[73] states that using larger ships will only reduce per unit transportation costs as long as port time is low and there is sufficient volume, and no competition (these points were not fulfilled for the United Kingdom–India routes).

Increasing ship capacity from 300 to 3000 containers reduces per unit costs by 42 per cent on the North Atlantic route as compared to 55 per cent on the United Kingdom–Australian route, that is relative reduction in per unit costs are greatest for the longest voyages.

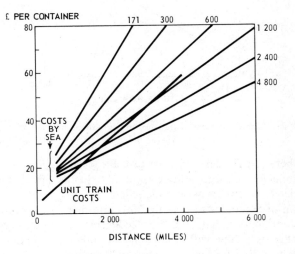

Figure 4.6 Costs per container as a function of number of containers per ship/unit train. Unit trains can be competitive with container ships in some situations

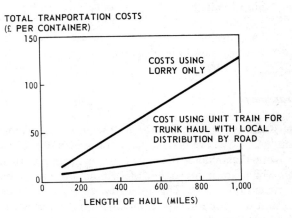

Figure 4.7 Cost per container lorry/unit train

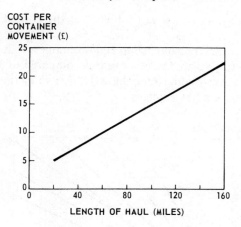

Figure 4.8 Cost of transporting containers by road

Break-even between Feeder and Port-of-Call Services
For a given mileage the cargo volume required to justify a port of call increases
with the capacity of the trans-oceanic ship.

A diversion of 500 miles to pick up 300 containers is economic for a ship
with a 1000 container capacity, whereas feeder services are more economic in a
similar situation for ships with a capacity of 2000 containers or above.

Finally the cost distribution of moving 5000 tons of mixed general cargo on
the U.S.A.–Europe route is shown as an example:

Receipt and storage at port	14%
Ship loading	36%
Voyage	23%
Discharging	16%
Receipt, handling, delivery	11%

4.2.4 Rail Transport

Swedish State Railways give (1968) the following rail transport costs for a
speed of 60 km/h: 2–4 Sw. øre per available ton km, 50 000 ton km/h, 20–60
cars of 20 tons with a load factor of 50 per cent, or 1 cent per ton mile (1 – 5d).

Fixed costs, which are independent of volume, are an important part of
railway cost structures. [87,89] The majority of railway investment costs
represent expenditures for long-lived facilities that have been sunk in the
costly plant facilities they use, in contrast to water, highways and aircarriers,

which use publicly owned rights of way and facilities. For these three modes payments are mainly through charges for use, which make their costs variable. Rates for railway services should never fall below incremental costs, that is, the existing and the prospective investments including depreciation, interest on capital and the cost of new rolling stock. There is, however, no single cost formula which will always and automatically be appropriate.

British Rail's track cost is the cost of providing, maintaining and operating the fixed plant used for traffic purposes. In 1961 these costs were as shown in table 4.11. Not all these costs are fixed costs, independent of traffic volume. With a track-carrying density of traffic between 1000 and 100 000 tons per day, B.R. considered that a 100 per cent increase in traffic is accompanied by an increase in permanent way maintenance cost of only about 20 per cent.

TABLE 4.11   British Railways track costs (1961)

1. Maintenance of way and structures, including renewals:	
Administration	6
Earthworks, bridges, tunnels, drainage	14
Track	50
Sidings	8
Stations and buildings	14
	£92 million
2. Signalling:	
Administration	2
Maintenance	18
Operation	23
	£43 million
Total	£135 million

With 20 000 route miles, the B.R. route costs per mile are £6000–£7000 per year. The long run fixed cost is only £2000 per mile per year; of that cost £1000 per mile is represented by the cost of the permanent way. With 2–4 million traffic units per route mile per year the cost per traffic unit varies between 0.7p and 0.35p, corresponding to a train density of 30–80 trains per day per route mile, or 20–50 trains per day per track mile. This goes for Switzerland, Germany, Holland, Belgium, Italy and France too; however, the United States seems to have 0.1p per traffic unit, but actually serves only freight traffic.

Rail passenger journey cost can then be calculated as follows:

$$\text{Vehicle operation cost/passenger mile} \times \text{distance} + \frac{\text{station cost/year}}{\text{passengers/year}} +$$

$$\frac{\text{track costs/mile/year}}{\text{passengers/year}} \times \text{distance}$$

where vehicle operation cost = 3p per passenger mile and
Station costs =£1 million or depreciation 4.5 per cent

for 50 years	£ 50 000/year
plus maintenance and operation	£100 000/year
	£150 000/year
Further track costs £1 million/mile, or depreciation	£ 50 000/year
plus maintenance	£ 10 000/year
per mile	£ 60 000/year

4.2.5 Road Transport

Samuelson[8] gives the following road transport costs for a speed of 60 km/h:

20–25 Sw.øre per available ton km,   100 ton km/h,   2 ton vehicle

10 Sw.øre per available ton km,   500 ton km/h, 10 ton vehicle

5–8 Sw.øre per available ton km, 2000 ton km/h, 30 ton vehicle

inclusive of vehicle and fuel taxes, that is, road costs. Approximately 2 cents per ton mile (1–5d) (1968).

The figures are of the same order for other countries: for example, in the United States the higher wages for drivers are balanced by lower fuel and original prices.

Fuel costs amount to about one-sixth of the total costs of road haulage operations and about one-quarter of private car operations (table 4.12).

TABLE 4.12   Road operating costs (percentage) 1961

	Road haulage	Private car
Standing costs	24	60
Fuel	17	24
Materials	9	3
Maintenance and repairs	3	13
Vehicle hire	2	
Wages	45	

Costs per vehicle mile (1961)[92] can be shown thus

$$C = 4.6 + \frac{80}{v}; \ 35 < v < 45 \text{ miles.}$$

where C is total average cost per vehicle mile in pence, and v is average running speed of traffic in miles/h

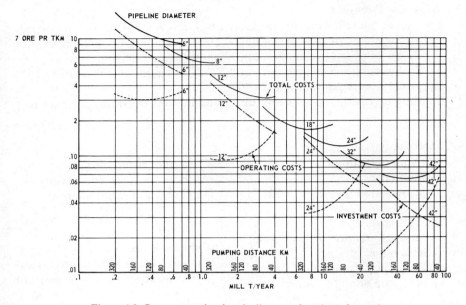

Figure 4.9 Cost per ton km by pipeline as a function of capacity

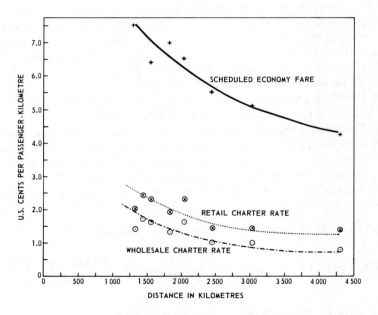

Figure 4.10 Air transport costs from Stockholm (I.C.A.O.)

4.2.6 Air Transport

Elle[8] gives the following air transport costs (F.A.A. 1964: U.S. domestic):

105 Sw.øre per available ton km,   500 ton km/h, DC3 400 km/h
 70 Sw.øre per available ton km, 3000 ton km/h, DC6 600 km/h
 35 Sw.øre per available ton km, 12 000 ton km/h, DC8 900 km/h

(approx. 12 cents per ton mile (6–30p).)

Splitting up operating costs into direct and indirect operating costs we find

Direct costs
  Flying operations   25 %⎫   (Crew, fuel, insurance)
  Maintenance   15 %⎬52 %(Airframe, engines, equipment)
  Depreciation   12 %⎭   (Aircraft, equipment, interest)

Indirect costs
  Passenger service   8 %⎫   (Cabin attendance)
  Station and ground   16 %⎬48 %(Aircraft, passenger handling) (fees)
  Sales and promotion   18 %⎪   (Booking, advertising, commission)
  General and administration 6 %⎭

Direct costs are closely associated with the aircraft, whereas indirect costs are associated with traffic, commercial and organisational circumstances.

The differences in operating costs are great between the U.S. trunk and local carriers, from about 16 cents per available ton km to about 32 cents. This is not because of differences in wages, fuel, price, etc., however; the trunk carriers handle 60 million passengers per year, whereas the local ones handle only 10 million passengers per year. Again, the average length of haul is 1100 km and 340 km, respectively, and the number of airports served is 185 and 560. This means that the local carriers have higher direct operating costs because of the use of smaller aircraft and short flying distances; they also have higher indirect operating costs, because of the many airports served. This description is also applicable to domestic airline traffic in Europe.

At present, helicopters tend to be twice as expensive to operate as conventional aircraft.

Air passenger journey cost is calculated as follows:

$$\text{Vehicle operation cost/passenger mile} \times \text{distance} + \frac{\text{airport costs/year}}{\text{passengers/year}}$$

where vehicle operation cost = 6p/passenger mile and

Airport costs = £20 million, or depreciation 4.5 per cent
for 25 years   £1.4 million/year
plus maintenance and
operation   £2   million/year
        _____
        £3.4 million/year

If C_r describes *en route* costs per available ton km and P the vehicle productivity in ton km/h, one has:

$$C_r = aP^{-0.33}$$

where $a = 10$ for sea transport, $a = 80$ for land transport, and $a = 800$ for air transport.

Summary of Operating Costs

For the figures given in table 4.13, E.E. Marshall[72] is the main source. These are average costs in England for 1968. The figures can vary considerably with type of vehicle, road, utilisation and wage rates, and so on. The cost of licences and taxation is included. The cost of pipelines varies with throughput, line diameter and pumping pressure.

TABLE 4.13   Operating costs by means of transport

	Operating costs (pence* per passenger mile)	Operating costs (pence per ton mile)
Sea	0.5d	0.1–0.5d
Railway	1–3d	1–5d
Bus–private car	1–8d	
Big truck–small truck		1–5d
Air	3–6d	10–50d
Pipeline		0.25d

*Note: pre-decimal currency

4.2.7 Indirect Costs of Transport Systems

In passenger transport, time, accident and noise costs should be mentioned. In goods transport, losses of interest on valuable goods in transit and damage loss should be mentioned.

Time Cost

Time costs are normally made up of cost of time for vehicle, driver, passengers and goods; they include depreciation plus interest on the investment in the vehicle. In public transport the value of the driver's time is set by the wage rate of the driver, and the value of vehicle time is the earning power of the vehicle per hour; it is obvious that there exists a money equivalent of cargo time. Delay time is also included.

The Danish Road Directorate[93] in 1970 gave the following recommendation for the value of 1 hour:

In 1968 the national income was 74 000 million Kr. which, divided by 2.4 million gainfully employed inhabitants, gives an average income per employee of 31 000 Kr.

With 2100 working hours per year, the average income per hour is 15 Kr. With 1.3 persons per car, one gets a value of 20 Kr per car hour, if the persons in the car are 'working' (*cf* page 34).

By questioning people driving cars on Danish mainroads the following was found:

Driving in 'work' and 'from home to work': 25 per cent of all cars
Driving in 'leisure time':   75 per cent of all cars

We then get the following value of time per person in cars calculated per car:
If leisure time is evaluated at   0 Kr: 5 Kr per car per hour
If leisure time is evaluated at 20/3 Kr: 10 Kr per car per hour

See also Searle: Beesley, Quarmby, Stopher, Watson, Hornville and Dawson.[10]

Cost of Accidents

The cost of road traffic accidents is considerable. According to a Danish investigation the cost per personal accident is 75–100 000 Kr (this includes also cost of accidents with no personal injury). In Denmark there are 20 000 accidents with personal injury per year and about 1000 fatalities. The total costs are then 1500 to 2000 million Kr per year.[93]

The United States had 54 700 people killed in 1971 in highway accidents. The social loss, estimated by the National Highway Traffic Safety Administration, was $46 000 million. This could double by 1980. Average lifetime earnings losses in ground surface accidents were assumed as $92 000 (1970), with injury costs of $350 per person. Property damage costs per accident were projected at $400 for automobile, $800 for bus and $3000–5000 for rail. Average lifetime earnings losses per air passenger mortality were $250 000 (1970), injury costs were $540 per person and property damage $500 000.

Lloyds estimates, for ships bigger than 500 G.R.T., an amount of £34 000 per ship casuality. The U.S. Department of Transport estimates £40 000 per ship damage.

Traffic Noise Cost

Some investigations have been made into the social costs due to noise. The costs involved in reducing the effects of noise have been described as follows.[94]

For a motorway a reduction in noise level of 30 dB(A) could be achieved by an additional cost of £50 000 per km of road (double glazing).

A reduction in noise level of 5 dB(A) could be achieved with a 3 m screen costing £30 000 per km.

The Resource Management Corporation in the United States found that when for motorways the outdoor perceived noise level (PNdB) fell from 82 to 68 dB (that is, a 17 per cent decrease in noise level), then the land value increased 1–4 per cent for surface/depressed and for elevated highways, respectively. For railways a 100 per cent increase in noise level diminished residential property values by 10–20 per cent.

The Roskill Commission found depreciation percentages as a function of noise level and house property values, in their study of noise at Heathrow Airport (see table 4.14a).

TABLE 4.14a   Percentage depreciation due to noise

House property (1968)	Noise exposure		
Value (£)	35–45 N.N.I.	45–55 N.N.I.	> 55 N.N.I.
< 4000	0%	3%	5%
4000–8000	3%	6%	10%
> 8000	3%	13%	23%

House-price depreciation figures should be complemented with endurance costs, moving costs, and modified moving costs (that is, people who do not move). These average minimum costs in sterling (1968) are shown in table 4.14b.

TABLE 4.14b   Endurance costs (£) due to noise

1968	Noise exposure		
	35–45	45–55	>55 N.N.I.
Endurance costs	570	690	950
Moving costs	1790	2190	2600
Modified moving costs	3610	4130	4400

Richards[13] found that the annual loss in relative house values around Heathrow Airport was £30 million; the 0.5 million inhabitants who are seriously disturbed could move out for £30 million per annum.

The full annual value of Heathrow was, however, £300 million: £120 million in passenger time savings: £100 million in freight time saving and £80 million in salaries of people working at or in association with Heathrow, together with taxes and rates paid on the buildings they occupy.

A very rough estimate to retrofit (alter the engine bypass to reduce noise) 1500 DC8, DC9, B707, B727 and B737 aircraft varies in price from $1000 to $3000 million.

Traffic Pollution Costs
A kit to reduce vehicle emissions in the United States costs about $20.00. A 100 per cent increase in air pollution level will decrease property values by about 5–10 per cent.

4.3 Prices, Fares and Charges
Prices should equal or exceed the marginal social opportunity cost of the resources used to produce each unit of output.[52] The opportunity cost is the 'escapable' costs saved, if one less unit of output is produced.

Fixed costs are costs which cannot be escaped and are not covered in opportunity costs. Some costs are inescapable in the short term, but not in the long term. Some costs are joint costs, and inescapable in that sense (return). Some costs are inescapable for small, but not for large changes of output. Indivisible expenses will not be covered in marginal costs. Since demand may fluctuate, so may marginal costs (high peak hour costs).

Private and social costs are often different, because of externalities. The social opportunity cost measures the cost of the alternatives forgone in using some resources to transport instead of other. In practice, the principle of charging a price that only covers escapable costs usually means that the company shows a loss. The loss can then be covered by general taxation or surplus from other companies. However, competition between public and private companies would be disturbed if all public companies used a marginal cost pricing policy.

Congestion, accidents, noise, air pollution, smoke, visual intrusion, and so on, give substantial social costs which are not reflected in the marginal private cost. The marginal vehicle will suffer a speed reduction during its entry on to a highway—a private marginal cost—but it will cause many other vehicles on the highway to slow down—this is a social marginal cost that the marginal vehicle does not bear. This requires taxes and subsidies.

The real difficulty in price-setting occurs where, as in the case of roads, airports and ports, government owns the transport network or terminal, but the transport means—vehicles, aircraft and ships—are privately owned.

In the case of roads, accountability is most difficult to establish. Normally, fuel tax is used and fixed costs are often recovered by means of an annual fee or licence, related to what the traffic will bear.

Another distortion lies in the difference between the private and the social rate of interest.

Models are used by the economists to explain the quantity sold in a market by the interaction of supply and demand. The behaviour of demand is summed up in a demand curve, which states the amounts sold at the market at various prices. Similarly, the supply curve states amounts offered for the various prices; the point of intersection of the curves then indicates the price at which demand equals supply. 'Elasticity of demand' is the degree of responsiveness of demand to changes in price.

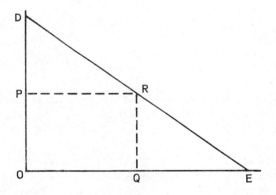

Figure 4.11 Price *E* as a function of the demand for travel *D*. *DPR* consumers' surplus

In mathematical economics it is possible to derive useful quantitative knowledge from general information about the shape of the demand curve based on knowledge of the effect of price changes and the quantity of demand.

Depuit[3] pointed out that the total gain resulting from construction of a road cannot be measured merely by total charges collected from users, since many users would, if necessary, pay rather more than they actually do ('consumers' surplus').

The consumers' surplus cannot be applied to such things as food in general, but items such as wine, tea, as well as transport, etc., which do not form a large part of an individual's total expenditure.

4.3.1 Ships' Charges

Ships' charges are dealt with at shipping conferences. Fixed costs are 60 per cent of the total for scheduled transport, but only 20 per cent for tramp. If the load transported is less than 50 pound/foot^3, the price is charged according to volume for ships, otherwise by weight. Although international inland shipping is uncontrolled with respect to both movement and prices, the establishment of international pools in Rhine shipping has led to uniform prices (*cf.* page 196).

TABLE 4.15   Ship charges

Japan–Europe	Price ($/ton)	Trim factor*	Price ($/40 foot^3)
Car tyre	28	4 : 1	112
Toy	33	7 : 1	231
Cotton	41	2 : 1	82
Television	50	3 : 1	150

* $\dfrac{\text{volume}}{\text{weight}}$

4.3.2 Railway Charges

Railway tariffs and fares can be calculated in order to achieve maximum profit and return on investment, or to cover variable costs. The United States used principle number one from 1830 to 1910, and after 1918 the second principle, 5.5 per cent.

In England the first railway charges were made in accordance with inland waterway charges, which was wrong because private people did not travel on the railways by their own vehicle. Charges were later made in accordance with road practice. There were three classes for passengers and goods (fast, normal and cheap) with distance tariffs, which was illogical since high terminal costs gave low charges for long distances. Later zone (or belt) charges were used with a fixed price per km inside the zone. Furthermore, goods of low value were given low charges. There were several intermediate charges, and special tariffs.

Fixed national tariffs have been used for railways in Europe. In 1934, the Netherlands replaced the fixed tariff with a maximum tariff; in 1957 the same happened in Great Britain. In 1962, Great Britain ceased to adhere to maximum tariffs; the railway is now free to fix the charges. Before 1957 about 80 per cent of all British rail traffic was at exceptional rates; the same goes for Germany and the Netherlands. The British Transport Commission was required to prepare a charge scheme for the whole inland transport.

The international railway tariffs consist of two parts, comprising a fixed charge and a variable charge. The fixed charge is intended to cover the costs of terminal facilities, and the variable charge the costs of the carriage. Besides the increase in rates resulting from changing rates at the frontier (often a 25 per cent increase over the inland tariffs, because terminal costs are levied twice), rates are also increased because of the increase in operating costs incurred through customs formalities: frontier charge, import and export charge, delay charge, etc.

Frontier charge is based on weight or per wagon, and different charges are used in various countries. The removal of this discrimination and the simplifying of frontier formalities under the Treaty of Rome has been of great help for the E.E.C. members.

4.3.3 Road Charges versus Rail Charges
In Germany the basic rail and road haulage tariffs were divided into seven goods classes with uniform rates throughout the country and based on a what-the-traffic-will-bear policy. With the railway being a national monopoly the effects of this average pricing were not marked. But cross subsidisation has, since road competition, been undermining the finances of the railways. The result was that the road haulier, who was under no obligation to carry freight began to specialise in the highest tariff goods.

In 1960, 80 per cent of the tonnage carried by the Deutsches Bundesbahn (D.B.) was in a new 20 ton class (cheaper than road haulage), but 50 per cent of the road haulage tonnage was also in the 20 ton range.

The favourable positions of the road hauliers in the face of lower rail tariffs is explained by the fact that road tariff is door to door, whereas rail tariff is station to station; furthermore the rail service is slow over short distances and keeps to a schedule. Two-thirds of rail traffic was private siding traffic in 1960 (for example coal traffic), but of a kind in which road hauliers have not specialised.

In 1960, 50 per cent of the D.B. traffic was for distances under 100 km, but only 12 per cent of the road hauliers' traffic was under 100 km. In 1961 a new German commission on tariffs was empowered to establish fork tariffs, with maximum and minimum limits.

In France the 1961 road haulage tariff was most complicated, making allowance for type, weight, loadability, distance and return load. It is believed that the tariff was based on market prices ruling at the time and not operating costs. It was to protect the railways (S.N.C.F.) against possible reductions in the road haulage pricing.

In Britain all consignments for road haulage transport were divided into the old railway classifications, at least for the Midlands Division. The three goods classifications, with six weight classes, gave eighteen alternatives for each distance, with rates increasing with distance. In the Scottish Division, on the other hand, each group (there were 207 road haulage groups in Great Britain) had freedom to form its own charges; there was no goods classification, and charges were based on destination, not distance.

In road haulage the operating costs of the tramp haulier vary, depending on factors such as ability, size of group, merchandise, length and direction of journey, type and size of vehicle, time of the year and weather. Two viewpoints exist on international tariffs for road haulage. The first applies those tariffs which exist in the country where a haulier may find himself (for example Germany). The second applies the prices which exist in the haulier's country of origin for the whole of the journey (for example the Netherlands). The first principle leads to a reduction of price competition.

By use of the Transport International Routier (T.I.R.) carnet system, established by two U.N. conventions, goods carried in sealed road vehicles are not subject to payment of import or export duties at customs offices *en route*.

In West Germany Mr Leber[95] presented a plan in 1967 to transfer long distance bulk road traffic to the railways, partly to decrease the annual deficit of the German Federal Railways of 1600 million DM, partly to decrease the number of people killed on the roads (17 000 per year).

In Great Britain Mrs Castle[96] presented a plan in 1967 to make the maximum economic use of railways as well as roads by promoting the transfer of all suitable traffic from congested roads to the railways. This was partly to decrease the number of people killed on the roads (8000 per year), partly to decrease the then annual deficit of British Rail (£160 million).

4.3.4 Investment in Infrastructure; Subsidies and Discrimination

Road haulage and inland shipping are dependent on the state for extension and improvement of their infrastructure. The railway companies are able to modify their infrastructures, but as the networks are state owned and in poor financial condition, such action implies government approval and aid.

In table 4.16 investment in infrastructure has been taken as a percentage of the G.N.P. (1960). Although relative investment in road transport in Germany is nearly four times greater than in the United Kingdom, the costs of building a normal road in Germany are $2\frac{1}{2}$ times as great.[53] The lack of investment in inland waterway structure in the United Kingdom, France and Germany is obvious.

TABLE 4.16 Transport investment in infrastructure as a percentage of G.N.P.

	Inland shipping	Railways	Roads	All transport
France	0.04	0.30	0.84	1.2
Germany	0.07	0.56	1.30	1.9
U.K.	—	0.29	0.35	0.6

In Germany, France and Great Britain the Governments were forced to grant the railways substantial financial aid after the Second World War, a policy which Italy always has followed. In 1961 S.N.C.F. showed a loss of £7 million but subsidies were £125 million (maintaining permanent way £60 million, pension fund £40 million, etc.)

As there is no standard form drawing up accounts, comparisons of profits and losses cannot be drawn between countries.

In the Netherlands the railway has normally not made a loss, but the depreciation is calculated on a replacement cost basis which, with rising prices, means that their depreciation is proportionately higher than in Great Britain and France, where depreciation is calculated according to earlier costs.

Any discrimination in transport charges could severely distort an economic union; for example, the charge for carrying German coke 60 km in France was nearly as high as the charge for home-produced coke carried 340 km.

Differences in internal rates are mainly caused by subsidies.

4.3.5 Taxation

When queueing problems occur on a road, the costs of such congestion are borne by all cars equally, irrespective of who was first or last on the road. The averaging of queueing costs means that the marginal user is paying far less than the marginal cost. The reduced costs for the marginal user mean that one will make use of road transport, when shipping, railway or air would be cheaper. Taxation should therefore be used to make up the difference between average and marginal costs.

There are three main types of taxation that are levied on transport undertakings: taxation on income; on vehicles and on petrol and the network.

Inland waterway carriers in Belgium pay waterway tolls and a turnover tax of 6 per cent. This is not the case in the Netherlands and Germany. The State railways in Belgium pay no tax, while the railway tax in the Netherlands and Germany is 3–7 per cent. In France, light goods vehicles paid much more in taxation than the track costs they incurred, whereas heavy vehicles paid substantially less, 258 against 66 per cent.

According to a study[53] made in Great Britain in 1964 the taxation of lorries and buses should be about four times greater than on cars in urban areas. In Belgium, Germany and the Netherlands road haulage undertakings pay turnover taxes of 6, 7 and 3 per cent, respectively. In France a special tax calculated on fully laden vehicles weights is levied. In Great Britain there is a tax on profits. Vehicle taxes are calculated in relation to unladen weight in Britain, Belgium and the Netherlands, to maximum weight in Germany and to engine capacity in France.

The taxation of fuels is given in table 4.17 (1961 data). The price of diesel oil is seven times as much in Britain, France and Italy as in Belgium.

TABLE 4.17   Taxation of fuels and road hauliers (1961)

	Sfr per litre petrol	Sfr per litre diesel oil	Taxation (NFr) road hauliers per ton km
France	0.64	0.40	0.02
Germany	0.37	0.35	0.03
Britain	0.37	0.37	0.02
Belgium	0.46	0.05	0.02
Netherlands	0.32	0.01	0.01

The differentiation in taxation is intended to offset state railway losses of unremunerative services. However, direct subsidies or customs tariffs are preferable.

4.3.6 Transport Costs in Industry[77]

A common dictum in transport economics is that, if rates reflect costs, shippers will make modal choices which allocate traffic to the most efficient mode for given transport requirements. The meaning of reflect is unspecified. Because of the large gap between average and marginal costs in the case of railways, it is unlikely that this dictum equals rates and costs. This cost–rate dictum represents an extreme oversimplification.

The movement component, including elapsed time of a shipment, packaging outlays, schedule frequency and reliability, completeness of the service, etc., is tied in with other components, such as production scheduling, inventory control, packaging and storing. Failure to recognise the cost interdependence among components may lead to suboptimisation.

The system view requires that movement costs be weighed against the effect which alternative modes of transport have in other components of the system.

The key is found in the effect which alternative modes of transport have on total distribution costs: the non-transport costs. The truck has the advantage in over-all distribution cost if the difference between price (truck) and price (rail) is less than the difference between non-transport cost (rail) and non-transport cost (truck), while shippers will presumably be attracted by lowest distribution costs, transport price plus non-transport cost. This sum does not necessarily measure the lowest real costs; these are measured by marginal costs plus non-transport cost.

Edwards[78] makes some interesting remarks in a discussion of the British census of transport costs in industry covering establishments engaged in manufacturing, construction, mining, gas, electricity and water. The coverage applied only to the larger establishments, employing 25 or more persons, within the United Kingdom, normally for the outward movement of goods only.

In 1963 the British industry mentioned spent about £1000 million on transport, of which about £500 million was paid to other organisations, mainly road hauliers and the railways, and nearly £500 million was spent on own road transport.

For 35 industries, out of 128, the cost of own road transport is more than half the total transport cost. Three of these industries gas, electricity and water supply are special cases because their products are carried by pipe or wire and their demand for other forms of transport is mainly related to the servicing of their supply channels; they make extensive use of their own road vehicles. This goes for food, drink, tobacco and furniture too. Other industries, such as aircraft construction and shipbuilding, are abnormal since much of their output transports itself. The same goes for the construction industry (the output is already 'on site').

For 59 industries the percentage cost of own road transport was 30–50 per cent (chemicals, engineering, vehicles, textiles, clothing, paper). For 26 industries, the percentage of own road transport was 10–30 per cent (metal, bricks). For 8 industries, the percentage cost of own road transport was less than 10 per cent (ores, coal, coke, iron and steel).

It is shown that transport costs are over 15 per cent of the value of net output for industries, such as bread, milk, sugar, animal food, mining, quarrying, coke, fertilisers and bricks.

Table 4.18 shows railway transport costs as a percentage of the wholesale market price in the United Kingdom, based on 400 miles transport.

TABLE 4.18   Rail transport costs as percentage of wholesale market price for a distance of 400 miles

Products	%
Ore, tin – copper	1–2
Wool – cotton	1–4
Tea – meat	4–6
Grain, barley – oats	22–28

4.3.7 Passenger Transport Fares

In Sweden ship fares are 33–50 per cent of rail fares per passenger km at 3–5 Sw.øre per passenger km (1968 prices).

Swedish State Railways received the following average revenue:

9.5 Sw.øre per passenger km for a mean travel distance of 77 km
  (2.9 cents per passenger mile) and with 33 per cent load factor (1–3p), which can be broken down as follows
      The number of seats per train 300, (30 tons)
      Average floor space of seat 0.6 m², (6m²/ton)
      En route costs per seat km is 2 Sw.øre.
that is revenue per passenger km is 6 Sw.øre, thus terminal and administration costs are 3.5 Sw.øre.

Interurban bus traffic received approximately the same revenue as the railways, 9.0 Sw.øre per passenger km, with lower capacity, lower seat space, and terminal costs (2.8 cents per passenger mile).

For domestic airlines in the United States revenue in 1960 was 18 Sw.øre per passenger mile (5.6 cents or 3–6p per passenger mile).

However, for European air traffic, the cost level is substantially higher due to unfavourable traffic conditions and a smaller scale of operations.

4.3.8 Budgets

Railways
The new Tokyo–Osaka railway line in Japan, designed for a travel speed of 200 km/h over a 500 km line, has an investment cost of 5600 million Sw. Kr or 11 million Sw. Kr per km inclusive of vehicles, track and terminals.

Assuming the annual financial costs to be 7–8 per cent of the investments, the recovery per day per km track is about 2000 Sw. Kr. If the number of passengers per day is 20 000 and the revenue 10 Sw.øre per passenger km, the financial situation will be balanced.

Roads
The governmental expenditure on roads in Sweden is about 1000 Sw. Kr per car per year, irrespective of increase in vehicle stock and traffic volume. This corresponds to about 20 per cent of the over-all costs for road traffic, that is 5000 Sw. Kr per car per year. With 8 million inhabitants and 250 vehicles per 1000 population we arrive at 2 million vehicles, that is, 2000 million Sw. Kr of road investments per year. To compare this with the railways it is necessary to include cost of vehicles, etc., that is 10 000 million Sw. Kr over-all road investments per year. With 40 000 km road network this means 250 000 Sw. Kr per km per year or 600 Sw. Kr per km per day.

Airports and Air Traffic Control
The governmental expenditure on airports in Sweden was 320 million Sw. Kr ($62 million) in 1965 (capital plus interest), and the account value 225 million Sw. Kr ($44 million).

A German study[8] shows that for European countries a typical rate of new investments is about $2 for travel between European countries for each passenger, arriving or departing, and about twice that for domestic passengers. The operating costs (excluding depreciation) amount to 40 million Sw. Kr per year. Approximately 50 per cent of these costs were for traffic control and weather service. In 1965, the F.A.A. budget was $734 million, of which $551 million were for operating costs. The costs for air traffic control were about 9 Sw. Kr ($2) per passenger in Sweden, but in the United States about 30 Sw. Kr ($6) per passenger. It is seen that the costs for air traffic control per passenger are substantially higher in the United States than in Sweden. Per landing the figures were 150 Sw. Kr ($30) in the United States and 100 Sw. Kr ($20) in Sweden.

The total costs for an air passenger in Sweden, taking into consideration domestic passengers (with a weighting factor of 2), depreciation and interest, are then $4 + $4 + $4 = $12 per passenger. This corresponds to the costs of transporting one passenger 200 km.

Modal Choice
Fares and rates charged by transport operators vary with distance travelled, capacity and type of service.

For aircraft on long-distance routes, the operating cost is about 1p per passenger mile, and for short-range aircraft the operating costs are about 2p per passenger mile, if the aircraft is full. Taking into consideration the usual load factor it will be more correct to reckon on 3p per passenger mile for long-distance routes and 6p per passenger mile for short-range aircraft. The comparable cost for railways is 3p per passenger mile.

Air is cheaper than rail for low traffic volumes, less than 2 million passengers per year, and longer haul routes of more than 500 statute miles. The calculation is based on a cost of 3p per rail passenger mile and 6p per air passenger mile, giving no value to time saving. The percentage of operating costs that varies with traffic is for rail and air only 25–50 per cent, whereas a bus service can have 80–90 per cent variable operating costs.

For situations where rail and sea distances are equal, rail costs for freight are always below those of ships with a capcity of 600 containers or less. For ships above 600 containers capacity, the break-even depends on the mileage involved. For a 1200 capacity container ship, sea becomes cheaper for distances above 3300 nautical miles. Similarly for a 2400 capacity container ship, sea is cheaper above about 1900 miles.

At a distance of over 100 km and a capacity of about 3 million tons per year the pipeline is the cheapest means of land transport.

For container transport in unit trains, rates for a distance of 600 km are only 25–40 per cent of conventional goods rates.

TABLE 4.19   Distances where, according to Swedish experience, rail is cheaper than truck transport[97]

Number of transfers of goods from truck to rail and vice versa	Carrying capacity of truck		
	8 tons	13 tons	21 tons
0		all distances	
1	>50 km	>80 km	>200 km
2	>200 km	>250 km	>400 km

McKinsey[73] gives the following rail cost in £ sterling per container: 500 miles about £10 compared to a road cost per container for 500 miles of about £75.

4.4 Location Theory and Transport Networks

There would be no need for transport, if there were no limits of cost; equally, unlimited space would be available, if transport was costless. However, while the cost and effort involved in transport limit the extent to which distant localities can be linked, transport costs determine the scale of production, size of cities and so on.[9]

Much of people's transport and life pattern is determined by the decisions made to locate roads, railways, ports and airports. Transport systems are designed to overcome the distances and obstacles imposed by geography. As such, they shape the distribution of activities and influence the share which each region contributes to the national product.

In many instances, the problem of transport is not to extend the system but to manage it, by imposing an efficient fare and rate structure and adapting its technological characteristics to an ever-changing demand. So changes in industrial output and location appear to alter the structure of transportation rather than the converse.

It is in the system of exchange, through the process of distribution, that the supplies of producers and the demand of consumers are brought together. Exchange takes place in markets. Markets exist where a number of buyers and sellers communicate. It is in the cities that intercity exchanges take place. People are willing to travel only short distances to obtain items they need frequently, but longer distances to obtain less frequent purchases.

Central-place theory is the theory of the location, size, nature and spacing of these market centres and their trade routes.[14] The basis of central-place theory was established by Lalanne (1863),[15] Christaller (1933),[17] and Lösch (1940).[18]

The ideal trade area of a market centre is a circle. If one adds the requirement that all consumers be served, then the trade areas will become hexagons for the most common commodity. If it is assumed that a large number of goods has to be provided for each of the consumers, who are distributed at uniform densities over an unbounded plain, and the goods are ranked in descending order of the minimum-sized market areas, it is necessary to make each of them just profitable. Lösch gives a solution to the spatial arrangement of market centres and transport; he takes the lowest-order good and derives an optimal hexagonal arrangement of centres and market areas.

In the first place Lösch lays his nets in such a way that all of them have one centre of production in common. Secondly, he turns his nets around this centre, so that he obtains six sectors where centres of production are frequent and six others where they are scarce; this arrangement provides for the best lines of transport. It can be shown that the aggregate of freight distances is a minimum. As more centres of production coincide, more consumers are able to buy from local stores, so that not only the mileage of transport, but also the mileage of lines of transport is reduced.

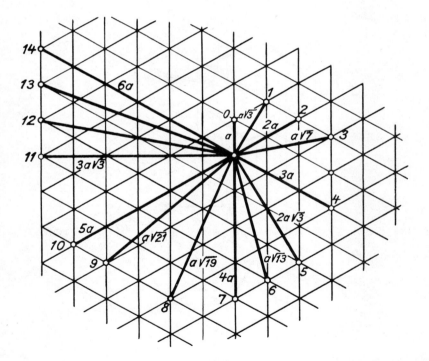

Figure 4.12 Distances from production centres (Lösch)

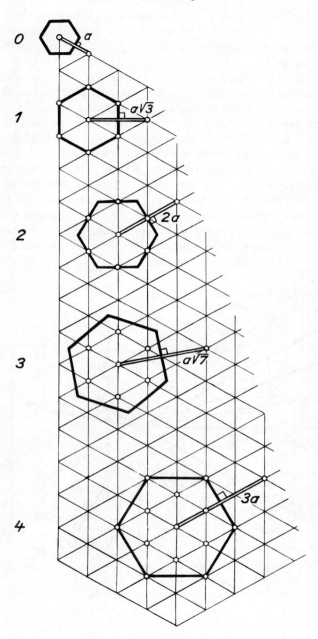

Figure 4.13 Hinterlands (Lösch)

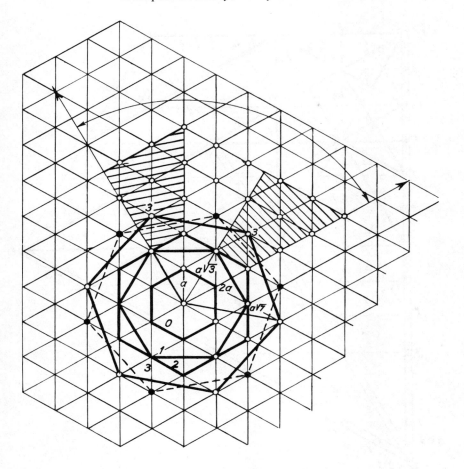

Figure 4.14 Location of hexagons (Lösch)

The construction of the Lösch model for the distribution of central places has always appeared particularly difficult. The prospect of rotating independently ten or more hexagonal nets into a merely infinite number of positions so as to arrive at a maximum coincidence of centres is daunting. However, rotation need not take place for many of the *K* networks, and for those rotated there are only two or four possible solutions: the construction of a city-rich sector is one of the constraints, the maximum coincidence of centres is another. If in a triangular network the distance between two nodes is *a*, the next distances will then be between production centres of next common commodities.

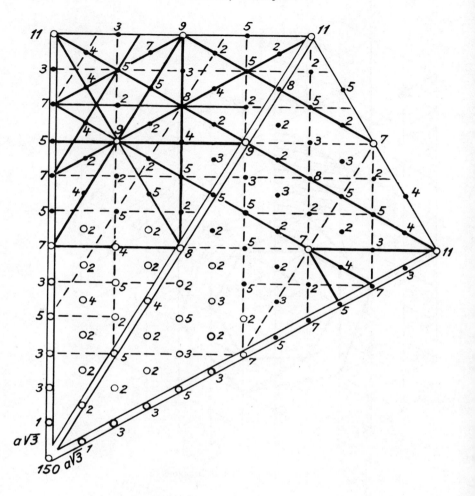

Figure 4.15 Transport network hierarchy (Lösch)

$a\sqrt{3}$, $2a$, $a\sqrt{7}$, $3a$, $2a\sqrt{3}$, $a\sqrt{13}$, $4a$, $a\sqrt{19}$, etc.

The hinterlands will then have areas $H = \sqrt{3}/2\ a^2$, $3H$, $4H$, $7H$, $9H$, $12H$, $13H$, $16H$, $19H$, etc. The number of common production centres will in these areas be 1, 3, 4, 7, 9, 12, 13, 16, 19, etc. The network with hinterlands equal to H, $3H$, and $4H$ can be placed around a main centre, without difficulty. However, the network with hinterland $7H$ can be placed in two positions, one of which is chosen. Once this has been done, network hinterlands $9H$, $12H$ can be placed, but $13H$ is to be placed in a sector with many production centres, the same goes for $19H$, $21H$, etc.

The number of production centres in a heavy sector' and a 'light sector' can now be counted. Omitting production centres with distance a, one finds, in the main centre 150 units, 11 units in the three radials at a distance of $24a$. Transport lines can now be drawn according to the number of production units per km: for example main radial roads will have $2n$ units per km; secondary roads will have $1.5n$ units per km, that is mostly ring roads; tertiary roads will have $0.5n$ units per km—this road network tends to be a rectangular road network, although one started at a triangular basis with radials and rings. There are more roads in the heavy sector than in the light. From each town six radials start, a pattern which is well known from transport patterns around big towns, such as highways and railways around London and Paris.

Often a system of production centres, whose numbers can be divided by 3, 4 or 7, is found in practice. Of the hinterlands mentioned, one can then choose only those with for example, 1, 3, 9, 27 . . . production centres or those with 1, 4, 16, 64, ... In a system $K = 3$, one will then find 1 capital city, 2 next-order cities $(3-1)$, 6 third-order $(9-3)$, 18 fourth-order cities $(27-9)$, 54, 162, 486, etc. If the minimum distance between villages is 9 km, the next distances will be 16, 27, 47, 81, 140 and 240 km. The hinterland areas will be approximately 70, 210, 660, 1890, 5670, 17 000 and 51 000 km^2.

In Denmark, Copenhagen has a hinterland of approximately 50 000 km^2, and the distances to Hamburg and Gothenburg are about 240 km. The next order cities, Odense and Aalborg, have hinterlands of approximately 17 000 km^2 and distance of 140 km. The third-order cities, Esbjerg, Randers, Viborg, Slagelse, and Vejle have hinterlands of approximately 5700 km^2 and distances of 80 km. The fourth-order (18) cities have 1890 km^2 hinterlands and distances of 50 km. The fifth-order (54) cities have 600 km^2 hinterlands and distances of 25 km; the sixth-order (162) cities have 200 km^2 hinterlands and distances of 15 km, and the seventh-order (486) cities have 70 km^2 hinterlands and distances of 9 km.

Peter Bjørn Andersen (1972)[20] found airport hinterlands of 6000–2000 km^2, and Buskgaard (1972)[21] found railway station hinterland of 1200–100 km^2.

In Iowa with its relatively equal distribution of production, the distances between towns increase with their size, just as in the theoretical picture. The regional substructure can also be identified in Europe: the ring of Frankfurt, Nuremberg, Munich, Zurich, and Strasbourg around Stuttgart are very regularly distributed. There should be one more centre to the south of Munich, but the Alps make this impossible. The rise of Munich over Augsburg, which had the advantage of an earlier start, is worth noting. See

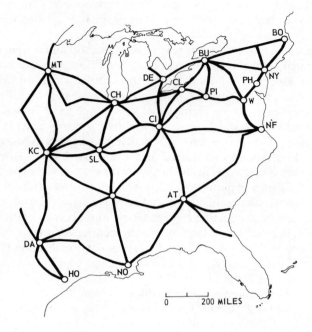

Figure 4.16 North American railway network (Philbrick)

Christaller 1933,[17] and *cf.* List's railway planning.[2]

Philbrick (1957)[23] distinguishes between areal units of organisation. The first order covers consumption conducted in the household; the second order covers retail trade conducted in a village; the third order covers wholesale conducted in a small city; the fourth order covers regional transport handling conducted in a bigger city; the fifth order covers national transport handling conducted in a big city, and the sixth order covers world transport handling conducted in a capital city. The seventh order covers world functions conducted in a world capital.

Philbrick and Harris have analysed some areas in the United States and found that:

(1) New York was a seventh-order world capital (leadership).

(2) New York, Chicago and Los Angeles were sixth-order capital cities (control).

(3) Chicago, Detroit, Toledo, Milwaukee, Columbus, Indianapolis, etc.—a total of 16 big cities—were fifth-order capitals (exchange).

(4) South Bend was, among 63 other cities, a fourth-order centre for Chicago (trans-shipment).

(5) Kankakee was, among 255 other cities, a third-order centre for Chicago (wholesale).

(6) Boswell was, among 1023 other cities, a second-order centre for Chicago (retail).

(7) A farm was, among 4095 other farms, a first-order centre for Chicago (consumer).

The railway system in North-east America is built up according to this theory.

In the middle of the nineteenth century, sea traffic was the expanding sector of transport, but towards the end of the century the railways accounted for the expansion. Nowadays road and air transport are dominating sectors (*cf.* chapter 1).

The seed for the analysis of general location problems can be found in von Thunen:[24] *Der isolierte Staat in Beziehung auf Landwirtschaft und National-okonomie, 1826.* According to him, production of farm commodities will tend to take place in concentric zones around a centre. To each zone there will correspond a particular agricultural product depending on demand, transport, cost and price.

Launhardt, 1882,[25] who presented the first significant treatment of industrial location theory, distinguished between determining the site of production within a polygon, whose corners, represented raw material sources and a one-point consumption place, and the supplying of a consuming area from a given point of production. However, Weber, 1909,[26] emphasises three basic location factors—transport-cost differentials and labour-cost differentials as well as agglomeration economies; and five historical development states—the agricultural, the primary industrial, the secondary industrial, the primary service official and the secondary service official (village, city, regional, national and world economy).

Let us take first the location of a firm where neither the production cost, nor the demand will vary with location. Here the only variable is the delivery costs, which should be minimised, so as to maximise the profit. If the firm is selling 200 units in one city, 300 in a second and 600 in a third, the location is often suggested as the mean location, or centre of gravity, which minimises the sum of the squares of the distances. However, this location is wrong; the right one is in the median location, which minimises the weighted sum of the distances, and this will be in the third city.[27]

We now take the location of a firm with one market and one production point, where neither production cost, nor demand will vary with the location. Here the only variables are the distribution costs and the assembly costs, that is the total transport costs should be minimised. These costs, C, are the sum of the assembly costs per mile, a, multiplied by the distance, d, from the production point to the firm and the distribution costs per mile, b, multiplied by the distance, e, from the firm to the market. Thus, $c = (a \times d) + (b \times e)$. If assembly costs are higher than distribution costs, the best location is for the firm to be at the production point, that is $d = 0$, and vice versa.

Introducing lower costs with increasing distances will be more realistic. Introducing a variety of carriers: ship, train, truck and pipeline will also give more realistic results. Usually trucks have lower terminal costs, but higher per mile costs than trains, as do trains with respect to ships. Terminal costs, lower costs with increasing distances and use of ship and rail reinforce the attractiveness of the location of the firm, either at the production point or the market point, because midway points are costlier than these points, even if assembly and distribution costs are even. Introducing exchange points or terminals, such as ports and railway stations, often turns out to provide a good location, depending on the particular values of the components in each case, such as, among others, the new loading and unloading costs.

Thirdly, we take the location of a firm with one market and two production points. It is now necessary to standardise the quantities per unit of product; one may then carry out the location analysis graphically. One draws around one production point lines representing the transport costs for the tons needed per unit of product; these curves are called isotims. The total transport costs at any point will be the sum of the isotims. Points with the same total transport costs may be joined by curves called isodapanes. To locate the firm one has to find the point of least transport costs; this point should be checked against location at the production points of the markets. This technique has been developed by Palander and Hoover (1935; 1948).[28] Variations from site to site in other costs, such as labour and power, must be assumed too. Therefore, Weber introduced a labour coefficient. Introducing alternative production sites gives rise to determination of market boundaries by the same technique except that the cost of production as well as that of transport is considered.

There are other realistic features that may be considered by the use of isotims, for example, assuming that transport is not equally possible in all directions, or taking into account tariff barriers and so on.

For a firm which is refining oil, the best location is near the supply centre or transport centre, while a firm manufacturing cakes, would have its best location near the demand market. If the production lies between these two extremes, the optimal location depends on factors such as transport, labour pool and factor-cost differentials.

Transport costs depend on distances and the transportability of products, but also on the mode of transport. The use of trucks brings a relative reduction of short-distance transport costs, and this means a decentralisation. Containerisation means a relative reduction of long-distance transport costs, and this means a centralisation.

Neither trade, nor location theories have been successful at incorporating agglomeration factors in analytical models. Agglomeration, which Lösch has treated, results from three factors: economies of scale, localisation and urbanisation economies. Economies of scale refer to the advantage of producing in large quantities. Localisation economies refer to the advantage of locating firms within a single industry (automobiles) near each other, and urbanisation economies refer to the advantage of closeness of different industries (common electricity, transport, labour pool, etc.).[9]

Isard[30, 31] (1960) has for some industries determined in what region the industry could achieve the lowest total cost of producing and delivering its product to market. Location of such industries as petrochemicals (Monroe, Cincinnati, gas), iron and steel (Fall River, Boston, ore, coal) and aluminium (Seattle, aluminium, power) have been treated.

Economic base, trade multiplier, scaling and factor analysis have been used (Guttman, Stouffer),[32] as well as input—output technique (Quesnay, Walras, Leontief).[35, 36] Goodwin[33] pioneered the multiplier concept (1949), using an input—output developed earlier by Leontief. Metzler (1950)[34] was the first to introduce the regional dimension. In 1953 Leontief and Isard published an analysis of regions using input—output techniques.

Morrill[37] simulated transport and town development in Sweden (1963) and suggested that major railway developments imply marked reductions in transport costs. Such reductions lead to the reallocation of market areas, the revaluation of existing resources, and redistribution of industrial production to the benefit of the most efficient and best located firms.

Kresge and Roberts[38] at Harvard have constructed an economic simulation transport model consisting of two connected submodels: an economic model based on input—output tables provides the transport model with data, and this last model assigns commodity flows to the transport network. It is seen how an improvement in the transport system reduces the cost of production.

Clark, Wilson and Bradley (1969)[70] from a study of economic potential in Western Europe showed a distinct change in the distribution of regions of greatest attraction to manufacturing industry. Before the Treaty of Rome, three discrete areas of high potential were found: Britain, North France and the Ruhr. After the first establishment of the E.E.C. only one area is found around the Ruhr. The enlarged Common Market including Britain and Denmark showed again one area around the Ruhr. A predicted situation of improved transport by containers still shows one area around the Ruhr. The same goes for improved transport by a possible Channel tunnel.

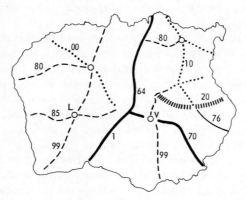

ACTUAL

SWEDISH
RAILWAYS

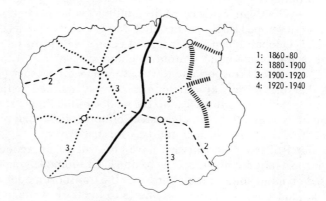

1: 1860-80
2: 1880-1900
3: 1900-1920
4: 1920-1940

SIMULATED

Figure 4.17 Swedish railway development (Morrill)

The potential P was found as

$$\frac{I}{M} + \left[\frac{I}{M + T_t + F} \right]$$

where I is regional income, M is minimum cost, T_t is transport cost and F is tariff.

Ventura[71] investigated the planning of an optimal structure for the French oil refining industry. Alternatives were evaluated and compared in terms of the total annual cost of making oil products available at consumption points based on forecast consumption levels:

(a) Establishment of new refineries in Strasbourg or Mulhouse or Montereau or Chalon.

(b) Construction of a pipeline Marseille–Paris or Marseille–Chalon, or no pipeline constructed.

Figure 4.18 Economic potential for an enlarged Common Market. The potential is calculated, as the regional income divided by costs ($, 1962) for moving a 10 ton load of heavy commodity a set distance, for 103 regions in Western Europe ($28 per region plus 28 cents per mile road, 12 cents per mile rail and 25 cents per mile sea). For example, maximum potential in the Rhine Valley:

Pre-Treaty of Rome	2800
E.E.C.	3600
Enlarged E.E.C. including containerisation	3800
Channel Tunnel	4000

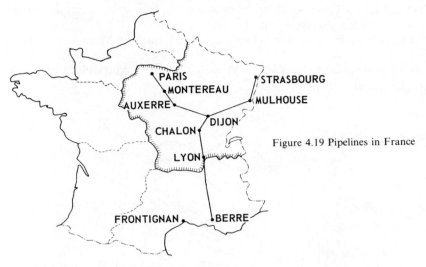

Figure 4.19 Pipelines in France

(c) The price of crude oil
(d) The level of exports for refined products.
(e) The cost of pipeline transport.

The calculations will not be referred to in detail. However, the result was that besides a new refinery recently established near Lyon there should be established a new refinery in Strasbourg supplied by a crude oil pipeline from Marseille. Furthermore the refinery in Dunkerque has been extended as suggested in the report.

Location of routes in practice often deviates from a straight line between the two points to be connected. If the route is lengthened in order to collect more passengers, it is a positive deviation as described by Wellington (1877),[39] who planned a railway from Mexico City to Vera Cruz. If the route is lengthened because of the need to avoid certain barriers or to minimise cost, it is a negative deviation.

Lösch found a route by which a product can be shipped as cheaply as possible between two points crossing a coastline, assuming cheap ocean freight and more costly rail freight. His law of refraction indicates that the land route should be shortened, assuming the entire coastline is favourable for port construction. The barrier consideration can be any necessary construction of a mountain tunnel or an isthmian canal.

Bunge (1962)[40, 41] handled the problem of connecting five centres, and came up with six route network solutions: (1) the postman's route; (2) the star routes; (3) the salesman's route; (4) the complete network; (5) the shortest route (soap-bubble), which has intersections that do not include any of the

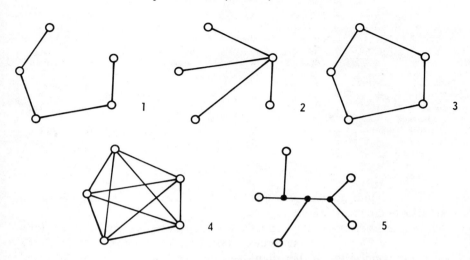

Figure 4.20 Five ways of connecting five towns

original centres; and finally (6) the general topological network (by Beckman) which adds two new intersections to the three in network (5), that is introduces a circuit inside the five centres.

Dantzig and Fulkerson (1954)[43] found for N centres $(N-1)!$ different salesmen's routes. For $N = 13$ there are 479 million solutions. It is obvious that users of a road network prefer solution (4), the complete network, whereas the road directorate prefer solution (5), the shortest route, which is cheapest to build.

Cooley (1894)[44] stressed the factors of politics in understanding route patterns. Taafe (1963)[45] investigated route development.

Knowledge of the relationship of network geometry to the development of regional resources has been greatly extended by Kansky (1963)[46] who introduced accurate comparisons between connectivity and shape of networks by use of graph theory.

The number of routes in a network with v points (centres) is called e. The network is disconnected, if it contains p isolated subnets.

A path is defined as a finite set of routes e. A circuit (ring) is a finite path in which the initial point coincides with the last point of the path. A tree is a connected network of at least two points such that the net does not contain any circuit. The number of circuits in a network m is $e - v + p$. The maximum number of routes in a completely connected network is

$$e_{max} = \frac{v}{2}(v - 1)$$

TABLE 4.20

Case	Number of edges e	Number of vertices v	Number of subgraphs p	Index			Average edge length d
				a	b	c	
Danish network	15	10	1	0.40	1.50	0.63	96 km
Network Netherlands	10	10	1	0.07	1	0.42	90 km
Network Belgium	9	8	1	0.18	1.13	0.50	90 km
Network Switzerland	8	8	1	0.09	1	0.45	50 km

See figure 5.2

The minimum number of routes (in a tree) is $e_{min} = v - 1$, the maximum number of circuits (rings) is e_{max}/e_{min}.

The a-index is $m/2v - 5$, the b-index is e/v, the c-index is $e/3(v - 2)$ $a = 0$ for a tree and $a = 1$ for a complete connected network. $b < 1$ for a tree and > 1 for a degree of connectivity higher than one ring. $c = 1$ for a complete connected network. m is also called the cyclomatic number or first Betty number.

Table 4.20 gives e, v, p, a, b, and c for transport networks in Denmark, The Netherlands, Belgium and Switzerland.

The a-, b- and c-indices are given for planar networks.

A d-index can be given as total net length divided by l, a route length.

A p-index can be given as total net length divided by diameter length.

A t-index can be given as total traffic volume divided by v nodes.

A θ-index can be given as total net length divided by v nodes.[47-51]

4.5 Scheduling and Location

Transport systems were studied by Hitchcock[74] and Koopmans[75] (1941; 1947). They formulated the problem of the most economical transport programme between a number of locations (unit cost of transport being independent of the amount transported). Dantzig (1951) and Flood (1954) solved the problem by linear programming. Further, relative costs of possible changes in the programme and the relationship of these cost ratios to freight rates formed in competitive markets were investigated, as well the relationship of freight rates to inter-regional price differences and movements of goods. The result was that private firms solved the most economical routing problem as efficiently as a public authority could. However, this model ignores congestion both of terminals and *en route*.

Arne Jensen (1954)[80] worked out an allocation scheme that will result in a minimum of 'empty' voyages for the available ships n_o in transporting given amounts of commodities along given sea routes. His programme leads to the smallest possible total accumulation of goods in the ports. First he found the production function for the shipping network. The average amount of goods transported per unit time N multiplied by the average time spent in ports b. This gave the average number of waiting shiploads. It is now possible to determine the optimum number of ships in the route network. The problem as formulated here was not linear, in good agreement with the theory of economies.

Beckmann (1953)[69] studied the supply side of railway freight distribution by investigating marshalling yards. Some of the problems were: the wagon time spent waiting for enough freight to accumulate so that a train can economically be formed, sorting wagons to minimise cost of these factors, together with scheduling. These models helped railways in computing capabilities of a given freight railway network and the rolling stock requirements, especially the best routing of empty wagons. (The network in the United States is divided into 12 regions.) More recently (1970), Law and Petersen from the Canadian National Railways have treated the wagon time problem by use of bulking queues.[98]

Each year British Rail distribute 200 million tons of goods between 2500 terminals in 50 different wagon types and in 17 commodity groups. The network is 22 000 km long and there are 500 000 wagons. The number of loaded distributed wagons per year is 14 million, that is, 1 million per month and 40 000 per day, a total of 25 000 million ton km per year.[99]

Between 2500 stations 100 000 different routes are possible. However, 80 main goods centres have been chosen and between these only 6000 routes are possible, of which only 4500 are used. After forecasting traffic in two-month periods, goods are divided into trainload flows and wagonload flows.

Wagonload flows are divided into local distribution or transit categories. Wagonload transit flows are divided into short-distance and long-distance flows; the latter must conform to staff regulations. The demand to be satisfied is the movement of a given number of loaded and empty wagons from their originating marshalling yard to their destination marshalling yard within a predefined maximum transit time, and in such a way that there is no undue congestion on any section of route or in any marshalling yard and the cost of the operation is the minimum consistent with these restraints.

It was necessary to break down the problem into six stages involving a degree of suboptimisation:

(1) Creation of a route library which gives cheapest route taking into consideration running time, staff and traction.

(2) Creation of a terminal library which gives direct service criteria.

(3) Route selection which gives also the fastest route.

(4) Creation of a timetable which gives priority to passenger trains.

(5) Train load calculation which shows whether a train can be saved.

(6) Simulation of period which gives variation in traffic and supplementary trains.

The determination of the optimum bus service has been based on the assumption that passengers choose the routes which minimise their expected total journey cost, and further that the cost of providing the bus service should be a minimum. It is now possible to find:[84]

> s = route spacing, the distance between adjacent parallel bus-routes in a route network forming a square grid
>
> i = service interval (that is the average time interval between successive buses on a route)

and m = number of buses per unit area

It is found that the optimum values of s, i, and m, are given by

$$s^3 = \frac{bhu^2}{jkv} \qquad i^3 = \frac{b}{jkh^2uv} \qquad m^3 = \frac{j^2k^2h}{b^2uv}$$

where j = number of journeys originating per unit area per unit time; k = value of unit time; b = cost of bus service per bus per unit time; u = walking speed; v = bus speed (including stops); w = average waiting time for a bus; h = a constant depending on the irregularity of the buses, defined by $w = hi$ (h = 0.5) are the parameters known.

For a Danish bus network the following constants were used for long distance buses in Jutland:

j = 0.04 trips per km^2 per hour; k = 8 Kr per hour; b = 45 Kr per bus per hour; u = 5 km/h; v = 20 km/h; h = 0.5

The results were an optimal route spacing of 20 km, and a service interval of 1 hour.

An algorithm for optimal aircraft scheduling[85] concerns the daily routing of each aircraft which maximises profit and satisfies capacity, service and other restrictions. Given a network of cities served by the airline and an origin–destination matrix for passengers, the link capacities are variable because the routing of the aircraft, which limits the flow, is a variable.

This is a mixed-integer programming problem and the decomposition technique by Dantzig – Wolfe can be used. The solution procedure involves solving sub-problems, bringing these into a maximum problem and then computing dual prices which form the basis for resolution. If the aircraft are scheduled within 10-minute intervals during a 16-hour day, then there are 6 × 16 = 96 time intervals. The number of aircraft is about 200, and the number of aircraft types 5. The number of cities for each time period is about 50, which means about 5000 nodes. The number of routes $50 \times 49 \times 100$ = 245 000 or more, depending on the routing time for different types of aircraft. The number of types of passengers is $50 \times 49 = 2450$ types. The inputs are aircraft availabilities/non-availabilities, aircraft capacities, passenger travel arrivals and departures at time t, flying times, waiting times, ground times and gate capacities. Further considerations are revenue loss, operating cost, passenger service cost, etc.

The variables are aircraft scheduling, passenger loadings, passengers *en route*; passengers dropped. The constraints are maximum passengers *en route*, maximum passenger load, flow balance for passengers and aircraft and maximum aircraft on ground in a city. The objective function is to minimise fare cost, operating and late arrival costs.

Taylor and Jackson[86] have given the relationships between the number of spare aircraft, the probability of a breakdown and the utilisation of the hangar repair facilities using queueing theory.

Neufville and Gordon[100] have worked on air transport networks (*Transport Research*, 1973). Their model optimises the level of service of a given air transport network for any given budget. Specifically the model minimises the total delay experienced by passengers being served by a fleet with a given number of aircraft, over a given set of routes. It indicates what load factors are optimal for different links of the network.

In view of the general interest in satellite airports, it is possible to investigate how many air-route links should be established between two regions. It is shown that the schedule is minimised when the number of links equals one. This result may change if travel distances are significantly different, because of greater congestion or distance of the airport from the town centre, or if smaller aircraft could be used to provide higher frequency at equivalent cost.

It is also shown that the network with least connections has the least delays. Results show that a tree is preferable for networks with more direct service.

The immediate effect of introducing larger aircraft on a network is in general to increase delays. This effect can be somewhat mitigated if the larger aircraft are more economical to operate. In the United States the past twenty years have witnessed a significant decrease in the number of points served by regular air carriers, as the size of aircraft has grown.

Improvements in service to remote communities must be paid for, either in terms of degraded service or increased cost, by the rest of the system. Technical analysis alone cannot hope to answer the political or ethical questions that must be answered to define what is fair to all groups.

This model is in accordance with the Danish air route tree, actually a star from Copenhagen, it also confirms some doubts about the use of large aircraft and the service to remote communities. However, it does not answer questions of hinterland size.

The Federal Aviation Agency (F.A.A.) requires airport regional studies for two air-carrier airports within 50 miles and one hour's driving time from one another and where one of the airports has originated fewer than 10 000 annual passengers.

The problem of locating airports for interurban services is no longer to get as close to the city centre as possible, but to ensure convenient access by automobile from the whole hinterland, according to Elle.[8]

An increasing availability of cars has made it easier to get to the airport, but the increasing local dispersion of persons to be visited has made it difficult to reach people by public transport from a terminal.

Elle compares four alternative development stages for Swedish domestic airports including 22, 40, 63 and 118 airports respectively. Sweden has an area of 440 000 km^2 and a population of 8 million. The basis for the geographical model is a division of the country into 100 regions. On this basis 80 hypothetical airports have been defined ($> 25\,000$ inhabitants). The 80 airports combine into $(80^2 - 80)/2 = 3160$ pairs of airports or routes.

Engstrøm and Sahlberg[102] in their publication from Lund University (1973) touched on these problems by using a so-called contact-supply possibility index defined as

$$\frac{\text{number of contacts (function of population,}}{\text{labour force and traffic accessibility)}}{\text{cost of travel} + \text{cost of travel time}}$$

The material used for the analysis of contact possibilities is data of contact requirements in the private and public sectors, in trade, industry and in administration. The contact-supply profiles are sensitive to distance and local accessibility (contact per Sw. Kr). The effects of changes in the transport system on the contact-supply profile are very small. Engstrøm and Sahlberg calculated indices for contact possibilities in Swedish cities. These are shown in table 4.21

TABLE 4.21   Contact possibilities indices

	Sweden 1970	With better air network	With major city density	With decentralisation
Stockholm	100	100	100	100
Malmø	33	35	33	45
Gothenburg	43	45	43	57
Jønköping	25	27	23	38
Karlstad	22	24	20	34
Eskilstuna	27	28	26	36
Norrkøping	27	30	25	42
Sundvall	17	21	11	21

High index value is associated with low contact cost.

An important factor is the stay time, which is defined as the time a person can spend in a place having left his home at a given time in the morning, and returning at a given time in the evening.

By means of this model it is possible to compare future development patterns and airport networks by use of a contact-supply index serving access needs of passengers on a regional basis. In the same way contact cost profiles can be used assuming a variable average speed for car travel, etc.

In chapter 5 the demand models and evaluation procedures will be given special attention.

References

1. Smith, A. (1776). *An Inquiry into the Nature and Causes of Wealth of Nations*, Edinburgh.
2. List, F. (1841). *The National System of Political Economy* (translation), Longmans, London
3. Dupuit, J. (1844). Utility of Public Works, *Annales des Ponts et Chaussées*, **8**
4. Pigou, A. (1912). *Wealth and Welfare*, Macmillan, London
5. Baumol, W. J. (1965). *Economic Theory and Operations Analysis*, Prentice Hall, New Jersey
6. Foster, C. D. (1963). *The Transport Problem*, Blackie & Son, Glasgow
7. Thorburn, T. (1960). *Supply and Demand for Water Transport*, Business Research Institute, Stockholm
8. Elle, B. (1968). *Issues and Prospects in Interurban Air Transport*, Almqvist & Wiksell, Stockholm
9. Kraft, G., Meyer, J. R. and Valette, J. P. (1971). *The Role of Transport in Regional Economic Development*, Lexington, Massachusetts
10. Searle, G. *et al.* (1973) Value of travel time saving, *Int Symp. Transp. Environ.*, Southampton
11. Tessier, M. (1973) Très Grande Vitesses Ferroviaires *1st Int Conf. Transp. Res.*, Bruges
12. Hirst, E. (1972). *Energy Consumption for Transport in the U.S.A.*, Oak Ridge National Laboratory, Tennessee
13. Richards, E. (1970). The cost of airport noise, *New Scient.*, **47**
14. Bendtsen, P. H. and Rallis, T. (1961). Lösch theory for an urban structure in Denmark, *Stads- og Havneingenioren*, **51**
15. Lalanne, L. (1863). Essai d'une Théorie des Reseaux de Chemin de Fer, *C. r. hebd. Séanc. Acad. Sci., Paris*, **42**
16. Galpin. D. J. (1915). The social anatomy of an agricultural community, *Research Report 34*, University of Wisconsin
17. Christaller, W. (1933). *Die Zentralen Orte in Süddeutschland*, G. Fischer, Jena
18. Lösch, A. (1940). *Die Räumlishe Ordnung der Wirtschaft*, G. Fischer, Jena
19. Illeriis, S. (1967). Functional regions in Denmark *Geografisk Tidsskrift*, **66**
20. Andersen, P. B. (1973). *Airport Hinterlands in Denmark*, Report 17, IVTB, Copenhagen
21. Buskgaard, O. and Rallis, T. (1973) Modal Distribution for Business Travelling *Dansk Vejtidsskrift*, **50**
22. Baggendorff, H. (1966). *Harbour Transport Hinterlands*, Danish Society for Civil Engineering, Copenhagen
23. Philbrick, A. K. (1957). Principles of areal functional organisation in regional human geography, *Econ. Geogr.*, **33**
24. Thünen, J. H. von (1826). *Der isolierte Staat in Beziehung auf Landwirtsch ünd National Okon*, Hamburg.

25. Launhardt, W. (1882). Die Bestimmung des Zweckmassizstten Standorts einer gewerblischen Anlage, *Zeitschr. d. Verein. Deutsche Ing. Berlin*, **26**
26. Weber, A. (1909) *Über den Standort der Industrien*, Tübingen
27. Friedman, J. and Alonso, W. (1964). *Regional Development and Planning*, MIT Press, Cambridge, Massachusetts
28. Berry, B. J. L. (1967). *Geography of Market Centres and Retail Distribution*, Prentice Hall, New Jersey
29. Kuhn, T. E. (1962). *Public Enterprise Economics and Transport Problems*, University of California.
30. Isard, W. (1960). *Methods of Regional Analysis*, MIT Press, Cambridge, Massachusetts
31. Isard, W. (1959). *Location and Space Economy*, MIT Press, Cambridge, Massachusetts
32. Stouffer, S. A. (1940). Intervening opportunities mobility and distance, *Am. Soc. Rev.*, **5**
33. Goodwin, R. M. (1949). The multiplier as matrix, *Econ. J.*, **59**
34. Metzler, L. A. (1950). A multiple region theory of increase and trade, *Econometrica*, **18**
35. Leontief, W. (1953). *Studies in the Structure of the American Economy*, Part II, Oxford University Press, New York
36. Walras, L. (1874). *Elements d'Economic Politique Pure*, Paris
37. Morrill, R. L. (1962). Simulation of central place patterns over time, *Geographical Series B*, **24**, Gleerup, Lund
38. Meyer, I. R., Kresge, D. and Roberts, P. O. (1971). *Techniques of Transport Planning*, Vol. II, Brookings, Washington
39. Wellington, A. M. (1887) *The Economic Theory of the Location of Railways*, New York
40. Bunge, W. (1962) Theoretical geography, *Studies in Geography Series C*, Gleerup, Lund
41. Haggett, P. (1965) *Locational Analysis in Human Geography*, Arnold, London
42. Dunn, E. S. (1954). *The Location of Agricultural Production*, University of Florida Press, Gainesville, Florida
43. Dantzig, G. B. (1963). *Linear programming and extensions*, Princeton University Press, New Jersey
44. Cooley, C. H. (1894) The Theory of transport, *Am. Econ. Ass. Publ.*, **9**
45. Taffe, E. J. and Gauthier, H. L. (1969). *Geography of Transport*, Prentice Hall, Englewood, Cliffs, New Jersey
46. Kansky, K. J. (1963). Structure of transport network, *Geographical Papers*, **84**, University of Chicago
47. Yau, S. S. (1961). Structures of a communications network, *IRE Trans. Circuit Theory*, **CT8**
48. Gomory, R. E. and Hu, T. C. (1961). Multiterminal network flows, *J. Soc. Industr. Appl. Math.*, **9**
49. Ford, L. R. and Fulkerson, D. R. (1962). *Flows in Networks*, Princeton University Press, New Jersey
50. Mayeda, W. (1960). Terminal and branch capacity matrices, *IRE Trans. Circuit Theory*, **CT7**
51. Neufville, R. de (1971). *Systems Analysis*, McGraw Hill, New York
52. Heggie, J. (1972) *Transport Engineering Economics*, McGraw Hill, London
53. Bayliss, B. T. (1965). *European Transport*, London
54. Bohm, P. *et al.* (1974). *Transportpolitiken och Samhällsekon*, Liber, Stockholm
55. Hirst, E. (1973). *Energy Intensiveness of Passenger and Freight Transport Modes*, Oak Ridge National Laboratory, Oak Ridge, Tennessee
56. Glück, H. (1973). Energy consumption at high speeds, *Railway Gazette International*, **129**, December
57. Breimeier, R. (1970). Der Energie aufwand des Massengut Transportes auf Binnenwasser−Strassen und Eisenbahnen, *Eisenbahn Technische Rundschau*, **19**
58. *Teknisk Ukeblad* (1973). nos 12 and 39, Oslo
59. Bendtsen, P. H. (1962) Influence of gradient on the traffic running costs of a new road, *Indian Builder*, Annual
60. Cambell, E. (1973) The energy outlook, *Traffic Quarterly*, **27**
61. IRU (1974). The Energy Crisis and Road Haulage Industry, Geneva
62. Andersen, P. Bj. (1975). *En Metode til Belysn. af forhøjede Oliepriser*, IVTB, Copenhagen

63. SOU, 75 (1974). *Energiforsyning C. Transporter and Samfund*, Liber, Stockholm
64. Koranyi, L (1966). Energy requirements of high-speed trains, *Railway Gazette*, **122**
65. Illich, I. D. (1974). *Energy and Equity*, Calder & Boyars, London
66. Mesarovic, M. and Pestel, E. (1974). *Mankind at Turning Point*, New York
67. Orski *et al.* (1974) *Transport. Res.*, **8**, no 4/5
68. Nordtrans, 13 (1969). *Norden as a Region for coordinating location and transport*, Stockholm
69. Beckman, M, McGuire, C. B. and Winsten, C. B. (1956). *Studies in the Economy of Transport*, Yale
70. Clark, C., Wilson, F. and Bradley, J. (1969). Industrial Location and Economic Potential in Western Europe, *Regional Studies* 3, London
71. Ventura, E. M. (1968) L'Industrie de Raffinage et des Transport de Produits Petroliers, *Annales des Mines*, **00**
72. Marshall, E. E. (1969).The role of aircraft in future transport systems, *Flight*, **94**, July
73. McKinsey (1967) *Containerization, the Key to Low Cost Transport*, British Transport Dock Board, London
74. Hitchcock, F. L. (1941). The distribution of a product from several sources of numerous localities, *J. Math. Phys.*, **20**
75. Koopmans, T. C. (1949). Optimum utilisation of the transport system, *Econometrica*, **17**
76. Dorfman, R., Samuelson, P. and Solow, R. (1958). *Linear Programming and Economic Analysis*, McGraw Hill, New York
77. Roberts, M. J. (1969). Transport Pricing and Distribution Efficiency, *Land Economics*, **45**
78. Edwards, S. L. (1970). Transport costs in British industry, *J. Transp. Econ. Policy*, **4**
79. Mathematica (1969). *Studies in Travel Demand*, vol. 4 Princeton University Press, Princeton, New Jersey
80. Jensen, A. (1954) *A Distribution Model*, Munksgaard, Copenhagen
81. Feldstein, M. S. (1964) *Net Social Benefit Calculation*, Oxford Economic Papers no. 16
82. Marglin, S. A. (1967) *Public Investment Criteria and the Public Investment Decision*, Allen & Unwin London
83. Neuman, J. and Morgenstern, O. (1944). *Theory of Games and Economic Behaviour*, Princeton University Press, Princeton, New Jersey
84. Holroyd, E. M. (1965). *The Optimum Bus Service*, Road Research Laboratory, London
85. Agin, N. I. (1972). An algorithm for optimal aircraft scheduling, *Proc. Nato Conf.*, Sandefjord
86. Taylor, J. and Jackson, R. R. P. (1954). *Operational Research Quarterly*, **5**
87. Lewis, W. A. (1949). *Fixed Costs*, Allen & Unwin, London
88. Baumol, J. C. *et al.* (1962). Minimum pricing of railroad services, *J. Business*, **35**
89. Joy, S. (1964). British Rail track costs, *J. Ind. Econ.*, **13**
90. Fugl-Meyer, H. (1957). *The Modern Port*, Technical Press, Copenhagen
91. Saggar, R. K. (1970). Turn round and costs of conventional cargo liners, *J. Transp. Econ. Policy*, **4**
92. Davies, E (ed.) (1963). *Traffic Engineering Practice*, S.P.O.N., London
93. Road Directorate (1970). Transport Economics and Evaluation of Road Plans, *Report on Economy*, Copenhagen
94. Walter, R. A. (1970). Environmental Quality, *Regional Studies*, **4**
95. Hamm, W. (1968). *Grundsätzlische Aspekte des Leber Plans*, Bern
96. Munby, D. L. (1968) Mrs Castle's transport policy, *J. Transp. Econ. Policy*, **2**
97. Bendtsen, P. H. and Rallis, T. (1971). Transport outside towns, Topic II, 2, *4th Int. Symp. CEMT*, Hague
98. Law, E. and Petersen, E. R. (1970). *Bulking Queues.*. . . . *Canadian National Railways*, Queens University Ontario
99. Alexander, N. J. B. (1970). *Symposium on Freight Transport*, P.T.R.C., Amsterdam
100. Neufville, R de and Gordon, S (1973). Design of air transport networks *Transp. Res.*, **7**
101. Choguill, C. L. (1973). Airport systems planned by spatial demography, *Proc. 1st. Int. Conf. Transp. Res.*, Bruges
102. Engstrøm, M. G. and Sahlberg, B. W. (1973). Travel demand, transport systems and regional development, *Studies in Geography* **B39**, Lund

5 Transport Demand and Planning

While the gross national products in the industrialised countries have increased by 4 per cent a year since the 1950s, industrial production by 6 per cent and world trade by 8 per cent, most traffic volumes have increased even more. Thus a very important point in intercity transport planning is the forecasting of future traffic volumes. In the following we shall first describe simple forecasting models, using the method of extrapolation.[1]

5.1 Forecasting Growth Curves

5.1.1 Arithmetical Forecast (extrapolation)

In order to estimate a future increase from the knowledge of the increase of previous years, a straight line is often drawn through the points observed. The differential equation for the increase is of the type:

$$\frac{dy}{dt} = k \text{ in a system of co-ordinates } (t, y)$$

where the abscissa is the time t, the ordinate y is the quantity, the increase of which is to be estimated, and k is a constant. By integration a straight line $y = kt + k_0$ is obtained, k_0 being another constant. It appears that the increase per time unit dy/dt is, from a mathematical point of view, independent of the previous state as well as of the time.

From this kind of extrapolation a picture is formed of the present limit of the development, that is the method is suitable for the near future only. If this method is used to establish the capacity of an airport during the next twenty years, there is a risk that the layout designed may be too small. The method is called arithmetical forecast (annual increase at a constant difference). It was first used in 1718 by De Moivre to represent the increase in population.

5.1.2 Geometrical Forecast (exponential extrapolation)

An increase curve, the differential equation of which contains the increase y of the past, may be of the type:

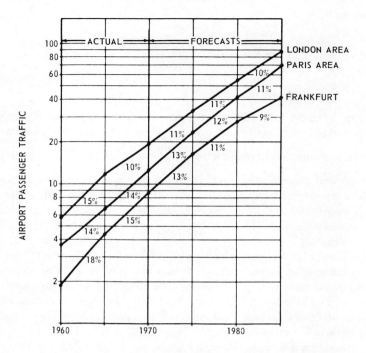

Figure 5.1 Growth curves for European airports (I.C.A.O.)

$$\frac{dy}{dt} = k \times y$$

By integration of this type of equation the curve $y = c \times e^{kt}$ is obtained—an exponential function in which e is the base of the natural logarithm and c and k are constants, other symbols as before. This method of prediction is called a geometrical forecast (annual increase at a constant quotient).

This curve represents an increase to infinity more rapidly than the increase found by arithmetical forecast.

It was first used in 1760 by Euler and in 1798 by Malthus to represent the increase in population. By means of logarithms we obtain

$$\log_e y = \log_e c + kt$$

that is the curve will be a straight line in a semi-logarithmic system of co-ordinates, $\log_e y$ being the ordinate and t the abscissa.

5.1.3 Logistic Forecast (gradually declining increase)
If the differential equation of the increase curve is

$$\frac{dy}{dt} = \frac{b}{a}y(a-y)$$

integration will result in the curve

$$y = \frac{a}{1+c\exp(-bt)}$$

where a is the upper limit of y, b is the rate of development (the development being degressive at $b < 0$), and c is an arbitrary constant. The curve is symmetrical about a point of inflection $\left\{\dfrac{\log_e c}{b}, \dfrac{a}{2}\right\}$ and has the t-axis as lower asymptote and the parallel $y = a$ as upper asymptote, that is, horizontal tangent to the infinite branch of the curve. It is seen that the increase per unit time is proportional to the total previous increase y as well as to the number of still unutilised possibilities $a - y$, $y = a$ being the saturation limit, that is, satisfied demand.

This method of prediction, which is also called a logistic forecast, is the most recent of the graphic increase curves. It was first used in 1838 by Verhulst to represent the increase in population which he, unlike Malthus, presumed to be rising towards a saturation limit, the asymptote. The logistic method is often used instead of the geometrical method to obtain an annual, gradually declining increase percentage.

The three constants of the curve, a, b and c, can be found when we know the co-ordinates of three points on the curve at reasonable, equal time intervals. Wilson points out that three such arbitrary points of observation, y_0, y_1 and y_2 will make it possible to determine the asymptote only if the following conditions are fulfilled

$$\frac{1}{y_1^2} < \frac{1}{y_0} \times \frac{1}{y_2} \quad \text{and} \quad \frac{2}{y_1} < \frac{1}{y_0} + \frac{1}{y_2}$$

We then have

$$a = \frac{\dfrac{1}{y_0} + \dfrac{1}{y_2} - \dfrac{2}{y_1}}{\dfrac{1}{y_0} \times \dfrac{1}{y_2} - \dfrac{1}{y_1^2}}, \quad c = a\frac{\left[\dfrac{1}{y_1} - \dfrac{1}{y_0}\right]^2}{\dfrac{1}{y_0} + \dfrac{1}{y_2} - \dfrac{2}{y_1}}$$

and

$$\exp(-bt) = \frac{\dfrac{1}{y_1} - \dfrac{1}{y_2}}{\dfrac{1}{y_0} - \dfrac{1}{y_1}}$$

This extrapolation seems suitable for representing the increase in the number of journeys within a certain period and area in which no appreciable structural changes are being made; it seems unsuitable for a period of sudden changes as regards service, politics and the economy.

In 1931 theories of probability were used in prognoses of population; and in prognoses of traffic an attempt could also be made to explain the distribution laws applying to the time intervals between the discontinuous jumps in traffic of observed developments.

The problem of making predictions is actually to determine the probability of a certain event, for example reaching a certain traffic volume, taking place in a certain time interval. This kind of extrapolation may be susceptible to error as a result of insufficient information concerning the development and the increase factors by which it is influenced. In the following, simple methods are given which take some important parameters into consideration.

Table 5.1 compares the 1970 traffic in the networks mentioned in previous chapters. It is seen that the density of transport in networks increases as the area of networks decreases.

TABLE 5.1   Trip generation and freight transport generation as a function of population and area

Networks (1970)	Passenger transport		Goods transport	
	journeys/ inhabitant/ year	journeys/ km^2/ year	tons/ inhabitant/ year	tons/ km^2/ year
(1) Intercontinental	0.01	0.6	0.5	30
(2) European	0.25	16	3	200
(3) Danish	20	2 000	6	600
(4) Copenhagen	2 000	20 000 000	600	6 000 000

5.2 Forecasting Growth Formulae For Passenger Traffic

5.2.1 *Estimation of Passenger Traffic Volume Between Cities.*[2]

The amount of travel between pairs of cities will depend primarily on the size and commercial character of the cities and the distance between them, because of the well-known theory of the inherent relationship between traffic and the length of haul. This postulates that the traffic potential between pairs of cities is related to the product of their populations and a 'community of interest' factor, and is inversely proportional to the distance between them. This is the gravity model, used in railway planning (Lill, 1880).

5.2.2 *Distribution of Traffic Between Modes*

The distribution of traffic between travel modes in intercity traffic can be calculated by the following formula

$$T_M = k \frac{\text{Frequency}}{\text{Fare} \times \text{Time}}$$

The trips with a given mode are, therefore, proportional to the service frequency and inversely proportional to the fare and the travel time.

A simple formula to forecast intercity traffic was developed by Björkman. He maintains that the rate of increase in traffic is proportional to the rate of increase in population PU, to the rate of increase in purchasing power I and to the rate of improvement of traffic service S. Using rates of 1.25, 2 and 2.5 per cent per year, one finds a tenfold increase in traffic in 30 years.

Björkman considers that the following factors influence air traffic: increase in the population P and increase in the urban population U, increase in the national income I, improved surface traffic service S, improved air traffic service A, reduction in air fares F. He believes that the air traffic to and from an area increases in proportion to the product of the said factors, and that some of the factors can be given greater weight by means of power indices.

Björkman's formula reads as follows. The increase factor in the number of passengers

$$T = PUI^{1 \cdot 2} F^2 \frac{A}{S}.$$

T is the figure by which the number of passengers in the basic year (index 1) shall be multiplied in order to reach the desired number, for example, 15 years later. If $P = U = S = 1$ after 15 years, whereas A has risen to 1.4, I to 1.8 and F to 1.2 in relation to the basic year, the total increase

$$T = 1 \times 1 \times 1.8^{1 \cdot 2} \times 1.2^2 \times \frac{1.4}{1}$$

The formula was set up by analysing the influence of each particular factor on T, while keeping the other factors constant.

The power indices 1, 1.2 and 2 were thus determined as the slope of the regression line of a number of observation points from a previous period in a semi-logarithmic system of co-ordinates, measured traffic multiplied by constant factors being the ordinate and the particular analysed factor alone the abscissa. Using Björkman's formula, the increase percentage of the factors mentioned must be fixed in each region.

5.2.3 *Network Flow*

The problem of forecasting flow equilibrium in transport networks is solved by supply and demand functions. The supply function for a link indicates how cost increases as flow increases up to capacity. The demand function for a pair of regions relates how volume decreases as the cost increases.[3]

Furthermore, there exist flow distribution rules: individuals choose a minimum cost route (Wardrop's first principle, 1952); public services choose routes that maximise their total consumers' surplus (Wardrop's second principle); minimum journey time.

Solutions to the problem can be divided into three categories: (1) traffic assignment; (2) mathematical programming; (3) algorithms with fixed and variable demands. Traffic assignment does not prove equilibrium convergence; mathematical programming (linear and dynamic) cannot handle the large-scale problems; algorithms with fixed demand are not realistic—those without fixed demand were worked out by Manheim 1968, and Gilbert 1968 (the latter proved the equilibrium convergence).

The trips between every pair of zones are assigned to the fastest route. Traffic is added up on each link.

The travel times of the links are adjusted according to the formula

$$t^i = e^{\left[\frac{q^i}{C} - 1\right]} t^0$$

where t^i = travel time after the i'th step of iteration

e = 2.718 (basis of Napier's logarithm)

q^i = the flow on the link after the i'th iteration

C = the practical capacity of the link

t^0 = initial travel time corresponding to flow equal to C

Using the adjusted travel times a new set of fastest routes between all pairs of zones is found. The process is repeated until the changes in the link flows and in the travel times are sufficiently small from one step of iteration to the next one.

5.3 Forecasting Models for Passenger Transport

5.3.1 Sequential Models

In this approach, the trip production function was assumed not to be dependent on supply such as travel time, price and frequency. The trip distribution on regions was normally a gravity or intervening opportunities model not dependent on travel price and frequency. The trip mode distribution was normally a function of simply the differences in travel time or generalised cost. The assignment of flows to the network was often of the types: all or nothing, with or without capacity restraint.

They were 'aggregate demand models' and 'deterministic'. Other major recent developments in traffic models are described below.

Behavioural Models with a Disaggregate Approach (Stopher, Lisco)
They use discriminant, logit and probit functions and are mostly concerned
with mode distribution and are 'stochastic' in nature. They are almost
impossible to use in intercity transport because of lack of data and complex
mathematics.

Entropy Models of Aggregate Approach (Wilson)
They often give the same result as the gravity model.

Simulation Models (Kresge, Roberts)
These have already been discussed in chapter 4.

5.3.2 Transport System Models

These are simple applications of economic theory to transport situations. One
finds equilibrium in the transport market by setting up a supply function and a
demand function and solving for the equilibrium flows. The consumer
considers many service factors in the supply function when he makes a choice,
for example travel time, travel cost, travel frequency, by each mode. The
demand function should include population, income, etc. The equilibrium
occurs in a network affected by capacity restraints, topology, structure, etc.

   The basic transport model for intercity transport should include several
variables.

   (1) Estimation of the total transport volume T_{12} between two regions 1 and
2, depends on the population size, P, and purchasing power I.

   (2) Distribution of the total transport volume between three or four modes
of travel T_R, depends on travel time H, fare F, and service frequency S.

   (3) Distribution of the transport volume for mode R, T_R, between three, four
or n routes of that mode between the two regions.

These are the steps in the model which Manheim calls the general share model.
   The four-step approach known from urban transport models is here
changed into a single step. Such a model was developed for forecasting
intercity passenger transport in the North-east Corridor of the United States
by Kraft,[4] McLynn,[5] Quandt[6] and Baumol. In the Manheim and Ruiters
DODOTRANS system (Decision Oriented Data Organized Transport Analysis System) of computer models from MIT (Massachusetts Institute of
Technology) and ICES (Integrated Civil Engineering Systems), these models
are available as an application of systems analysis to intercity transport
problems.[7]

Baumol–Quandt Model
The relationship that is used is

$$T_{R,n}^{12} = a_0 P_1^{q_1} P_2^{q_2} I_1^{q_3} I_2^{q_4} H_{\min}^{a_5} \left[\frac{H_R}{H_{\min}} \right]^{a_6} F_{\min}^{a_7} \left[\frac{F_R}{F_{\min}} \right]^{a_8} S_{\max}^{a_9} \left[\frac{S_R}{S_{\max}} \right]^{a_{10}} \tag{5.1}$$

This is an abstract mode model, without cross elasticity, in which the variables are all vectors. Here $a_0, \ldots a_{10}$ are the empirical constants, elasticities, to be found by calibration. The variables I, F should include several income groups or travellers broken down into business and non-business trips, or car owners and non-car owners.

The variables H, S should include several door-to-door combinations, that is movements to and from the main haul mode termini (access–egress links). Furthermore the travel time over a link is a function of the transport volume over the link, and of the capacity. In practice most of these factors are difficult to achieve, as the quality of available data will not usually support such a level of detail, and some averaging is necessary. An advantage of the abstract mode model is that it can be used to forecast the traffic for new modes without changing form or constants.

McLynn Model
In the McLynn model the supply variables are gathered in a general impedance of travelling $\sum W_{ijR}$. Here W_{ijR} is the 'composite utility' of travel from i to j by mode R, where W again is a function of H, F and S, and

$$\frac{T_R}{\sum T} = \frac{W_R}{\sum W} \tag{5.2}$$

Kraft Model
In the Kraft model there is one equation for each mode R

$$T_R = a_0 (PU_i PU_j)^{a_1 R} (I_i I_j)^{a_2 R} (O_{ij})^{a_3 R} \times \pi \tag{5.3}$$

Where PU is population multiplied by an urbanisation factor, O is ownership of cars

$$\pi = \pi H^{a_4 R} F^{a_5 R} S^{a_6 R}$$

It is seen that all cross-elasticities are non-zero.

The criterion used to compute the model constants is to minimise the square of the error, defined as the difference between the observed and the estimate variables. Normally a stepwise multiple regression is used. If some variables are highly correlated, constants may not be plausible. Sometimes constrained regression is used if the problem of collinearity of variables is present.

The constants can be taken as elasticities. As the McLynn model is a ratio model, the elasticities of W vary with mode distribution.

'Self-elasticity' is the change in mode R traffic, because of a change in W_R, cross elasticity is the change in mode R traffic because of a change in another mode W impedance.

Example 1

The McLynn model has been used in Denmark[8] to forecast traffic across a new bridge at Great Belt. The number of zones used was 60 and data were collected from a sample of 130 000 travellers' origin–destination information. Two alternatives of growth during the period 1970 to 1985 were assumed: alternative 1 was that the economic growth continues as in the period 1955–70; alternative 2 was that the economic growth decreases.

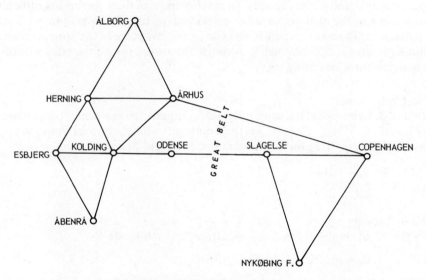

Figure 5.2 The Danish network

TABLE 5.2   Average daily traffic (passengers) across Great Belt (1985)

Mode	1970	*Status quo* Alternative 1 1985		Decreased growth in G.N.P. Alternative 2 1985	
		Ferries	New Bridge	Ferries	New Bridge
Railway	8 000	7 000	7 000	34 000	38 000
Road	16 000	36 000	54 000	8 000	11 000
Aircraft	2 000	1 000	1 000	1 000	1 000
Total	26 000	44 000	62 000	43 000	50 000

The resulting average daily traffic (rounded) across Great Belt (in passengers) is shown in table 5.2.

Example 2

In Denmark[8] an investigation of the long-run sensitivity of intercity passenger travel behaviour to a petroleum shortage has also been carried out. It gives the modal choice and travel volume when prices of fuel are altered for the three modes automobile, air and rail for 60 city pairs in Denmark (40 west of Great Belt). The alternative cost assumptions are used as input to the abstract mode demand model given by McLynn. Table 5.3 shows the sensitivity.

TABLE 5.3   Effects of increased oil prices

	50% increase	100% increase
Causes an increase in rail traffic of	28%	45%
Causes a decrease in automobile traffic of	48%	70%
Causes an increase in air traffic of	17%	21%
Total traffic decreased 20%		

Such studies have also been carried out in the United States by Crow and Savitt (1974) using a Monsod model. However, this is a long-run forecast where other parameters such as highway speed, railway speed (that is Great Belt Bridge) and airline frequency are not given any variation.

5.4 Estimation of Freight Traffic Volumes Between Cities

Once it is recognised that trade patterns and the geographical distribution of activities mutually determine each other, there is no reason to treat trade and location theory separately. Trade economists have explicitly recognised the role of transport costs in trade patterns. The fundamentals of trade theory were set up by Ricardo (1817)[9] and applied to inter-regional trade by Ohlin (1933)[10] and Olsen (1971)[11].

Ricardo's theory states that two areas will exchange commodities in which they have a comparative advantage, that is, existence of absolute price differentials between different locations, a production advantage and a transport advantage.

The Swedish Ohlin school has explained international trade by national differences in relative factor endowments. If there are no costs for transport, no tariffs and no other barrier to trade, the capital-rich country will export the capital-intensive commodity and import the labour-intensive commodity. The labour-rich country will correspondingly export the labour-intensive commodity and import the capital-intensive.

The social Carey school (1858)[12] has explained international trade by use of gravity models, an analogy from physics used in social studies by Reilly (1929),[13] Stewart (1947)[14] and Zipf (1946)[15]. Stewart's formula of gravitational force is a constant times the product of the two masses (populations) divided by the square of the distance separating them. The gravitational energy is defined by dividing by the distance, and the gravitational potential at point *i* is defined by dividing population in area *j* by distance *ij*. Stewart stresses that there should be no significant differences among areas in preferences, income, age distribution, occupational structures, etc. of their population.

Lisard described the use of gravity models in the analysis of the exchange of letters, telephone calls, etc. In a study of trade between regions it is useful to weigh population with *per capita* income, to raise mass and distance to other powers than one and two and to measure distance in a unit other than physical distance, for example in time or money units.

Pöyhönen[16] and Tinbergen[17] have recently developed models for trade. Mass is included in their gravity model as national income, distance is measured as the cost of transport and new parameters—an export parameter for the country of export and an import parameter for the country of import—are introduced. Pöyhönen estimated the parameters of this gravity model in a study of the trade between Belgium, Denmark, Finland, West Germany, Italy, the Netherlands, Norway, Portugal, Sweden, and the United Kingdom in 1958. Later (1963) the Finnish group studied trade between 62 non-communist countries from all parts of the world. These countries were divided into eight market areas: United States, Canada, Central America, South America, Europe, the Middle East, Africa, and the Far East, and it was assumed that the trade between two countries was influenced by the size of the market areas to which they belonged, by geographical location and meteorological conditions.

Tinbergen (1958) and Linnemann (1966)[18] from the Netherlands Economic Institute have used 18, 42 and 80 countries in their analysis. The 18 countries were Pöyhönen's 10 countries enlarged by the addition of Austria, France, Switzerland, Australia, United States–Canada, Japan, South America and Africa. The Ohlin model then gives the composition of trade, while the gravity model gives the value of trade, that is, volume.

Econometric input–output models have been used to calculate the total amount of production and consumption for different commodity groups and regions. The production is determined from the regional distribution of employees and total production per commodity group per economic sector. The household consumption is made proportional to the size of the regional population. The investments in any region are proportional to the number of regional employees in each sector of the economy. Forecasting is carried out by solving the national input—output system corresponding to an exogenous G.N.P. forecast.

Once the regional production and consumption are known, the entropy concept devised by A. G. Wilson[19] can be applied to calculate the flows of goods between the regions. The distribution model is identical to the gravity model. The flow is proportional to the productions in the respective regions and inversely proportional to the transport costs (distance) between the regions.

The modal choice phase determines the distribution between road, rail and ship traffic for each commodity group and each pair of regions. A linear modal choice model (Noortman and van Es) has been developed with the following variables: transport cost, transit time and frequency and accessibility (depends on distribution, iteration). This was a summary of optimisation of transport networks as seen from the national planning point of view.[3].

Baumol and Vinod[20] have given some interesting suggestions for freight transport models (1967) in the north-east corridor of the United States. One mode distribution model is of microeconomic type, called the inventory model, another model is of macroeconomic type, called the behavioural model in aggregated form.

5.4.1 The Inventory Model
This is given by the following:

Total annual cost of handling equals shipping cost + in transit cost + order cost + inventory cost

$$C = rT + utT + a/s + ws\frac{T}{2}$$

where r is shipping cost per unit

T is total amount transported per year

t is average time in transit

u is cost per unit of time (interest + deterioration + pilferage rate)

a is order cost per shipment

s is time between shipments, $s = (2a/wT)^{\frac{1}{2}}$

w is warehouse carrying cost per unit per year

The mode m then carries

$$\frac{T_m}{T_m + T_n} = \frac{1}{1 + (C_m/C_n)^d}$$

if there are two modes m, n. For commodity K, unity value V_K, d constant

TABLE 5.4 Formula constants corresponding to commodity groups

	(1) Food	(2) Textile	(4) Paper	(5) Plastic	(6) Petrol	(9) Furniture	(10) Stone	(11) Metal	(13) Machine	Total
u_{truck}	0.07	0.14	0.64	0.24	0.21	0.26	0.68	0.10	0.36	0.08
u_{air}	5766	1.6×10^7	9279	6574	943	97	3×10^6	0.7×10^6	3.39	0.3×10^6
H	5.3	4.7	22	1.48	11.37	5.52	55	4	18	4.35
h	0	0	0	0	0	0	0	0	0	0
d	8.8	2.9	1.7	5.3	6.68	2.55	1.4	1.8	1.7	1.95
K_r	0.001	0.81	3.57	0	0.02	0	0.09	0.50	2.41	2.76
K_i	6.7	4.1	19.4	3.25	2.63	2.06	0.34	0.64	4.18	2.18
H	100	262	219	798	−7.3	61	−0.07	75	452	53
h	0.19	0	0	0.29	3.86	0.06	0.20	0	0.02	0
K	3.85	1.14	0.63	0.48	0.2	0.91	0.71	0.76	0.05	0.15

$$C_m = r_{mk} + u_m t_m V_k$$

for rail $u_m t_m = u(H + hD)$ where H, h are constants and D distance. This cannot be used for air.

5.4.2 The Behavioural Model

This is given by (abstract commodity model):

The mode m carries $\dfrac{1}{1+w}$

where $w = \left(\dfrac{r_m}{r_n}\right)^{kr} \left(\dfrac{t_m}{t_n}\right)^{kt} \left(\dfrac{r_m^{\ln t_m}}{r_n^{\ln t_n}}\right)^{K}$

for rail $t = H + hD$. Table 5.4 contains the formula constants corresponding to a range of commodity groups.

5.5 Evaluation Procedures

5.5.1 Transport Systems and Cost–Benefit Analysis

Cost–benefit analysis is an important aid to public policy in order to avoid loss of consumers' surplus and to cover costs, both variable and overheads. Its aim is to extract revenue from those who benefit most, and encourage customers to travel or send goods at prices which at least cover variable costs.

It was not until the Federal Inter-Agency River Basin Committee's subcommittee on Benefits and Costs reported in 1950[30] that any real attempt was made to formalise the procedures for valuing costs and benefits in the United States. In Great Britain the earliest application was to the first motorway, the M1, the study being carried out by the Road Research Laboratory in 1960.[31] Since then the main application has been to transport projects—Maritime Industrial Development Areas, the withdrawal of rail services, proposed new airports and so on. Cost–benefit analysis has extended the idea of efficiency to public expenditures at a time when capital expenditures have become large.[34]

The decision-making levels are: projects (airport), programme (airport system), activity (air transport) and economy (transport).

Costs and benefits from actions can be divided into internal and external values, which can in turn be divided into market and non-market costs, the latter being not measured (N.M.) in money costs.

An example of a motorway project analysis is given below

	Cost	Benefits
Project	Right of way costs	User charge revenues (N.M.)
	Construction costs	Fuel tax, licence fees, parking revenues
	Parking space costs (N.M.)	Concession revenues
	Fixed cost of cars	Savings in door-to-door travel time (N.M.)
	Operating costs motorway	Quality of service, convenience (N.M.)
	Vehicle drivers time cost (N.M.)	
	Vehicle operating costs	
	Users accident costs (N.M.)	
Programme		
	Effect on other roads (N.M.)	Effects on other roads (N.M.)
	Effects on other road users (N.M.)	Effects on other road users (N.M.)
Activity	Effects on transport other than road (N.M.)	Effects on other transport than road (N.M.)
Economy	Environmental costs	Beneficial planning (N.M.)
	Accidents to non-users (N.M.)	Aesthetic effects (N.M.)
	Noise, pollution, aesthetic effects	
	Decrease in land values	Increase in land values (N.M.)
	Decrease in tax revenues	Increse in tax revenues
	Decrease of foreign aid	Increase of foreign aid

In cases where the benefits cannot be assessed in monetary terms, as is the position at the moment with most environmental changes, an alternative procedure is to carry out a cost—effectiveness study. If, for example, it is required to reduce the noise level but it is not possible to place financial values on the reductions, a cost—effectiveness study would compare the cost of schemes with the reduction in noise.

The evaluation procedures can vary as shown by Thygesen.[35]

(1) Partial planning, that is projects for a single activity in a department. The classical investment theory is used, the criterion being to maximise the present value of the net cash flow of alternative projects. The rate of discount should be the marginal rate of time preference. This goes for a perfect capital market, using the market rate of interest. The internal rate of return is

inconsistent. A normal interest rate is used to discount the net revenue to its present value. The investment rule is to accept any project having a positive net present value. In public planning a cost—benefit analysis must be used. First-year benefit can be used for optimal timing of an investment, even if the shadow value of capital in coming periods is unknown.

(2) Total planning in a department. Here the aim is to maximise the present value of the net payments from the department. Decentralisation is possible.

(3) Total planning under uncertainty. Here the aim is to maximise expected utility.

A road user benefit analysis for highway improvements is a comparison of annual costs of alternatives. For each alternative the annual road user costs and the annual cost of improving, maintaining, and operating that portion of the highway are determined for a selected period of time. Then the alternatives are compared arithmetically to express a benefit ratio or quotient of the cost differences as follows:

$$\text{Benefit ratio} = \frac{\text{Benefits}}{\text{Costs}} = \frac{\text{Difference in road user costs}}{\text{Difference in highway costs}} = \frac{R - R_1}{H_1 - H}$$

where R = the total annual road-user cost for the basic condition, usually the existing road

R_1 = the total annual road-user cost for the improvement, including travel on existing highways by the traffic directly involved or affected

H = the total annual highway cost for the basic condition, usually the existing road

H_1 = the total annual highway cost for the improvement.

A benefit ratio less than one indicates that in a road user benefit sense the basic condition is to be preferred over the alternative improvement.

5.6 Some Transport Plans

5.6.1 Reshaping British Rail

Beeching's reshaping of British Railways[22] (as it was then called) has been one of the biggest operations in Europe to evaluate unremunerative public transport services. The working deficit of British Railways in 1962 was £100 million.

The following measures were carried through:

(1) During the period 1962—68 the number of staff employed was reduced from 500 000 in 1962 to 300 000 in 1968.

(2) Closure of unremunerative lines and stations. The number of route

miles was reduced from 17 000 in 1962 to 13 000 in 1968, the number of stations reduced from 5000 in 1962 to 2700 in 1968 (30 per cent of the route miles had 1 per cent of traffic and the receipts were 10 per cent of the expenses). (Fifty per cent of the stations had two per cent of the traffic.)

(3) The rolling stock was reduced thus: from 14 000 locomotives in 1962 to 5000 in 1968 (including new diesel and electric locomotives); from 36 000 cars in 1962 to 20 000 in 1968 (including new passenger carriages); from 900 000 wagons in 1962 to 450 000 in 1968 (including new freight-container wagons).

(4) Reduction in train miles from 335 million in 1962 to 250 million in 1968.

All this has, however, not been able to eliminate British Rail's financial deficit. It may be attributed to the following factors:

(a) Labour earnings increased faster than labour productivity.

(b) Railway receipts per passenger mile and per net ton mile increased by only 4 per cent whereas working expenses rose by 22 per cent.

(c) It may be noted that subsidies to bus services substituted for unre-munerative passenger trains cost £500 000 in 1966.

(d) Available resources were used for modernising and developing main routes.

(e) Investment in signalling automation and electrification, amounting to £100 million.

(f) £100 million were spent on the electrification of the London–Manchester/Liverpool line over a period of 10 years.

Evans (University of Sussex)[21] analysed the benefits from the improvements of the London–Manchester/Liverpool electrifications (200 miles). He found that a 25 per cent reduction in travel time gave an increase in passenger traffic of about 40 per cent. The reduction in travel time gave a yearly benefit of £2 million. The increase in traffic yielded a yearly receipt of another £2 million. Money saved by use of rail instead of air gave a yearly benefit of £250 000.

The passengers having transferred from air to rail in that British example saved £250 000 per year. Those people who used the railway both before and after the electrification gained £2 million per year in saved time.

5.6.2. *The Channel Tunnel*[23]

Today sea and air services are carrying passengers, goods, road vehicles and trains across the Channel. Instead of expansion to meet the needs of increasing traffic, a tunnel or bridge was proposed to be built before 1980.

This would be a tunnel for rail only, having a length of 50 km (40 km under the sea) and linked with 2 terminals, 70 km apart. A rail tunnel is being

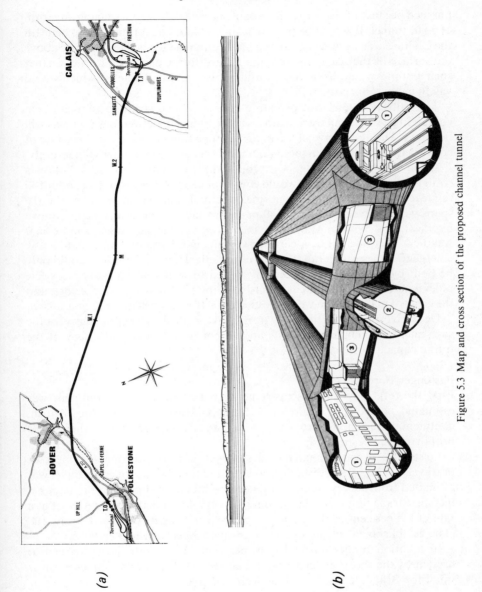

Figure 5.3 Map and cross section of the proposed channel tunnel

pursued because of the very considerable practical difficulties facing any form of road tunnel. It would be impracticable to ventilate a road tunnel beneath the Channel except by shafts driven up through the sea bed to protrude above the surface of the sea, constituting a hazard to the dense sea traffic; further such a tunnel would have to be considerably larger in diameter, which would vastly increase its cost.

The railway tunnel will probably consist of two separate tunnels, each containing a single rail track, with a service tunnel in between. All tunnels will be bored. The alternative of an immersed tube tunnel was rejected because of construction difficulties in the channel and because of its greater vulnerability.

As an alternative a bridge was proposed for road and rail use, to follow a straight route 34 km long. It would consist of metal spans resting on about 140 reinforced concrete piers. The normal length of span would be 225 m, but 10 spans would have a length of 440 m and would give clearance height above high water of 70 m, so as to allow the passage of the largest ships in normal weather. There would be a carriageway giving 6 lanes of traffic, flanked by emergency lanes with a rail track on either side. However, a bridge could only be built by international agreement; added to which its supports every few miles would constitute a great hazard to shipping. Finally, its initial costs and the costs of maintenance would be enormously greater than those of a tunnel.

Detailed estimates of the likely traffic have formed an essential basis for the assessment of comparative costs and revenues and of the adequacy of the traffic capacity offered.

Passenger Forecast
First the total flow of passengers between Britain and the Continent was estimated, based on leisure and business travel, divided into British, continental and non-European traffic, and by mode. Later the tunnel proportion was estimated.

Leisure travel was estimated from surveys taking into account income, cost of travel, value of time, distance travelled and travel time. Business travel was estimated from surveys taking into account managerial population, regional incomes, trade flows, etc. The annual growth of national income was set at a rate of 2.8 per cent in Britain and 4 per cent in France, Germany, Italy, etc. (The establishment of the O.E.C.D. means 25 per cent higher rates.)

In addition tunnel tariffs 10–20 per cent lower than those charged at present by the short sea ferries were assessed. The capture of tunnel traffic is small for British leisure travel, as seen in Table 5.5.

Freight Forecast
The basic model relates trade flows to growth in national income and then takes note of the price effects of tariff changes. Surveys were used.

TABLE 5.5   Estimated passengers and freight tonnage crossing the Channel by tunnel (millions)

	1970	1980	1990
1. Without car			
Leisure	16	26 (7)	42 (10)
British, continental, other	10, 4, 2	15, 6, 5	21, 13, 8
Business	4	9 (2)	18 (3)
British, continental others	2, 1.5, 0.5	4, 4, 1	7, 9, 2
Total without car	20	35 (9)	60 (13)
2. With car			
Leisure	4	8 (5)	14 (10)
	3, 1, 0	5, 2.5, 0.5	8, 6, 0
Business	0.5	0.5 (0)	1 (1)
Total with car	4.5	8.5 (5)	15 (11)
All together	24.5	43.5 (14)	75 (24)

Million tons freight crossing the channel (in tunnel) (excluding petroleum) Import + Export	1970	1980	1900
Containerisable	3+ 2+ (2+)		
Bulk component	9+ 9 (1 + 1)		
TOTAL	12+11 (3 + 3)		
	23 (6)	(13) (5)	(20) (8)

Tunnel traffic in parentheses. 6 million tons through the tunnel (potential) for 1970 is only 15 per cent including petrol.

The travel time will be one hour from terminal to terminal against today's nearly 3 hours by ferry. The travel time London–Paris will be 3.5 hours with hourly departures. This travel time will be reduced to 2.5 hours by high speed trains. Vehicle ferry trains can depart every 2.5 minutes. With 24 trains per hour and 200 vehicles per train the capacity level is near 4800 vehicles per hour per direction, which comes close to a 6-lane motorway with 1600 vehicles per hour per lane (service level C).

(1) Estimated construction costs
   Construction capital cost (January 1973 figures)
      is   £468 million
Provision for interest and financing costs are   £192 million
Provision for escalation due to inflation is   £186 million
                                                           £846 million

(2) Estimated revenue	*1980*	*1990*
Passengers without vehicle	£ 35	£84 million
Passengers with vehicle	£ 50	£156 million
Freight	£ 16	£46 million
	£101	£286 million
which means with operating costs		£34 million
(3) Profit in operating		£252 million
Debt service		£89 million
net receipts		£163 million

The finance for the project will be wholly raised from the private sector. After paying the remuneration of the companies' share capital, the remaining profits belong to the British and French governments. The loans will be repaid by 2004, and governments will own the tunnel by about 2025.

The British Ministry of Transport made a cost–benefit analysis for an operating life of 50 years.

£ million

	Ferry	Tunnel	Bridge
A Initial capital cost		141	351
B Capital and operating costs 50 years	308	67	72
C Benefits of generated traffic		54	70
D Benefit of fixed crossing (308–67 + 54)		295	306
E Overall net benefit (295–141)		+154	−45

The benefit of a fixed crossing compared with the established means, that is the ferry, is shown above. (All figures are adjusted to 1969 value; discount rate 7 per cent per annum.)

Detailed explanation and comments on point:

£ million

		Tunnel	Bridge
A′	Initial costs at 1962 prices	142	298
	Tunnel/bridge	100	275
	Terminals, etc.	27	23
	Rolling stock + fire	15	0

B'	Difference ferry — tunnel/bridge	241	234
C'	Revenue (operator)	47	61
	Surplus (user)	7	9
		54	70

vehicle toll, ferry £10.10
vehicle toll, fixed £7.80

D' Comfort, view, etc. not included in money terms
Hovercraft not included in money terms
Area economy not included in money terms
National investment programmes not included
(availability of labour, materials, production cap-
acity)

5.6.3. British Air and Sea Links

Maplin
Britain is also preparing for a big development of its air and sea links with the
world over the next 20 years. In December 1972 the government introduced a
bill in Parliament which anticipated a new era in transport. It provided for the
setting up of the Mapling Development Authority and the building of a new
seaport. This would have involved the reclamation of 70 km^2 of land. These
projects would have cost more than £1000 million, but they have since been
cancelled.

The potential benefits of establishing Maritime Industrial Development
Areas (MIDA) in Great Britain have been studied by Peston and Rees:[26] six in
England, four in Scotland, and one in Wales.

(1) A port facility can be specified by: (a) location; (b) size; (c) transport
links; (d) internal transport; (e) types of cargo. The problems are optimum
location and optimum size, that is, optimum development through time.

(2) The costs and benefits of a port development can be classified as:
(a) direct receivers of benefits; (b) direct bearers of costs; (c) indirect
receivers of benefits; (d) indirect bearers of costs; (e) net costs and benefits to
the whole economy; (f) transfer costs and benefits. Some of these are
measurable,, some are non-measurable.

(3) The alternatives of port development are: (a) development of one or
more existing ports; (b) construction of one or more new ports;
(c) development of existing facilities other than ports: railway stations, road
haulage terminals or airports; (d) construction of one or more facilities other
than ports: railway stations, road haulage terminals or airports; (e) improved
utilisation without major developments of (a) or (c).

Concerning (1), the beneficiaries would be users of other ports switching to the new port, a net addition to users of ports. A second set of beneficiaries are those whose economic welfare is derived from the initial beneficiaries, again divided into two parts. A third set of beneficiaries are the owners of the land where the port is built, and other locations which will be favoured by the port, including owners of land over which new transport links will be built, as well as owners of land where factories, offices and houses will be constructed, (cf. MIDA concept). Users of existing facilities will benefit too, and local inhabitants may benefit from relatively less noise, smell and dirt as a result of developments elsewhere.

Concerning (2) the costs would be: construction costs, operating costs, costs of transport links, etc. A second set of costs derive from congestion, firms and houses. A third set of costs are the fall in land values from the existing facilities, relocation, etc., and indirect facilities.

The correct discount rate to be applied to the public sector investment projects should be discussed, as should the amenity and price of houses. Further the influence of lower port costs on the balance of payments should be examined.

The pricing of sea transport is, however, no simple matter. The freight rate which provides an internal rate of return equal to the opportunity cost of capital is a long-term equilibrium rate; it is generally referred to as a shadow price. Market freight rates will often be very different from the shadow price. However, the shadow price could be used in cost—benefit analysis of relative evaluations (see Benford).

It is obvious that port investments must be co-ordinated with whatever systems of national and regional planning may be in use in the nation concerned. This raises the question of which port or ports shall be invested in.[24, 33]

Goss and Pinochet[25] have treated these problems which also pose questions in the economics of international trade.

Third London Airport

The Roskill Commission on the third London Airport[32] has made a report concerning the siting of a new airport. The main elements considered were:

(1) Airport construction costs.
(2) Surface transport costs and benefits.
(3) Cost of dislocation of military facilities.
(4) Noise nuisance and amenity costs.
(5) Cost of land use changes.
(6) Air traffic and airport operations relocation costs.
(7) Labour benefits.

(8) Housing and town costs and benefits.

(9) Regional planning considerations.

In 1972 the British government decided to locate London's new airport at Maplin, after more than a decade of searching. However, the Maplin site was not recommended by the Roskill Commission. As noted above, the government has now cancelled the project.

Maplin would have required the establishment of a new town of 250 000 inhabitants, because it is some 90 km from London. A motorway and rail link would have been constructed. The airport was to be designed to handle 125 million passengers per year, 50 per cent using the railway to and from London. This would necessitate a traffic of 12 000 passengers/hour in each direction. The area proposed was 40 km², with a length of 12 km made up of four parallel runways capable of taking 150–170 aircraft per hour. The runways proposed were 3600 m long.

In fact the Roskill Commission's report recommended Cublington as the best site, although Buchanan favoured the coastal site of Foulness, the site later chosen by the British government.

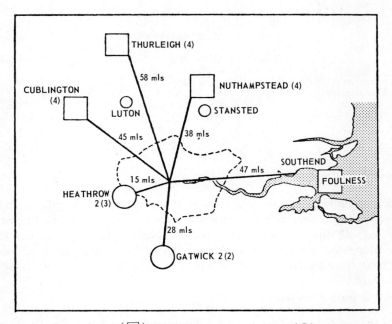

Figure 5.4 Possible sites (☐) for a third London Airport. (◯) The existing London Airports, (○) other airports in the area. Number of parallel runways in parentheses

The area disturbed by noise has been given by Masefield, following a 40 N.N.I. night index, low disturbance level, to be 270 km². The noise zones would extend 2 km outwards from the sides of outer runways and 20 km along the approach path, amounting to more than six times the area of the airport. The employment rate was estimated to be 64 000 primary and 15 000 secondary employees. To generate service employment a multiplier of 1.5 was used. This means that all together nearly 200 000 employees, or probably 400 000 inhabitants would have been involved in airport work alone, half of whom would have to live locally.

As already mentioned, London is served by two airports; at Heathrow and Gatwick, located 15 miles and 30 miles respectively from London.

The four potential sites investigated by the commission were Cublington, Thurleigh, Nuthampstead, and Foulness, located respectively 45, 58, 38, and 47 miles from London. The cost–benefit analysis was unusual because there was no valuation of the benefits of the airports, but valuation of some disamenity effects. The site with the lowest total social cost was selected. Costs were all discounted at a uniform rate of 10 per cent, as given by the Treasury.

The summary cost–benefit analysis, 1968 prices discounted up to 1982, gives the extra costs (not using Heathrow) as shown in table 5.6.

TABLE 5.6   Cost–benefit analysis of third airport sites

	Extra costs (£ million) using			
	Cublington	Foulness	Nuthampstead	Thurleigh
Airspace movement*	1 900	1 900	1 930	1 930
Passenger movement	2 900	3 100	2 930	2 920
Capital and other	640	630	640	650
Noise	20	10	70	20
Total	5 460	5 640	5 570	5 520
Difference	0	+ 180	+ 110	+ 60

*   Movements London area 450 000

The airspace movement costs are the costs of approaching the airport from a periphery with London in the centre, whereas the passenger costs are the costs associated with surface access from airport to London. The noise costs consist of the lump-sum figure which would be required to compensate those who suffer from noise nuisance in such a way as to leave them as well off as they were before.

The following assumption were made:

(1)   Effect of the channel tunnel: 5 million passengers lost to the tunnel by 1980.

(2) Effect of V.T.O.L.–S.T.O.L. aircraft not to be taken into account.
(3) No national airports policy.
(4) No advanced passenger trains.

The benefits were not quantified, but identified as:

(1) Benefit of international trade to business air travel.
(2) Benefit of social advance to business air travel.
(3) Income to the airport area.
(4) Extra air travel income.

These benefits should exceed the social costs at the chosen site, otherwise the airport should not be built; furthermore these benefits must be the same for all sites, otherwise it is not correct only to compare costs.

The forecasting of passengers for the period 1970–2000 was a major task. The costs were dependent on these figures. Prediction was divided into British leisure, British business, and non-British passengers. It was possible from surveys to find the number of air passengers per income group and the number of expected trips by this group and extrapolate these, when the future population, distribution by income group and change in the propensity to fly was known. A 3 per cent income growth rate was assumed, and a 5 per cent increase in propensity to fly was assumed, a population forecast being given.

TABLE 5.7 Forecasts for London Airport

	Passengers (million)		
	1972	1990 (high)	1990 (low)
U.K. charter	7.8	19.1	14.3
U.K. leisure short	2.0	10.1	7.3
long	1.2	5.4	3.9
Foreign leisure, short	2.1	17.7	10.8
long	4.6	26.0	16.1
U.K. business	2.0	9.13	6.9
Foreign business, short	1.4	9.3	5.9
long	0.9	4.4	2.9
Total	22.0	101.7	68.1
Non-I.P.S.* and Ireland passengers	6.0	30.0	22.0
Of this London area (Heathrow, Gatwick, Luton, Stansted) 70 per cent	23.6	106.6	72.2
Domestic	3.6	7.9	6.1
Total	27.2	114.5	78.3
With Channel tunnel		106.2	72.7†

* International Passenger Survey
† Passengers per aircraft average 225

The user benefits were split up into:

(1) Consumers' surplus:

$$\frac{1}{2}(T_i - T_f)(C_f - C_i)$$

where T is trips by passengers to airports, C is costs, behavioural, for the traveller including fares and time, index i is inland sites, f is Foulness

The constant $\frac{1}{2}$ was chosen as an average of benefit 0 and $(C_f - C_i)$

(2) Operators' surplus:
$$(T_i - T_f)(C_i - R_i)$$

where R_i is travel resource costs at inland site, $C_i - R_i$ is therefore profit to the transport undertaking.

(3) Resource cost savings:
$T_f(R_f - R_i)$ where R_f is travel resource costs at Foulness. This calculation gave the passenger movement user costs in table 5.6.

The Value of Time (1969)
Behavioural costs relate to the leisure passenger, resource costs relate to businessmen. The value of leisure time was 25 per cent of the passengers' income or 55d per hour. The value of business time was gross income plus overheads (50 per cent), 555d per hour. The value of paid drivers, accompanying adult and children was set to 128d, 39d, and 13d per hour respectively. These values were extrapolated to the year 2000 with 3 per cent growth per annum. Cost of operating vehicles was set to 4.5d per old rail mile and 6d for new.

The Value of Noise Nuisance
The N.N.I. index was used, without a night noise weighting. From the N.N.I. curves a correlation to property prices was found.

The residents' social costs were split up into: R removal costs; S consumers' surplus; D change in market price, and N compensation costs for H, households.

The projected number of households within a 35 N.N.I. contour in the year 2000 was for Cublington 29 000, for Foulness 20 000, for Nuthampstead 95 000 and for Thurleigh 25 000.

D represents the depreciation in house prices because of noise. D was set at 20 per cent on average for high-priced houses, rising 5 per cent per annum. $N = D$ for a median group of households. However, people with annoyance scores above the median value will move, giving cost R; people with annoyance scores below the median will stay, that is cost N. People moving will lose the consumers' surplus $S + R + D$. New entrants have social costs zero. The value of S and R was found by questionnaires, rising 3 per cent per annum (*cf.* chapter 4).

Carruthers and Dale[36] found the distribution of passengers (table 5.8) for London Airports in 1990 by the normal four-step procedure, based on gravitation and cheapest route and mode. They established 319 zones.

TABLE 5.8 Passengers (million) using the London Airports system with Cublington as the new airport

Total traffic	117
Made up of Heathrow	59
Gatwick	18
Luton	5
Manchester	5
New Airport	30
Percentage railway trips of new airport passengers	53 %

5.6.4 Intercity Transport in Europe 1970–2000.

We shall now examine the European intercity transport study (O.E.C.D.), initiated by COST (European Cooperation in Scientific and Technical research). Some 109 regions, 32 sectors and 16 countries have been studied. An area of 2.5 million km^2.

The total population of the study area amounts to around 345 million (region 88 which contains London has approximately 15 million inhabitants; region 26, Corsica, has 200 000 inhabitants).

Household surveys of long-distance travel from Toulouse, Linz, Valencia, Bruges, Lisbon, Geneva, Den Haag, Düsseldorf and Turin were made. (Some 5000 households and 100 000 trips were surveyed in May 1973–74.)

The modelling of the road network followed conventional methods. There were 1530 links and connectors in the base year network but many of them were long and not homogeneous in terms of geometric standards or traffic.

The network contained 791 nodes, consisting of nodal cities, important road junctions, zonal centroids or frontier crossing points.

There were 1020 links and connectors in the rail network. The 634 nodes of the network were the zonal centroids, large cities, mainline railway stations, railway junctions and frontier crossing points. It was necessary to take account of other types of traffic—that is, goods traffic, local passenger traffic and external traffic—using the network.

The air network was made up of about 400 direct links between origin and

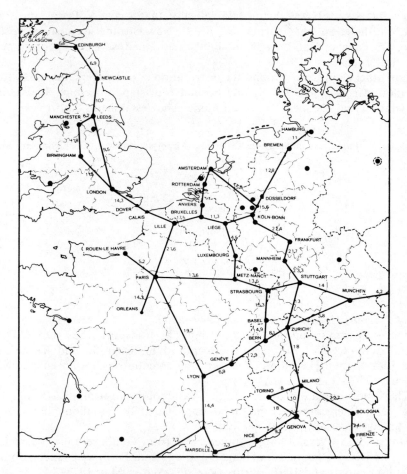

Figure 5.5 European high speed railways. Numbers are 1000 passengers per day (2000)

destination airports. The nodes of the network were the 84 airports together with zonal centroids.

Intercity transport trips in Europe consist of 25 per cent business travellers, 25 per cent holiday travellers, 45 per cent weekend travellers and 5 per cent other short duration travellers. Of these (1970 figures) 12 per cent go by train, 76 per cent by car, 5 per cent by bus and 5 per cent by air; these are increasing by 3 per cent per year (*cf.* chapter 1).

Models
Travel flows are calculated between the 109 zones by the three trip purposes:

business, holiday and short stay personal (S.S.P.). The model is structured differently for business and personal travel. The models for the two personal travel groups are conceptually similar, treating trip generation, spatial and modal distribution as separate phases, Business travel, on the other hand, is analysed by a direct, total demand model of the gravity type with the modal split closely related to the generation–distribution part.

Trip Generation and Distribution—Business Travel
On theoretical grounds a gravity function has been constructed to simulate the generation and spatial distribution of business trips. The function uses generation and attraction variables for zones i and j as a product and an impedance variable for the travel cost between the two zones. Variables and coefficients were calibrated using regression analysis with two sets of data: business flows between zones in the United Kingdom and the Continent, for international travel, and between selected zones in Germany for domestic travel. The result of the calibration process was the following function:

$$t_{ij} = (\text{G.R.P.}_i \times \text{G.R.P.}_j) \times \overline{T}_{ij}$$

where t_{ij} = number of yearly business travellers between zones i and j
  G.R.P. = gross regional product of the zone (in \$ thousand)
  $\overline{T}_{ij}$ = modally weighted travel time from zone i to zone j (in minutes).

Trip Generation and Distribution—Personal Travel
Household structure and income. The numbers of trips generated in each zone are estimated by means of category analysis, distributed to all other zones by a gravity type function, and then distributed between modes by diversion curves.

The variables used to determine personal trip generation are household structure, car ownership and income. As a result of the long-distance travel survey, trip generation rates for holiday and S.S.P. trips were found for 30 household categories, which are combinations of three household types (young adults, old adults and families), two car-ownership classes (car and non-car owning households) and five income classes (A, B, C, D and E).

Holiday and S.S.P. trips were generated for each zone by multiplying the trip rate by the number of persons in each category. The trip rates were applied on the assumption that they would not change in the future.
Trip generation. It was found that people living in rural areas take far fewer holidays than do people in cities. Since the survey was concentrated on cities the trip generation rates had to be varied according to the degree of urbanisation. From French and German holiday statistics, a factor of 0.425 was derived for the trip generation rates of people living in towns of less than

100 000 inhabitants and in rural areas. The number of trips generated by category and zone then became:

$$TG_c = POP_c \times TGR_c \times (0.575u + 0.425)$$

and the zonal trip generation:

$$TG_z = \sum_c TG_c$$

with POP_c = number of persons in category c
        TGR_c = trip generation rate of category c
        u = degree of urbanisation.

Trip distribution—trip attractions. Trips generated by residents in zone i are distributed to all other zones by means of a gravity type function, which can be formulated as:

$$t_{ij} = \frac{k \times t_i \times A_j}{R_{ij}}$$

Since

$$\sum_j t_{ij} = t_i,$$

therefore

$$k = \left(\sum_j \frac{A_j}{R_{ij}} \right)^{-1}$$

where A_j = measure of attraction of zone j
         R_{ij} = function of travel impedance from i to zone j.

Since no data existed on the number of tourists attracted by different zones, a special analysis was carried out to develop, for each zone, attraction factors for holidays and weekend trips. These attraction factors should be a measure of the inherent power of the zone to attract tourists. Since their sum is not identical to the total trip generation, constants had to be introduced in the distribution function to ensure that the number of trips distributed from each zone equals the number of trips generated in the zone. The impedance function in the distribution model should include variables which measure differences in travel resistance. To account for the varying marginal utility of money to travellers with different incomes, generalised time was taken as the impedance measure:

$$T_{ij}^* = T_{ij} + C_{ij}/\lambda$$

with T_{ij}^* = generalised time
        T_{ij} = travel time from i to j

C_{ij} = travel cost from i to j

λ = value of time (monetary units per unit time)

$T_{ij}{}^*$ varies both with the mode and with the type of traveller.

The perceived value of time of the traveller was assumed to be related to his declared household income: for holiday travel it was taken as 50 per cent of the declared income per employed person of the household, and for S.S.P. travel, 100 per cent.

The distribution function was estimated from the survey results as a power function of the variable $T_{ij}{}^*$:

$$R_{ij} = (T_{ij}{}^*)^\alpha$$

Since $T_{ij}{}^*$ is a mode specific variable, there are for each t_i to be distributed to zone j as many values of $T_{ij}{}^*$ as there are modes offered. The value applied in the distribution function is the minimum value, $T_{ij}{}^*$, min. The elasticity of demand with respect to travel impedance, α, was derived from the trip distance distribution as revealed in the survey.

The trip generation rates include only trips of over 80 km. Some zones, however, are rather large and some are islands, and a certain percentage of trips generated in such zones stay in the zone. This is particularly important for S.S.P. trips because their average distance is relatively short.

It has been assumed that on average the probability of a person making an intrazonal trip is the same as that of a person located at the centre of the zone.

The trip length distribution function has been shown to be:

$$p = aD^{\alpha D}(D > 80 \text{ km})$$

with $\displaystyle\int_{80}^{\infty} p\,\mathrm{d}D = 1$

Then the proportion of intrazonal trips becomes:

$$P_i = \int_{80}^{r} p\,\mathrm{d}D = \frac{a}{\alpha+1}(r^{\,\alpha+1}\,80^{\,\alpha+1})$$

The impedance function p has different coefficients for holiday and S.S.P. travel:

For holiday travel $\quad p = \dfrac{49\,700}{D^{1\cdot35}}$

For S.S.P. travel $\quad p = \dfrac{904\,000\,000}{D^{3\cdot37}}$

To calculate the percentage of intrazonal trips, each zone was classified as either circular or semi circular, its radius r was calculated from its surface area and the functions P_i were calculated separately for holiday and S.S.P. trips.

A positive correlation was found between income and trip length distribution: the distance exponent, α_{D*}, decreased from 1.38 for the lowest income group A to 1.18 for the highest income group E. α_{D*} represents the distance impedance of trips to all destinations around a zone. To derive from that an exponent α_D for each $i-j$ pair, one must discount for the fact that the number of possible destinations grows progressively as one proceeds further from the origin. A factor is applied to the distance exponent α_D as follows:

$$D^{\alpha_D} = D^{\alpha_{D*}} \times D = D^{\alpha_{D*}+1}$$

Then the relationship between the distance and $T_{ij}*$ impedance function becomes:

$$D^{\alpha_D} = (T_{ij}*)^{\alpha_{T*}}$$

Inserting for D the average travel distance, α_{T*} was calculated by mode and income group. Since the variation of α_{T*} between modes was within ± 4 per cent, a mean α_{T*} was taken for the distribution function which was applied separately by income class, $\alpha_{T*} = 2$.

Before the generated trips could be distributed to all other zones it was necessary to estimate the proportion of trips leaving the study area.

Modal Distribution of Holiday Trips

Five categories of holiday trips are assumed to use the car in the great majority of cases, with no serious choice offered by other modes. They are: camping and caravanning holidays (H1, H2), car trips by non-car-owning households (H3), trips of less than 250 km by car-owning households into rural areas (H4) or with a party size of three or more persons (H5). Bimodal choice cases are produced by trips under 250 km by non-car-owning households (H7) and by car-owning households with a party size of one or two persons (H6); the choice is between car and train, for car-owning households, and between train and bus for households without a car. Diversion curves give the probability of choosing the train as a function of the ratio of the generalised times of the train and the bus (or car):

$$\frac{t_{ij,\,\text{train}}}{t_{ij}} = f\left(\frac{T_{ij}*,\,\text{train}}{T_{ij}*,\,\text{bus}} \right)$$

with: $t_{ij} = t_{ij,\,\text{train}} + t_{ij,\,\text{bus}}$

The function is of a logistic type, which can be written as:

$$\frac{t_{ij,\,\text{train}}}{t_{ij}} = \frac{1}{1 + e^{U_m}}$$

with $U_m = a T_{ij}*,\,\text{train} / T_{ij}*,\,\text{bus}$

Since all curves are fitted by hand, the logistic function is not explicitly derived.

For trips of more than 250 km all modes are used by car-owning households (H8) and all public modes by non-car-owning households (H9). Diversion curves are used for each bimodal sub-choice, as described above.

The second part of the modal distribution analysis is the allocation of holiday trips to each category. Where the category is defined by a distance criterion the number of trips is automatically given by the distance of the t_{ij} pair (H7, H8, H9). In the other categories, additional factors or functions are needed to determine the allocation.

Modal Strategy

The first main strategy studied, was the *status quo* strategy in which the traditional ways of balancing demand and supply were followed. Under this strategy, more road and airport capacity is provided wherever existing facilities become congested, except for roads on the edge of large cities, subject to normal taxation of road users and conventional charging policies for air transport. Railways are subject to normal commercial criteria. This strategy led to a main road network of 229 000 lane km, against 140 000 in 1970, to an upgrading of rail speeds to an average of 115 km/h from 87 km/h in 1970, and to an air network of 448 direct air links, against 270 in 1970. The capital cost of roads, railways and airports was about $63 000 million.

The *controlled mode* strategy was based on the thesis that the main problems could be solved if the railways were able to attract a substantially larger share of the traffic. The chosen method of achieving this was to invest in a greatly improved rail system while reducing investment in roads. In the first variant of this strategy, CM(A), 3600 km of the rail network was upgraded to a cruising speed of 200–270 km/h and the rest of the network improved, giving an average network speed of 141 km/h. In the second, more costly variant, CM(B), a comprehensive new network of 9000 km with a maximum speed of 350 km/h was superimposed on an improved, existing network, raising the average network speed to 167 km/h. Fares were raised by 10 per cent on trains with speeds over 200 km/h and by 20 per cent on trains with speeds of 350 km/h. A road network of only 184 000 lane km was included. The capital costs were: CM(A), $58 000 million, CM(B), $69 000 million.

The *controlled demand* strategy was based on the thesis that excessive demand for car and air travel could not in practice be attracted to other modes of transport and must be restrained directly. The general aim was to use existing facilities to the full but not to create major new facilities if they entailed high economic and environmental costs. The same road network as in the controlled mode strategy was included. Motorway tolls around 59 cities and airport taxes at 19 major airports were used to reduce effective demand at critical points of congestion. The network of scheduled bus services was expanded to cover the whole study area. The capital cost of this strategy was only $45 000 million.

Finally, the *planned demand* strategy was based on the thesis that demand–supply relationships could be improved, not by redistributing demand from air and car to rail, nor by limiting demand to the capacity that could be supplied without undue economic and social cost, but by redistributing demand over space and time. This was achieved by (a) a planned location of future growth of population and employment in selected development regions rather than in already overdeveloped regions, and (b) a planned rearrangement of holiday and weekend travel in order to even out the sharp peaks in traffic demand (but this was not modelled). This strategy included a road network of 203 000 lane km, with emphasis on regional needs, a much improved conventional rail network, a comprehensive bus network and a decentralised air network. The capital cost was $75 000 million.

Forecasts for 1970–2000 show a population increase from 340 million to 396 million (about 16.5 per cent) but with an annual growth rate declining to possibly zero. Household size is expected to continue falling, from an average of 3.09 to 2.72, and urbanisation to continue rising, from 41.8 to 49.8 per cent. The gross national products have been assumed, as a central hypothesis, to multiply by 2.1–3.1 in the eleven countries with relatively developed economies and by 4.3–5.0 in the other five, the precise amounts depending on population growth. The labour force for the study area is expected to increase by 26 per cent, with changes of −41, 28 and 46 per cent in the primary, secondary and tertiary sectors, respectively. Car ownership, although likely to be subject to increasing restraints in urban areas, is expected to rise from 60.4 million to 142.7 million (+136 per cent), and the number of car-owning households from 47.0 million to 113 million (+140 per cent). Average working hours are expected to come down but not so far as to make a 4-day week normal. Average holiday entitlement is expected to grow, mainly through the extension of the four-week annual allowance, plus public holidays, to those workers who do not yet have it. The O.E.C.D. anticipates upward trends of 0–30 per cent in the cost of rail transport, depending on the country, downward trends of about 10 per cent for air, and varying trends from −12 to +13 per cent for the car.

Central assumptions (O.E.C.D.) are that oil prices will remain at their January 1975 level, in real terms, and that electricity prices will fall by 1 per cent per annum after 1980. No development of strategic importance can be foreseen in the technology of road transport, for application during this century, unless it be the electric car.

Results
The number of long-distance trips is predicted to rise from 1163 million in

1970 to 2305 million in the year 2000, under *status quo* conditions.

The predicted growth is greatest for business trips, being 188 per cent, compared with 63 per cent for holiday trips and 90 per cent for S.S.P. trips. The large growth in business trips results from economic growth, transport improvements and evolution of the Common Market.

The number of holiday trips is exactly proportional to the number of holidays, which is expected to grow steadily but not spectacularly. Holiday trip generation is not significantly influenced by the transport system itself (within the range of service relevant in Europe) and is therefore determined by demand factors alone. A population growth of 16 per cent is one factor. The trend towards urbanisation is another, since the urban population takes more holidays (per head) than the rural population; but this factor in itself accounts for only a 2 or 3 per cent growth. Income growth is the main factor; the elasticity of holiday-taking to income is about 0.3–0.4. These three factors in combination indicate a growth of about 60 per cent, which compares with 63 per cent given by the model.

The growth of S.S.P. trips is closely related to household car ownership: the survey showed that car-owning households made nearly three times as many short stay trips (*per capita*) as non-car-owning households, at all income levels. Income is a minor factor, apart from its influence on car ownership itself; an income elasticity of less than 0.1 was found for S.S.P. trips. In the whole study area the population in car-owning households is expected to increase by about 78 per cent, and that in non-car-owning households to decline by about 34 per cent. This indicates a net increase in S.S.P. trips of about 46 per cent, which is further increased to about 60 per cent when higher incomes are taken into account. The improved transport facilities anticipated in 2000, under *status quo* conditions including cheaper air services, are predicted to lead to a generation of new long-distance trips, of the order of 8 per cent. Under *status quo* conditions there are increases of 15 per cent in the average length of business trips, and 6–7 per cent for personal trips. All the alternative strategies for the year 2000 produce slightly higher average trip lengths than in the *status quo* condition.

The *status quo* forecast gives the magnitude of current trends. It shows increases in passenger trips between 1970 and 2000 of 275 per cent by air, 74 per cent by train, 28 per cent by bus and 78 per cent by car.

The Air Forecast

Although the predicted number of air trips in 2000 (*status quo*) is nearly four times its 1970 level, this represents a lower growth rate than that generally forecast within the aviation industry itself, where growth of six, eight or ten times is commonly expected. The difference is not in the business trips but in the personal. Other forecasts do not normally distinguish between holiday and short stay personal trips but since the forecast growth of short stay trips is very high—nearly twelve times—it is clearly in the holiday market that the difference lies. The methods used here are very different from those used in the aviation industry. The O.E.C.D. have adopted, for the first time on a European scale, a comprehensive transport analysis incorporating all modes and basing the demand for travel on the personal conditions that give rise to it.

Consequently the central forecast is that the model distribution of holiday trips within the study area will tend to stabilise at about 65 per cent by car, 20 per cent by train, 10 per cent by air and 5 per cent by bus. Holidays outside Europe are another matter.

The Rail and Bus Forecasts
An overall increase of 74 per cent in long-distance trips by rail represents a continuation of the trend during the past 20 years. It is largely attributable to the strong growth of business trips, although personal trips also show an increase. It is predicted that the percentage of business travellers on intercity trains will grow from 22 to 37 per cent, which implies an increasing demand for high quality of service.

The Car Forecast
The car will remain the dominant means of long-distance transport although its share is forecast to decline from 66 to 63 per cent. Its share of business trips falls from 53 to 45 per cent, partly because of the improved air and rail services assumed to be available in 2000 (*status quo*), and partly because of the relatively large growth of longer, international trips. The car also drops its share of S.S.P. trips, from 75 to 71 per cent, entirely because of the success foreseen in this market for cheap air services (see table 1.5).

Traffic growth is expected to be much greater in every way in the southern parts of Europe than elsewhere. The lowest growth rates are predicted in Germany, where the population is expected to fall and where a highly developed transport system already existed in 1970.

If the railway services do not improve, or are allowed to deteriorate, while road and air competition grow steadily stronger, the volume of railway traffic might start to decline in the spiral (familiar on urban and rural railways) of rising fares and falling standards. It must be remembered what happened to passenger rail services in the United States. Higher speeds and larger volumes of traffic cause capacity problems on some lines and imply investment in track improvements (including signalling) and sometimes in new track.

Analysis of airport traffic and capacity suggests that only a few airports will clearly need new runway capacity by the year 2000 if they are to handle their predicted traffic within the permitted level of peak hour delays: they are Barcelona, Madrid, Athens, Frankfurt and Munich.

The impact of a much faster rail network, together with a somewhat worse road network than in the *status quo* condition, is substantial: CM(A), with a maximum cruising speed of 250 km/h, raises the number of rail trips by 18 per cent; CM(B), with a maximum cruising speed of 350 km/h, raises it by 29 per cent. But whereas CM(A) draws 63 million trips away from the road (that is 6 per cent of the latter) CM(B) does no more, and the impact of both strategies on the volume of air traffic is negligible.

The controlled demand strategy proved remarkably ineffectual in reducing road traffic, but much more successful in reducing air traffic. The net result was only a small loss of 10 million trips from the system as a whole, but a substantial shift from air (43 million) and car (25 million) to train (32 million) and bus (26 million).

The planned demand strategy generates 3–8 per cent more traffic than the other strategies because the decentralisation of employment away from the biggest cities leads to the substitution of intercity trips for intracity trips. The newly generated trips tend to go by air or train. The volume of air traffic is much larger in this strategy than in any other but it is more evenly divided between airports and gives rise to few cases of airport congestion.

This strategy is the only one which significantly relieves the problem of a road congestion near large cities.

TABLE 5.9   User costs (2000) by strategy and mode ($ millions, 1973)

	1970	Strategies				
		SQ	CM (A)	CM (B)	CD	PD
Car	4 860	11 700	11 250	10 920	12 900	10 800
Bus	182	251	259	249	384	338
Train	2 062	4 162	5 465	6 391	4 513	5 055
Air	3 061	9 145	8 650	8 307	9 166	10 046
Total	10 165	25 258	25 624	25 867	26 963	26 239

Evaluation

The results of the estimates are shown in tables 5.9 and 5.10. Table 5.9 gives the user costs (that is, the expenditure by transport users) for each mode and strategy. The difference between these user costs and the operating costs (net of taxes and subsidies) represents the producers' surplus which is given in table 5.10. The producers' benefit in each strategy is then the difference between the surplus in that strategy and the surplus in the *status quo* strategy (this having been defined as the yardstick).

The sum of users' and producers' benefits gives the total internal benefits relative to the *status quo*, as shown in table 5.11. It must be remembered that the calculations of users' benefits are dependent on arbitrary values of time.*

TABLE 5.10   Producers' surplus and benefit (2000) by strategy and mode ($ millions, 1973)

	1970	SQ	CM (A)	Strategies CM (B)	CD	PD
Producers' surplus:						
Car: tolls	190	860	785	765	2300	620
fuel tax	1357	3160	3039	2948	3088	2944
Bus	−80	−130	−134	−128	−201	−176
Train	−19	59	597	1760	−75	524
Air: operating surplus	367	987	446	361	382	1508
tax	−	−	−	−	2088	−
Total	1623	4936	4733	5706	7582	5420
Producers' benefit:	n.a.	−	−203	770	2646	484

n.a. not applicable

TABLE 5.11   Internal benefits (2000) relative to the *status quo*, by strategy
($ millions, 1973)

	Strategies			
	CM(A)	CM(B)	CD	PD
Users' benefit	162	1158	−4296	1100
Producers' benefit	−203	770	2646	484
Internal benefits	−41	1928	−1650	1584

These internal benefits may be compared with the investment costs to give the basic cost benefit structure, as follows:

* Here $14.4 per hour for business trips
       $ 4.8 per hour for short stay trips
       $ 2.4 per hour for holiday trips.
Operating costs
       car and air trips 5 cents per passenger km
       bus and rail trips 2.5 cents per passenger km

$ millions (1973)

	New benefits relative to the *status quo*	Investment cost	Investment relative to the *status quo*
SQ	—	71 800	—
CM (A)	−41	68 600	−3 200
CM (B)	1 173 to 1 928	83 600	11 800
CD	−1 650	52 700	19 100
PD	1 584	84 800	13 000

It is clear that the large investment costs on CM(B) and PD, relative to the *status quo*, are matched with high net benefits of the order of 10–16 per cent in the CM(B) and 12 per cent in the PD, and the big investment saving in the CD is matched by a big shortfall in benefits, of the order of 9 per cent, while the CM(A) costs only slightly less and gives only slightly less benefit. There is no clear reason for preferring any one strategy to any other on the basis of these aggregate results.

The number of casualties (9300) on the intercity road network can be held in check and actually reduced. There are three reasons for this: first, the proportion of motorway and dual carriageway, on which accident rates are universally much lower than on ordinary single carriageways, will increase (under *status quo* conditions) from 41 to 78 per cent; secondly, accident rates have already been reduced by a large degree in some countries and brought down to a level less than half that of other countries, suggesting that in due time the same might be done in the latter; and thirdly, even in the countries with the lowest accident rates, new safety measures are expected to bring further important savings in lives and injuries.

The regulation of noise and air pollution from road vehicles, though designed primarily for the benefit of urban areas, will also be effective on intercity roads.

As regards air transport, despite the growth of traffic, there are reasons to expect that the noise levels will actually begin to diminish in the near future when the next generation of aircraft appears. The numbers of people severely affected by noise from the intercity transport network appear from the O.E.C.D. survey to be about 3 per cent of the non-urban population of the study area (170 million).

It is estimated that energy consumption in 1970 on the defined intercity network, for all three modes, was 10.8 million tons of oil equivalent. The source of energy was almost wholly oil, of course, and represented 2.5 per cent of oil consumption in the study area.

5.6.5 *Transport in the North-East Corridor of the United States*[38]

The north-east corridor covers 67 000 miles², and the population is expected to be 60 million by 1995. The family median income will rise to $15 000 by 1985, 49 per cent with more than this income, 23 per cent with $10 000–$15 000, 18 per cent with $5000–$10 000 and 10 per cent with less than $5000 (see also chapter 1).

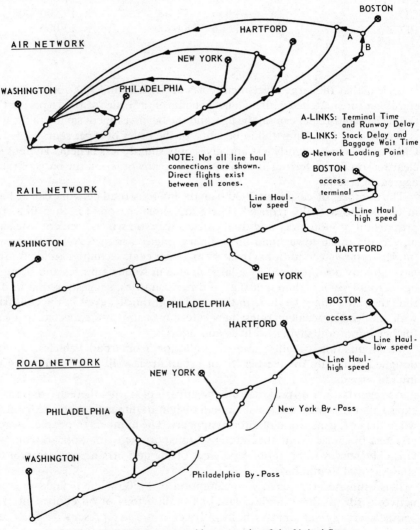

Figure 5.6 North-east corridor networks of the United States

Among the transport problems are congestion, safety, noise, air pollution, land requirements, etc. The following alternatives in transport improvement will be described:

(1) A high-speed railway system
(2) A highway system
(3) A S.T.O.L.–V.T.O.L. aircraft system

All the above will be examined from the point of view of environment, capacity and economic analysis. Finally a multi-modal evaluation is given.

Railway System
The network would serve Washington, Baltimore, Philadelphia, New York, New Haven or Hartford and finally Boston. The rolling stock could be Metroliner (speed 70–120 miles/h), high-speed 1 railway (speed 150 miles/h) with intermediate possiblities, high-speed 2 railway (speed 200 miles/h), like the Tokaido line in Japan, and finally a tracked air-cushion system (speed 300 miles/h). The number of seats per car will be 70–100, the number of cars per train 6–10 and the right of way width 30–60 m. Table 5.12 gives travel times with station stops for Washington–Boston.

TABLE 5.12   Travel times Washington–Boston

Metroliner (1970)	7 hours
High speed 1	5 hours 20 min
High speed 2	3 hours
Air cushion	2 hours 20 min

In 1968 there were more than 20 million intercity passenger trips (of more than 100 miles, *cf.* chapter 1) made within the north-east corridor region and of those about 10 per cent were made by railway. By 1985 the number of intercity trips is expected to double, assuming a growth rate of 4 per cent per annum which corresponds to the national annual transport growth rate experienced during 1950–65. If the railway was able to maintain its percentage of the travel market some 4 million trips would be made by railway; however, a growth rate of 2 per cent per annum is more likely to be true, giving about 2 million trips. If high-speed trains were developed, the railway passenger forecast could be 20–45 million by 1985 (including short-distance trips). As simple trend analysis is not useful over long-term periods where new technologies are introduced, a mathematical model in the form of a McLynn model was used. This model gave the results shown in table 5.13.

TABLE 5.13   Estimated railway passengers in 1985 (million) for the Washington–Boston corridor

Metroliner	20
High-speed 1	30
High-speed 2	35
Air cushion	40

The comparison of the systems for long-range planning required cost estimates.

Investment costs in $ million for 1970 are shown in table 5.14.

TABLE 5.14   Railway investment costs ($ million, 1970) for the north-east corridor

	Rolling stock	Land acquired	Terminals	Signals	Electrification	Track	Total*
Metroliner	78	–	–				100
High-speed 1	90	214	100	80	70	1050	1600
High-speed 2	84	472	214	150	80	1460	2500
Air cushion	165	261	250	100	210	1600	2700

* Including research and development $30–110 million

Operating costs are given in table 5.15 in dollars (1970). Indirect operating costs are not related directly to running a train, but represent service costs, including terminal operation and maintenance.

TABLE 5.15   Railway operating costs ($, 1970) for the north-east corridor

	Energy per car mile	Crew per train mile	Vehicle maintenance per car mile	Track maintenance per car mile	Signal maintenance ($ million per year)	Indirect (per pass. mile)
High-speed 1	0.04	0.90	0.20	0.04	1.90	0.017
High-speed 2	0.05	0.20	0.20	0.09	4.60	0.015
Air cushion	0.16	0.17	0.66	0.36*	13.00	0.013

* or $7.600 per track mile.

Equations for total operating costs were derived from a system-optimising model and are given in table 5.16. The model documentation provides a linear relationship between costs and traffic, the constant being the fixed annual operating cost, the coefficient to P being the marginal cost per passenger, which includes components varying with demand: energy, crew and vehicle maintenance.

TABLE 5.16   Annual operating costs. C ($ million, 1970).

Metroliner	$C = 3.40 + 4.587\,P$
High-speed 1	$C = 11.36 + 3.614\,P$
High-speed 2	$C = 14.78 + 3.239\,P$
Air cushion	$C = 34.48 + 3.362\,P$

P = number of passengers (million per year)

Annual costs in cents per passenger mile are given in table 5.17. The annual investments were found, assuming an interest rate of 10 per cent and an economic life of 35 years for fixed plant, 14 years for vehicles and infinite life for land. The annual operating costs are added. Taxes are not included in the costs.

TABLE 5.17   Annual costs in cents per passenger mile

	P passengers (million per year)
Metroliner	$C = 4.73 + 4.92/P$
High speed 1	$C = 3.38 + 153.31/P$
High speed 2	$C = 2.75 + 288.78/P$
Air cushion	$C = 2.84 + 296.20/P$

The evaluation procedure was given by net present value, the basic structure of which may be shown as

$$NPV = R - C - I_f - (I_v - S_v) + S_f$$

where NPV is the net present value
R is the discounted annual revenue
C is the cumulative discounted annual operating costs
I_f is the discounted investment in land and fixed plant
I_v is the discounted vehicle investments
S_v is the discounted vehicle salvage value
S_f is the discounted salvage value of land and fixed plant.

System profitability is measured by the calculation of the present value of revenues minus present value of costs. A fare level of $1.50 per passenger plus $0.075 per passenger mile is used (for example, $18 from New York to Washington); in addition a 10 per cent discount rate and 3 per cent annual growth rate in traffic is used. The net present values in $ million (1970) are shown in table 5.18.

TABLE 5.18   Net present values ($ million, 1970)

	NPV	R	C	I_f+I_v	S_v+S_f
Metroliner (1972–85)	449	1067	509	29+80	7+0
High-speed 1 (1972–85)	−72	1220	462	1163+67	11+269
(1972–99)	102	1912	716	1163+93	5+37
High-speed 2 (1972–99)	60	1153	299	869+30	7+98
Air cushion (1972–99)	124	1363	385	902+58	13+94

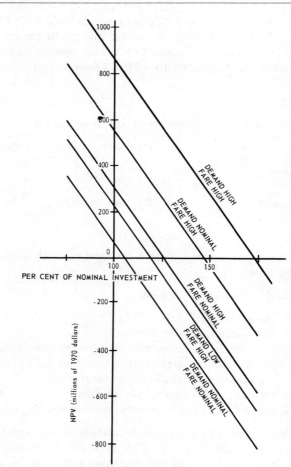

Figure 5.7 Net present value as a function of the nominal investment for the north-east corridor (High-speed 1)

It is seen that a high-speed 1 system for the period 1972–85 appears to give a substantially negative net present value. This suggests that a choice somewhere between metroliner and high-speed 1 would permit a reasonable trade-off between reduced travel time and net present value.

If a high-speed 1 system were to operate until 1999, the situation improves to a point where the nominal set of assumptions for demand, fare and investment gives a surplus of $102 million in net present value. With higher fares, $3 per passenger plus $0.085 per passenger mile, and a lower demand, minus 20 per cent, investment could exceed the nominal value by 20 per cent and net present value would still remain positive (figures 5.7, 5.8).

Air cushion shows an advantage in the net present value figures. It is better than the high-speed 2 system in speed, safety and comfort, but not in noise pollution. Table 5.19 shows noise and air pollution effects for air cushion vehicles.

TABLE 5.19   Noise and air pollution effects for air cushion rail vehicles (1985)

	U-shaped track at grade	All fossil fuel
Noise level 15 m from vehicle [dB(A)]	83	
Land area affected* [miles² (excluding right of way)]	2	
Air pollution† NO $_x$(g/passenger mile)		0.37

* $\geq$ 30 N.E.F.
† CO emission is not considered significant.

Highway System

Highways represent the principal means of intercity travel in the north-east corridor; automobiles and buses represent 74 and 5 per cent respectively, that is 14 million and 1 million passenger trips in 1968. In general, 20 per cent of all intercity highway traffic takes place during 10 per cent of the days of the year, which creates congestion of freeways. For 1985 the forecasts are 300 000–800 000 trips per day. Even allowing for a high speed railway/air system being in operation in 1975 the models gave an automobile passenger mile percentage of at least $55 + 7 = 62$ per cent.

The development of the highway system is limited to: (1) expansion to include new primary routes; (2) construction and upgrading of existing routes; and (3) improvement of the utilisation and efficiency of the existing routes. The cost of an intercity driver information system could vary from $6 to $60 million.

Travel times from Washington to Boston were calculated—a distance of 441 miles. The minimum travel time would be 8 hours, against 13 hours on the worst day. The New Jersey Turnpike with 12 lanes will have an average daily traffic volume of 160 000 vehicles in 1985. Of these, 50 000 will on average be intercity traffic; however, this figure is expected to reach 120 000 during the morning rush hour of the worst day. Taking the initial capital cost of freeway control to be $27 million the annual cost is calculated to be $23 million for 531 miles of freeways (assuming a 10 per cent interest rate and amortisation over 10 years). However, the benefits will be:

Operating cost savings by 1985, $27 million
Plus vehicle hours saved 127 million
Plus accidents avoided, 60 000
Plus extra vehicle miles of capacity, 2890 million

The land area exposed to excessive noise by the entire highway network (affected by mean night sound pressure levels greater than 64 dB(A)) was estimated to be 200 miles², against 140 miles², if the north-east corridor automobile traffic was eliminated.

Estimated air pollution emissions per vehicle mile for 1985 are given in table 5.20.

TABLE 5.20   Highway air pollution (1985)

	CO	HC	NO_x
g/vehicle mile			
Auto	6	0.1	0.4
Bus	3	3	1.6
g/passenger mile			
Auto	3.22	0.07	0.21
Bus	0.15	0.14	0.07

A S.T.O.L./V.T.O.L. Aircraft System

The characteristics of S.T.O.L. and V.T.O.L. aircraft in 1975 are given in table 5.21. Terminal design and location have the following characteristics. S.T.O.L. air ports are rectangular, the runway being 540 × 30 m. The width is 180 m in total providing an area for manoeuvring. There are 20 gates for 60 aircraft operations per hour. V.T.O.L. air ports are T-shaped; the landing pad covers 120 × 60 m and the total area required is 240 × 120 m, to allow for manoeuvring. There are 20 gates for 60 aircraft operations per hour. The network is covered by 18–24 terminals. Table 5.22 shows air port costs for the Manhattan area of New York.

TABLE 5.21 S.T.O.L. and V.T.O.L. characteristics (1975)

	S.T.O.L (DC210)	V.T.O.L. (SIK S65)
Passenger capacity	120	80
Cruising speed (miles/h)	400	300
Maximum range (miles)	500	300
Cost ($ million)	7	5
Take-off distance (feet)	790	0
Cruising altitude (feet)	20 000	8000

TABLE 5.22 Airport costs ($ million) for the Manhattan area

	S.T.O.L.	V.T.O.L.
Land	123	65
Runway	53	24
Passenger deck	15	22
Parking etc.	4	6
Maximum	195	117

The simulation of network operation for the year 1985 yielded the costs displayed in table 5.23 (excluding costs of air cushion construction).

TABLE 5.23 Air network operation costs (1985)

	S.T.O.L. system	V.T.O.L. system
Passengers/year (million)	29	42
% of total	13%	17%
Investment ($ million)		
Private	585	891
Public	629	698
Gross revenue	470	754
Private cost/year	304	514
Charges per year	91	98
Taxes per year	77	120

Present Value Analysis

For a S.T.O.L. system the present value accumulated does not become positive until 1990. In 2000 the discounted value is $86 million. For a V.T.O.L. system the present value accumulated becomes positive in 1983, and increases to $293 million in the year 2000 (figure 5.9).

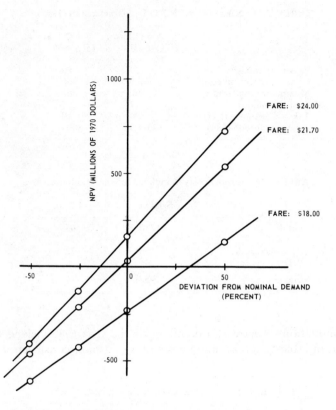

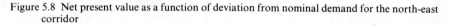

Figure 5.8 Net present value as a function of deviation from nominal demand for the north-east
corridor

Congestion

Although the number of conventional aircraft operations are predicted to
decrease by 1040 from 5500 operations per day in the New York air terminal
area in 1985, the addition of 3450 S.T.O.L. operations brings the total up to
nearly 8000 operations for New York air traffic control, a critical situation.
Noise and air pollution emissions are set out in tables 5.24 and 5.25. The land
area exposed to excessive noise for the conventional 8 big airports in the area
was 400 miles², and 350 miles² if the 1985 north-east corridor air traffic was
excluded.

The increase delay at conventional airports can be eliminated by diversion
of passengers to: (1) high speed railway; (2) fourth airport; (3) existing
airports; (4) S.T.O.L. system. Passengers' delays for New York's Kennedy

Airport in 1985 are forecast as in table 5.26. Alternatives are evaluated in table 5.27 with the aid of the calculations already given.

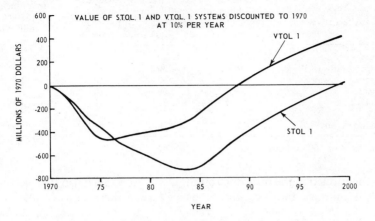

Figure 5.9 Extrapolated costs of S.T.O.L. and V.T.O.L. systems

TABLE 5.24   Airport noise

	Noise level [dB(A)] at 15 m	Land area affected* (miles²) excluding terminal
S.T.O.L.	85	14
V.T.O.L.	85	10

* ≥ 30 N.E.F. or higher

TABLE 5.25   Airport air pollution (g/passenger mile)

	CO	HC	NO$_x$
S.T.O.L. aircraft	0.42	0.32	0.12
V.T.O.L. aircraft	0.45	0.37	0.09
Conventional aircraft	0.24	0.17	0.07

TABLE 5.26   Passenger delay for Kennedy Airport (1985)

	1970	Alternative (1)	(2)	(3)	(4)
Passenger delay average (min)	34	13	13	4	6
Diversion to		new railway	new airport	existing airports	new S.T.O.L. system

TABLE 5.27   Evaluation of alternatives

1985 Alternative	New York – Washington block time (min)	Traffic (Million passengers/ year)	Costs (cents/ passenger mile)	Investments ($1000 million)
Highway	240	20	–	–
High speed railway 1	105	30	10	1.6
High speed railway 2	75	50	10	2.5
Air cushion	55	60	10	2.7
V.T.O.L.	40*	60	11	2.3
S.T.O.L.	35	70	14	4.3
Conventional aircraft	80	10	–	–

* Door to door 150 minutes

As mentioned in the introduction the evaluation must also take account of political, military and sociological, as well as aesthetic considerations.

References

1. Rallis, T. (1963). Airports, *Acta Poly. scand.*, **18**, Copenhagen
2. Bendtsen, P. H. and Rallis, T. (1971) Transport Outside Towns, Topic II, 2, *4th Int. Symp.*, CEMT, Hague
3. Rallis, T. (1973). *Intercity Transport Capacity*, Int. Conf. Transp. Res., Bruges
4. Kraft, G. (1963). *Demand for Intercity Passenger Travel Systems*, Analysis and Research Corporation for Department of Commerce, Washington
5. McLynn, J. M. (1973). *Modal Choice Models*, Davidson, Talbird and McLynn, Bethesda, Maryland
6. Quandt, R. (1970). *The Demand for Travel*, Princeton University Press, Princeton, New Jersey
7. Manheim, M. L. and Ruiter, E. R. (1970). *Highway Res. Record*, 314, Washington
8. Andersen, P. Bj. (1976). *Models for Forecasting Intercity Passenger Transport*, Danish State Railways, Copenhagen
9. Ricardo, D. (1817). *Principles of Political Economy and Taxation*, Dent, London
10. Ohlin, B (1933). *Inter-regional and International Trade*, Cambridge University Press, London
11. Olsen, E. (1971). *International Trade Theory and Regional Income Difference*, North-Holland, Amsterdam
12. Carey, H. (1858). *Principles of Social Science*, Lippincott, Philadelphia
13. Reilly, W. J. (1929). *Methods for the Study of Retail Relationships*, Bulletin, University of Texas, Austin
14. Stewart, J. Q. (1947). Rules concerning the distribution and equilibrium of population, *Geog. Rev.*, **37**
15. Zipf, G. K. (1949). *Human Behaviour and the Principle of least Effort*, Cambridge University Press, London
16. Pöyhönen, P. (1963). A model for volume of trade, *Weltwirtschaftlisches Archiv.*, **59**
17. Tinbergen, J. (1962). *Shaping the World Economy*, Appendix VI, Twentieth Century Foundation, New York
18. Linneman, H (1966). *An Economic Study of International Trade Flows*, North-Holland, Amsterdam
19. Wilson, A. G. in Chisholm, M. *et al.* (1971). *Regional Forecasting*, London
20. Baumol, W. J. and Vinod, H. D. (1967). *Studies in the Demand for Freight Transport*, Washington PB 176479, D.O.T.

21. Evans, A. W. (1969). London–Manchester electrification, *J. Transp. Econ. Policy*, **3**
22. British Rail Board (1963). *Reshaping British Rail*, H.M.S.O., London
23. *Proposal for a Fixed Channel Link* (1963). Cmnd 2137, H.M.S.O., London
24. *Major Ports of Great Britain* (1962). Cmnd 1824, H.M.S.O., London
25. Goss, R. O. (1967). Port investments, *J. Transp. Econ. Policy*, **1**
26. Peston, M. H. and Rees, R. (1970). *Maritime Industrial Development Areas*, National Ports Council, London
27. T.R.R.L. (1970) *Comparative Assessment of New Forms of Intercity Transport*, Special Report 1, vol. 1, 2 and 3, London
28. Canadian Transport Committee (1970). *Intercity Transport Study*, Ottawa
29. Horonjeff, R. and Kanafani, A. (1973). *Forecasting the Demand Potential for STOL*, I.T.T.E., Berkeley, California
30. Dasgupta, A. K. and Pearce, D. W. (1972). *Cost–Benefit Analysis*, Macmillan, London
31. Coburn, T. M. Beesley, M. E. and Reynolds D. J. (1960) *London-Birmingham Motorway*, Road Research Laboratory, TP46, London
32. *The Third London Airport* (1967) Cmnd 3257, H.M.S.O. London
33. Ministry of Transport (1966). *Portbury*, H.M.S.O., London
34. Kuhn, T. E. (1962). *Public Enterprise Economics and Transport Problems*, University of California
35. Thygesen, I. (1971) *Investeringsplanleegning*, Polyteknisk Forlag, Copenhagen
36. Carruthers and Dale (1969) *Traffic Engineering and Control*, **11**
37. Thomson, J. M. *et al.*, (1976) *COST 33, European Intercity Transport Study*, O.E.C.D. Paris
38. Cheslow, M. *et al.* (1971). *Northeast Corridor Transport*, Final Report, D.O.T., Washington

Glossary of terms

A.C.C.   Area control centre

A.C.C.	Area control centre
Acre	$= 0.4$ ha
A.D.R.	Advisory route
A.P.P.	Approach control
A.T.C.	Air traffic control *or* Automatic train control
B.C.	Before Christ
Bit	Amount of information
B.R.	British Rail (formerly British Railways)
Bushel	$= 36$ l $= 8$ gallons
Chaldron	$= 36$ bushels
C.N.R.	Composite noise rating
d	pence (pre-decimalisation)
db(A)	Noise measured by an A-weighted sound level meter
D.B.	German Federal Railways
DM	Deutschmark
D.O.T.	Department of Transportation, Washington
D.S.B.	Danish State Railways
D.W.T.	Deadweight ton
foot	$= 0.3$ m
F.A.A.	Federal Aviation Agency, Washington
F.I.R.	Flight information region
F.L.	Flight level
Gallon	$= 4.5$ l
G.M.T.	Greenwich Mean Time
G.N.P.	Gross national product
G.R.T.	Gross register ton $= 100$ foot$^3 = 2.83$ m^3

hp	Horsepower = 0.17 kcalorie/s
H.R.B.	Highway Research Board, Washington
Hz	Measure of frequency = 1 cycle/s
I.A.S.	Indicated airspeed
I.A.T.A.	International Air Transport Association
I.C.A.O.	International Civil Aviation Organisation
I.E.E.E.	Institute of Electrical and Electronic Engineers
I.F.R.	Instrument flight Rules
I.L.S.	Instrument landing system
J.N.R.	Japanese National Railways
I.T.A.	Institut du Transport Aerien, Paris
kJ	kilojoule = 0.278 kWh
Knot	= 1 nautical mile/h
kWh	kilowatt hour = 859.680 kcalorie
L_x	Noise level exceeded x per cent of the time
Mile	= 1.61 km
M.I.T.	Massachusetts Institute of Technology
$M/M/n$	Queue system: Random arrivals, random service, n channels
N	Newton
Nautical mile	= 1.85 km
N.E.F.	Noise exposure forecast
N.D.B.	Non-directional beam
NFr	New francs
N.N.I.	Noise and number index
N.R.T.	Net register ton
O.R.	Operational research
P.A.R.	Precision approach radar
PNdB	Perceived noise decibel
p.p.m.	Parts per million
SFr	Swiss francs
S.N.C.F.	French National Railways
S.T.O.L.	Short take-off and landing
T.A.S.	True airspeed

Glossary of terms

T.M.A.	Terminal area
tun	Wine cask containing 252 gallons (1134 l)
T.W.R.	Tower control
V.F.R.	Visual flight rules
V.H.F.	Very high frequency
V.O.R.	V.H.F. omnidirectional radio range
V.T.O.L.	Vertical take-off and landing

Index